VIOLENCE IN CAPITALISM

VIOLENCE IN

CAPITALISM

Devaluing Life in an Age of Responsibility

JAMES A. TYNER

UNIVERSITY OF NEBRASKA PRESS   LINCOLN AND LONDON

Library of Congress Cataloging-in-Publication Data
Names: Tyner, James A., 1966– author.
Title: Violence in capitalism: devaluing
life in an age of responsibility /
James A. Tyner.
Description: Lincoln: University of
Nebraska Press, 2016. | Includes
bibliographical references and index.
Identifiers: LCCN 2015033085
ISBN 9780803253384 (hardback: alk. paper)
ISBN 9781496206411 (paper: alk. paper)
ISBN 9780803284562 (epub)
ISBN 9780803284579 (mobi)
Subjects: LCSH: Violence. | Violent
crime—Social aspects. |
Crime—Sociological aspects. | Capitalism—
Social aspects. | BISAC: SOCIAL
SCIENCE / Violence in Society.
Classification: LCC HM1116 .T963 2016
| DDC 303.6—dc23 LC record available
at http://lccn.loc.gov/2015033085

Set in Lyon by M. Scheer.
Designed by N. Putens.

For Belinda

CONTENTS

ACKNOWLEDGMENTS

When my family asked about my current book project, they were mildly disappointed. A book on violence? Didn't you already write a book on violence? Yes, I must plead guilty. In an earlier book I applied a geographic perspective to the study of (mostly) direct violence; at the time, I believed that the geography discipline (as a whole) was largely silent on the subject of direct, interpersonal violence. In this book I remain concerned with violence—but violence of a different sort. Here, my concern is on the meaning and making of violence, for it is my argument that violence does not exist but rather is abstracted from particular, concrete practices. Violence, in other words, is very much a product of its time.

So too is this present manuscript. It was written during a time of my life in which various political and economic debates raged across the United States: debates over health care and terrorism, unions and voter representation, marriage rights and school shootings. I was, and remain, struck by the unevenness of media coverage and general public awareness of these topics, by the vicissitudes of violence, which seem to defy any consensus in our comprehension of them. Where I saw violence, others saw justice, or nothing. It became all too apparent that much violence was hidden in plain sight and that there was a pervasive indifference to life in the abstract. Television programs, for example, were often based on individual pain and suffering; one person's misfortune was another person's source of amusement and entertainment. Tragedy and loss were increasingly commodified and capitalized, but rarely were these shows viewed as violent.

These observations formed the kernel of this work and provided the foundation for my initial proposal and contract with the University of Nebraska Press. Accordingly, I must first thank Derek Krissoff, as well as the entire staff at the University of Nebraska Press, for seeing this book through to completion. Derek in particular was exceptionally supportive at the beginning of the process, and I appreciate his insight and encouragement. Special thanks are extended to Courtney Ochsner, Ann Baker, and freelance copyeditor Maureen Bemko.

This book, of course, did not appear in isolation. Over the years I have benefited from my interactions with colleagues both at Kent State and beyond. These individuals have helped shape my understanding and interpretation of a wide range of topics and issues. Thanks are owed to Stuart Aitken, Derek Alderman, Gabriela Brindis Alvarez, Noel Castree, Pamela Colombo, Alex Colucci, Gordon Cromley, Michael Dear, Melissa Gilbert, Kathryn Gillespie, Sam Henkin, Joshua Inwood, Sokvisal Kimsroy, Scott Kirsch, Audrey Kobayashi, Philippe Le Billon, Patricia Lopez, Nick Megoran, Don Mitchell, Joe Nevins, Shannon O'Lear, Richard Peet, Chris Philo, Chris Post, Laura Pulido, Stian Rice, Estela Schindel, Savina Sirik, Simon Springer, Dave Stasiuk, Joel Wainwright, Bobby Wilson, and Melissa Wright.

I am grateful, also, to Richard Peet for permission to use a revised version of my previously published article, "Dead Labor, Homo Sacer, and Letting Die in the Labor Market," which appeared in *Human Geography: A New Radical Journal* 7, no. 1 (2014): 35–48.

Outside of academia I thank my parents, Dr. Gerald Tyner and Dr. Judith Tyner, for their ongoing support and encouragement, as well as my brother, David, and my aunt, Karen, for their interest and inspiration. As always, I thank my now fourteen-year-old puppy, Bond, and my fifteen-year-old cat, Jamaica. Together, these two remarkable individuals have never complained about my idiosyncrasies or the piles of books and papers that appear in my wake. Most important, however, I thank my immediate family. I am blessed with two wonderful daughters, Jessica and Anica. I am extremely proud of their academic success, as stellar sixth and eighth graders, respectively. I am even more proud of their kindness and generosity toward others. Lastly, I thank my friend and partner, Belinda. I am not easy to live with; as academics, writers, and husbands go, I am the embodiment of all clichés: the absentmindedness, the piles of books littering my desk and nightstand, the unexpected bill for a newly purchased book. Through it all Belinda has been my foundation, and it is for this reason that I dedicate this book to her and say, deeply, *mahal kita*.

VIOLENCE IN CAPITALISM

1

The Abstraction of Violence

Lives are legibly valuable when they are assessed comparatively and relationally within economic, legal, and political contexts and discourses, framed by a culture of punishment according to the market logic of supply and demand.

—LISA MARIE CACHO, *Social Death: Racialized Rightlessness and the Criminalization of the Unprotected*

Jessica Kate Williams was murdered on May 23, 2003.[1] Twenty-two years old and homeless, Jessica (an African American woman) had been living in a street camp in Portland, Oregon, with a number of other runaway youths, most of whom came from white, middle-class homes. Jessica, in many ways, was different from the other youths. For one thing, there was her size. At six feet, four inches tall and weighing 230 pounds, Jessica was bigger than most of the other residents of the street camp. For another, Jessica had been determined to have the mental capacity of a twelve-year-old, having been born with fetal alcohol syndrome. Jessica had been adopted by Sam and Rebecca Williams when she was just nine months old. As a child, and later as a young woman, Jessica had desperately wanted to be independent but also to fit in. In 1999 Jessica graduated from high school and learned to ride the bus. Although she continued to live with her parents, Jessica would on occasion run away, sometimes to a friend's house, other times to a homeless shelter downtown. But she would also always phone home, to let her parents know where she was.

Unbeknown to her parents, Jessica began to hang out with a group of street youths in Pioneer Courthouse Square in downtown Portland. The youths were led by James Daniel Nelson, a convicted murderer who had been released from prison in February 2003. At some point, Jessica was accused by members of the street camp of spreading lies; because of this accusation, approximately twelve youths, including Nelson, repeatedly beat and stabbed Jessica before spraying her with lighter fluid and setting her on fire.

Mark Price died on November 28, 2010, in a Tucson, Arizona, hospital from complications of leukemia.[2] Gravely ill, Mark was awaiting a bone-marrow transplant that would never come—not because a suitable donor could not be found but because of budget reductions. On October 1 of that year Arizona legislators imposed drastic reductions on state Medicaid services to help balance the budget. According to the *Arizona Republic*, "Benefit cuts to the 1.3 million adults enrolled in the Arizona Health Care Cost Containment System (AHCCCS) include certain liver, bone marrow, heart, lung and pancreas transplants, as well as annual physicals, podiatry, insulin pumps and emergency dental care." For 2011 savings were projected to be $5.3 million, with an additional $20 million in matching federal funds lost. Spokespersons for the AHCCCS explained that the cuts were calculated to "affect the fewest people or, in the case of transplants, represented the least effective treatment."[3] In other words, the treatments eliminated were the ones not considered cost-effective.

These two examples suggest that violence, although seemingly self-evident, is not always as it appears.[4] The brutal murder of Jessica Williams is readily grasped as a violent act; the death of Mark Price, perhaps less so. The difference, some might argue, lies in the fact that the killing of Williams was intentional; Nelson and his friends deliberately chose to take the life of the young woman. For Price, however, there is no apparent intentionality to his death; he was not singled out but rather was the victim of a tragic set of circumstances.

Or so it would appear, for in the same year Price was denied a life-saving procedure because of budgetary cuts, public officials in Arizona raised more than $23 million to support their political campaigns.[5] In other words, choices were made—by identifiable persons—to determine where monies would be spent. Could not sufficient funds have been found to maintain adequate medical services?

The deaths of Williams and Price provide insight into the vagaries of violence but also, by extension, criminality, for the killing of Williams was criminal, while the death of Price was not. This disparity relates, once more, to the notion that Williams's murder was intentional; it was an action committed by a perpetrator against a victim. Conversely, there was no readily identifiable person directly responsible for the death of Price. Moreover, Price was not killed, strictly speaking, although he was disallowed life through the denial of life-saving medical services. In the following chapters I argue that how violence and crime are constituted is intimately related to how lives are valued in society. The determination of violence, especially criminal violence, is neither neutral nor objective.

Too often, theories and models have fetishized violence, thereby obfuscating the fundamental socio-spatial relations and processes that give violence its meaning. Consider, for example, the definition provided by the World Health Organization (WHO) whereby violence is "the intentional use of physical force or power, threatened or actual, against oneself, another person, or against a group or community that either results in or has a high likelihood of resulting in injury, death, psychological harm, mal-development or deprivation."[6] As Etienne Krug and his colleagues explain, this definition attempts to be inclusive, to encompass all forms of violence. With that definition of violence, acts such as murder, rape, and physical beatings are readily understood as violent. Statistics, in turn, indicate the prevalence of such actions. Worldwide, approximately 4,400 people die every day because of intentional acts of self-directed, interpersonal, or collective violence. In the year 2000, for example, an estimated 1.6 million people died violent deaths. About one-half of all deaths resulted from suicide, one-fifth were war related, and another third were homicide related.[7]

The death of Jessica Williams would be included in such statistics; the death of Price would not. But what if for the moment we consider violence to be any action (or inaction) that results in injury, maldevelopment, or death? In other words, what if we move beyond an individually oriented and biologically premised understanding of violence to consider how certain policies, practices, and programs may have the same consequences for human survivability? It is undeniable that, standing alongside the 4,400 people who are *directly* killed, are many millions more who die from other, *preventable* causes. Each year, for example, an estimated 3.5 million children worldwide under five years of age die from pneumonia and diarrhea.[8] Most (if not all) of these deaths could be prevented if those families affected had better access to clean water, medicine, and health care. In the United States alone (in 2010) an estimated 26,100 people between twenty-five and sixty-four years of age died prematurely due to a lack of health-care coverage; this figure translates to a death toll of 72 people—such as Mark Price—dying per day simply because they had no access to health care.[9] Deaths from breast and cervical cancers, for example, occur disproportionately among women who are uninsured; rates for women of color are especially high. In part, this high death rate exists because many women—especially those living in poverty or nearly so—are unable to obtain mammograms and Pap tests that may detect cancer at an earlier stage.[10] By way of comparison, an estimated 80 people die in the United States each day from gun-related violence. One form of premature death makes the headlines; the other does not.

Why such a gap exists, between the very visible (albeit highly contentious) debates surrounding gun-related deaths and the near silence on other forms of preventable deaths, such as those stemming from lax workplace safety regulations, is complex. In part, however, the explanation lies in the fact that gun-related deaths (and other forms of direct violence) are often very spectacular and very immediate. Furthermore, the promotion of (selected) acts of gun violence plays into the fears and insecurities that are used to eliminate social welfare programs. Contrast this drama to the sometimes agonizingly slow death attributable to hunger or disease that actually stems from the elimination of social programs or safety regulations.

To counter the prevalence of narrowly defined theories of violence that focused exclusively (if not entirely) on direct violence, Johan Galtung in 1969 introduced the concept of "structural" violence.[11] He began by noting six dimensions to violence, provisionally defined as being "present when human beings are being influenced so that their actual somatic and mental realizations are below their potential realization."[12] Galtung has argued that a key distinction among different forms of violence is "whether or not there is a subject (person) who acts."[13] Direct violence is therefore said to occur when there is an *identifiable* actor who commits an act of violence—defined as any action that reduces human potential; structural violence (also termed "social injustice" by Galtung) occurs when no such actor is identifiable. Galtung elaborates that whereas in the first case (direct violence) these consequences can be traced back to concrete persons or actors, in the second case (structural violence) this act of blaming is no longer meaningful. There may not be any person who directly harms another person in the structure. The violence is built into the structure and shows up as unequal power and, consequently, unequal life chances.[14]

Structural violence, in other words, "occurs as inequalities structured into a society so that some have access to social resources that foster individual and community well-being—high quality education and health care, social status, wealth, comfortable and adequate housing, and efficient civic services—while others do not."[15] Consequently, "to understand who is made most vulnerable where and how socially produced harms are naturalized discursively and materially, it is necessary to theorize specific economic, political, and social relations of oppression and domination and how they articulate (or intersect) in particular historical, geographic moments."[16]

Galtung's separation of direct and structural violence is a positive move; it highlights the myriad ways in which harm may occur. It is a mistake, however, to categorize structural violence a priori as either unintentional or as having no identifiable agent. Consider again the harm that may result from a denial of health care. Clearly some decision—made by knowable individuals—is rendered whereby some identifiable people have access while others do not. Is it not a fair assumption that the *intentional* slashing of health-care items in a budget will result in some level of harm? It is certainly worthwhile to contemplate both the intentionality and agency underlying the implementation of institutional structures that have the potential to cause knowable harm, suffering, injury, and death.

The work of Galtung can, however, be viewed as an ongoing attempt to expand the definition of violence, to move beyond what was viewed as an overly narrow and restrictive understanding of violence that neglected many processes and practices that harmed, injured, or killed people. Indeed, Edwin Sutherland, writing decades before Galtung, forwarded the concept of white-collar criminality, which ultimately led to engagement with what is now known as corporate violence.[17] Newton Garver, likewise, has attempted to broaden the concept of violence. A contemporary of Galtung, Garver has emphasized both the moral and political underpinnings of definitions of violence, observing that "those who deplore violence loudest and most publicly are usually identified with the status quo—school principals, businessmen, politicians, ministers." He has explained, however, that "what they deplore is generally overt attacks on property or against the 'good order of society.' They rarely see violence in defense of the status quo in the same light as violence directed against it."[18] Equating violence more with violation than with force, Garver has argued that it is insufficient to focus exclusively on murder, beatings, and rapes; instead, it is necessary to address other actions whereby a human may be violated.

Galtung, Garver, and other social scientists who have promoted more expansive definitions of violence have been met with stiff resistance—and the debate between those who champion minimalist or restrictive definitions as opposed to those lauding more expansive definitions remains as vibrant today as it was in the 1970s.[19] In an early critique of Garver, for example, Joseph Betz cautions, "If violence is violating a person or a person's rights, then every social wrong is a violent one, every crime against another a violent crime, every sin against one's neighbor an act of violence. If violence is whatever violates a person and his rights of body, dignity, or autonomy, then lying to or about another, embezzling, locking one out of his house, insulting, and gossiping are all violent acts." Betz concludes that "this enlargement of the extension of the term comes at considerable cost, for there is simply no extension left for the term 'nonviolent social wrong.'"[20]

C. A. J. Coady also guards against overly capacious definitions because they may be appropriated politically. Broad terms such as "structural violence," Coady argues, "tend to serve the interests of the political left by including within the extension of the term 'violence' a great range of social injustices and inequalities." This expansion poses a potential danger, Coady warns, because "this not only allows reformers to say that they are working to eliminate violence when they oppose, say, a government measure to redistribute income in favor of the already rich, but allows revolutionaries to offer, in justification of their resort to violence, even where it is terrorist, the claim that they are merely meeting violence with violence." Conversely, "legitimist" (and therefore narrower) definitions—that the word *violence* must refer *only* to the illegal or illegitimate use of force—are most often promoted by conservative or neoliberal right-wing groups.[21]

Advocating for a narrow definition predicated on direct, intentional force, Coady concludes (erroneously, I believe) that the "use of the wide definition seems likely to encourage the cosy but ultimately stultifying belief that there is one problem, the problem of (wide) violence, and hence it must be solved as a whole with one set of techniques."[22] Here, Coady misses the point, for the argument in favor of expanded definitions is just the opposite. Galtung, Sutherland, and Garver, in particular, argue that because violence assumes so many forms, it requires a multiplicity of solutions. Policies designed to address rape or murder, for example, will not address famine or lack of access to medical care.

I agree with Coady and other critics, however, in that *any definition of violence is necessarily political.* Also, I take issue with the fact that most, if not all, definitions seem to take violence as given, as some*thing* that exists. Consequently, I eschew both minimalist and expansive definitions of violence, for it is my contention that violence per se does not exist. This statement is not intended to deny the salience of particular concrete actions—and inactions—that result in harm, injury, or loss of life nor is it intended to provide a simplistic argument that violence is discursive. The shooting deaths of more than eighty people *per day* in the United States are ample testimony to the materiality of what we take as violence, just as the tens of thousands of occupational injuries and fatalities that occur yearly in the United States must be considered incidences of violence.

My argument unfolds as a series of propositions: two general and one specific. My first general proposition is that *violence is an abstraction.* Many scholars of violence argue that societal conflict is unavoidable, that humans are by nature competitive and aggressive. And while these arguments are most apparent in strands of evolutionary psychology—which postulates that there is a strong biological component to violence—there are many other positions in which the presumption is that conflict and violence are simply part of human nature. Violence, in short, is given its own reality: it simply exists. Conversely, I argue against the existence of a pre-given, pre-discursive ontology. Violence is not biological—at least, not in the genetic or molecular sense. Violence is most assuredly associated with the biological ability to live, reproduce, and die; there is necessarily a materialist foundation to behaviors we may recognize and agree are violent. Consequently, the biology of existence is conceived in the social. What we understand (and potentially criminalize) as violence is itself the outcome of political practice—practice that is conditioned by any given social formation. The constitution of violence, in other words, is internal to the social relations of any given society. Hence, "laying off workers, paying low wages, avoiding costly environmental regulations, avoiding taxes, skirting health and safety regulations, moving production to low-wage areas, can all be justified by the unavoidable imperatives of profit."[23] These practices are unique to capitalism, but to what degree are any or all of these intentional actions and inactions that lead to harm, injury, and death considered either criminal or violent? The answer depends on how violence and crime are politically abstracted.

In other words, in arguing against the existence of a transhistorical concept of violence, I postulate that violence (and, by extension, crime) is an internally derived abstraction that is a contingent and contextual product of human interaction.

My second general proposition, therefore, is that to theorize the broader salience of violence in society *one must abstract violence from dominant modes of production* that give rise to particular concrete acts. In the first volume of *Capital* Marx makes a distinction between "abstract" and "concrete" labor; he does so in order to focus attention on the valorization of capital: the generation of surplus value. For Marx, labor in general is an abstraction, because most people believe that the concept of labor has existed in all social systems—that labor is transhistorical and transgeographical.[24] In other words, outside of a Marxist perspective, labor is taken as given, as something that is ubiquitous in humankind and is natural. Violence, as the above definitions and approaches indicate, is similarly posited as something natural and essential. Consequently, there is a tendency to focus on measurable, mappable, concrete acts, such as rape, homicide, or suicide. This tendency is readily apparent in various empirical studies of crime and violence that are, in actuality, indirect studies of how certain acts are defined—counted—as criminal or violent. Those actions (and inactions) that are not considered violent, or have not been criminalized, are not counted. In the process, moreover, violence begins to assume the form of a static, independent variable (i.e., the likelihood of any given individual either perpetuating an act of violence or of becoming a victim of an act of violence). In turn, other abstractions, such as poverty, education, race, and so forth, are held as dependent variables. The relationship among these surface appearances assumes the form of causality. However, such studies provide insufficient attention to the hidden totality that internally relates the supposed disarticulated variables. By falling into this analytic trap, scholars make the mistake of conflating "real" concrete acts with specific abstractions, instead of seeing such acts for what they are: acts that are historically and geographically contingent and dialectically related to the dominant mode of production from which they emerge.

Combined, the first two general propositions lead to my third, and most specific, proposition: contemporary understandings of violence and crime within neoliberal capitalism are *predicated on a market logic of, in medical ethics terminology, "letting die."* Simply put, capitalism—but especially its neoliberal, neoconservative variant—is structured around a particular value system, a valuation of life that, in turn, contributes to a particular abstraction of violence and crime. This is not to suggest that all forms of violence under capitalism are subsumed under some generic notion of class struggle or that all other systems of domination and oppression that are manifest in violent actions (and inactions) are derivative of class. It is, however, meant to acknowledge that violence *appears* in different forms depending on the dominant mode of production.

These propositions require considerable explanation and are developed in subsequent chapters. Thus, in the remainder of this chapter I forward the argument that violence and crime must be viewed not as transhistorical or transgeographical categories but as abstractions. I also argue that violence and crime must be materially grounded in particular modes of production; chapter 2, therefore, provides an overview of materialism and the mode of production concept in general, followed by a discussion of the development of capitalism as a particular, concrete mode of production. In chapter 3 I theorize how capitalism itself is structured around a particular, abstract violence, namely, that of letting die. Through an engagement with the notion of positive and negative rights, I detail how the market logics of capitalism are determinant of a pervasive indifference to life whereby some individuals are disallowed life because they fail to conform to the dictates of capital accumulation. Chapter 4 provides an extended, historically grounded discussion of the market logics of letting die with respect to those individuals deemed redundant in society. A summary of my argument, and path forward, is provided in the final chapter.

DEVELOPING AN ABSTRACTION OF VIOLENCE

The social theorist Michel Foucault premised his writings on a very simple yet deeply profound assertion. In *The Birth of Biopolitics*, a series of lectures presented in 1978–79, Foucault ponders, "Let's suppose that universals do not exist." He continues, "How can you write history if you do not accept a priori the existence of things like the state, society, the sovereign, and subjects?" This was, he explains, the foundation of his previous research on the history of madness. Foucault's "method consisted in saying: Let's suppose that madness does not exist. If we suppose that it does not exist, then what can history make of these different events and practices which are apparently organized around something that is supposed to be madness?"[25] Following Foucault's cue, I begin with the premise that violence does not exist.

To propose that violence does not exist is not to suggest that there is no materiality. I am not proposing some form of idealism, claiming that violence is ultimately, and in a reductive sense, discursive. Rather, it is to acknowledge that our knowledge of violence—while experiential, in the sense of some*thing* that may be experienced—does not simply appear. Immanuel Kant, for example, presumed that all knowledge begins with experience; however, for Kant, experience merely provided the raw material for thought and reason. Grounded experiences—the concrete—cannot provide the methods by which empirical facts are ordered, classified, and related.[26] This can be accomplished only through thought. The crucial component, however, is how thought relates with objectivity. Kant therefore argued that a real, objective world—one that could be sensed (and measured)—did exist; where he differed from the empiricists was his assertion that empiricism alone could not provide an adequate understanding of that world. To do so required the use of rational concepts by which data—supplied from our senses—would be interpreted. Space, time, and causality, for example, are not empirical characteristics of the real world but instead are mental constructs; moreover, these constructs are the *preconditions* for interpreting reality.[27] To interpret the world, concepts must precede any knowledge derived from the senses.

When I look out my office window I see an objective world. However, my interpretation of that reality is conditioned a priori by a set of concepts. As a geographer—following a Kantian approach—I see a suburban landscape with various land-use patterns; a biologist, conversely, may see an assemblage of ecosystems. In either case, our understanding—our interpretation—of the view is predicated on our preconceptions. There is, therefore, no single interpretive reality, although there is a unique objective reality. As Peter Strawson writes, "What really emerges here is that aspect of [Kant's] transcendental idealism which finally denies to the natural world any existence independent of our 'representations' or perceptions."[28]

Kant, however, writes himself into a contradiction. He acknowledges that we respond to an external objective reality, which suggests that the real world *causes* our sense impressions of it. Stated differently, causality must be a property of empirically known objects. However, Kant also argues that causality is a concept internal to us, that is, causation is not a property of the thing itself.[29]

Hegel provided a possible way out of Kant's conundrum by forwarding a *dialectical* understanding.[30] According to Bertell Ollman, "Dialectics is a way of thinking that brings into focus the full range of changes and interactions that occur in the world."[31] This is counter to more conventional and pervasive epistemologies—of which empiricism is exemplary—that disaggregate the world into discrete and unrelated entities. So conceived, a disaggregated epistemology limits analysis to the surface appearance of objects. Dialectics, conversely, opens space for a deeper and more profound analysis. Reality, from a dialectical vantage point, consists not simply of disparate "things" but also *processes* and *relations*. In other words, reality is more than the epiphenomena that can be counted, classified, and mapped; it is more than the observation that strikes us immediately and directly, which masks the underlying structures and social relations. Dialectics therefore restructures our thinking and our ontological reality by replacing the commonsense notion of "thing" with notions of "process," "relation," and "change." This restructured thinking thus allows us to reconsider "how something works or happened while simultaneously developing [an] understanding of the system in which things could work or happen in just this way."[32]

Hegel maintained that previous philosophical thinking was inadequate, for it was based on an overly static form of logic derived from Aristotle.

Adhering to a *principle of noncontradiction*, this form of logic holds that an object cannot be both "A" and "Not-A."[33] In other words, objects exist as discreet, fixed *things*. Such a logic system underpins much of our contemporary way of understanding the world: one is presumed to be male or female, guilty or innocent, violent or nonviolent, living or dead. To be sure, many of these binaries have been destabilized. Developments in medical technology, for example, have introduced the "living dead" person—one who is technically, legally, brain dead yet still retains certain physiological properties that denote life. Such a blurring of previously fixed categories (e.g., dead or alive) is fundamental for contemporary systems of organ transplantation. In other areas, however, a more Aristotelian conception of nature holds sway. In the legal system, for example, one is still considered to be guilty or not guilty; it is generally not possible to be "just a little guilty." Likewise, one of the most contentious issues confronting contemporary society—and not just in the Western world—is the binary of male and female.

The idea that one can never step into the same river twice is held to originate from the ancient Greek philosopher Heraclitus. This proposition maintains that everything is in a state of flux and that while surface appearances suggest that the river, for example, is the *same* river, in actuality it is in constant motion, constantly changing. However, equally if not more significant is Heraclitus's contention that "unity" exists in apparent opposites. According to G. S. Kirk, "Heraclitus' unification of apparent opposites depended in its clearest form upon an unfailing reciprocal movement between extremes: night succeeds day and day night, therefore night-day is a single continuum; so too with the other pairs of opposites."[34] Combined, these two concepts—of constant, permanent change and the unity of opposites—would greatly inform Hegel and, in turn, Marx.

Hegel argued that the principle of noncontradiction distorted the complexity of how both the human mind *and* the objective world operated. For Hegel, the only permanent reality was the reality of change, and the key to understanding reality as process was to understand that everything in existence in some sense contained within itself its opposite or its negation.[35] To take an obvious example, children and adults are in many respects considered opposites. Indeed, a fundamental principle of many criminal justice systems is to determine the dividing line between childhood and adulthood. However, there can be no clear separation between one phase and another. Logicians, for example, distinguish between "phase sortals" and "substance sortals."[36] Following Jeff McMahan, a phase sortal designates a kind to which an individual may belong through only part of its existence; the concepts "infant," "adolescent," and "adult," for example, are phase sortals. Any given individual will at some point cease being an infant and become an adolescent; likewise, an adolescent will cease to exist, to be replaced by an adult. Conversely, a substance sortal designates a kind to which an individual necessarily belongs throughout its entire existence; these indicate what some*thing* or some*one* essentially is. The concept "human" is a substance sortal. A human cannot cease to be a human and still exist; an adolescent can cease to be an adolescent but continue to be a human.[37]

The concepts of both unity and sortals are extremely significant for the constitution of violence and crime. Criminal justice systems, for example, are often founded upon the temporal separation of humanity into distinct phase sortals, such as juvenile and adult. Indeed, different criminal justice systems have been developed in response to these philosophical distinctions. And yet, in contemporary society we see also the uneasy existence of substance sortals, for example, in the concept of career criminals and the attitude that some people are naturally and always evil.

Returning to the paradox of Kant, Hegel insisted on the unity of opposites—a position more akin to that of substance sortals. Any given society, Hegel maintained, would contain within it the seeds of change. Likewise, it was this notion of unity that combined the totality of human experience—a totality that had been split by Kant into "mind" and "outside reality." For Hegel, societies were composed of various institutions, laws, morals, and beliefs. These concepts embodied certain ideals that were related to a particular stage of development of reason, which Hegel termed the "spirit of the age."[38] For Hegel, it was the spirit of the age that informed one's preconcepts of reality; it was these ideals that informed how one understood reality. Our representations of reality, in other words, are internally related to our consciousness, which is both historically and geographically grounded.

Hegel argued that societies change because of contradictions that emerge within a collective consciousness. Such change may occur, for example, when people begin to take notice that increased surveillance techniques or repressive policing practices contradict their ideals of freedom and liberty. Hegel suggested that contradictions lead to societal transformation and that these contradictions are dialectic in that the conditions for potential transformation are found within society itself. Henceforth, contradictions, which may be said to drive change, are *internal* to society itself, and therefore any given society holds the potential for its own transformation. John Rees elaborates Hegel's view:

> The transition from one form of society to another [is] a result of a contradiction that emerges in the spirit of the age. When nations or historical epochs are born, they are free of contradiction. The contradiction between the total potential rationality and freedom of mankind (Spirit) and the particular social structure is not in evidence. . . . But when the "objective world, that exists and persists in a particular form of worship, customs, constitution and political laws" hardens and grows old, it ceases to represent the full potential for reason that has been developing among its citizens. Spirit leaves the people. Within society, some people begin to look at their own laws and institutions and question whether they really are rational or merely accidental, contingent, and irrational.[39]

Hegel therefore premised that: (1) societies must be viewed as totalities, (2) societies are in constant dialectic change, (3) change is predicated on contradictions that are internal to society, and (4) these contradictions originate in the collective consciousness of society. To the first three premises, Marx was in general agreement. Marx also shared Hegel's understanding that ideas or concepts did not have an independent existence, that laws, regulations, and institutions were not transhistorical but particular to any given society. It was with the notion that change is found in consciousness that Marx disagreed. Thus, in his critique of Hegel—and of those philosophers who followed Hegel's lead—Marx steadfastly refused to abide by something as mystical as "spirit."

The fundamental problem for Marx was that Hegel began with an abstraction—the "spirit of the age." Marx, writing with Engels, averred that

> in direct contrast to German philosophy which descends from heaven to earth, here it is a matter of ascending from earth to heaven. That is to say, not of setting out from what men say, imagine, conceive, nor from men as narrated, thought of, imagined, conceived, in order to arrive at men in the flesh; but setting out from real, active men, and on the basis of their real life-process demonstrating the development of the ideological reflexes and echoes of this life-process. *The phantoms formed in the brains of men are also, necessarily, sublimates of their material life-process, which is empirically verifiable and bound to material premises. Morality, religion, metaphysics, and all the rest of ideology as well as the forms of consciousness corresponding to these, thus no longer retain the semblance of independence.* They have no history, no development; but men, developing their material production and their material intercourse, alter, along with this their actual world, also their thinking and the products of their thinking.[40]

In another passage Marx inverts Hegel or, as he puts it, stands Hegel on his head: "My dialectical method is, in its foundations, not only different from the Hegelian, but exactly opposite to it. For Hegel, the process of thinking ... is the creator of the real world, and the real world is only the external appearance of the idea. With me the reverse is true: the ideal is nothing but the material world reflected in the mind of man, and translated into forms of thought." Acknowledging his debt—and critique—of Hegel, Marx then states that "the mystification which the dialectic suffers in Hegel's hands by no means prevents him from being the first to present its general forms of motion in a comprehensive and conscious manner. With him it is standing on its head. It must be inverted, in order to discover the rational kernel within the mystical shell."[41]

From this vantage point, Marx and Engels are able to assert, "It is not consciousness that determines life, but life that determines consciousness."[42] In other words, rather than succumbing to accepting the existence of a mystical, phantomlike abstraction—the spirit of the age— Marx declares that ideologies (e.g., the stuff of law, religion, morality, and so on) are materially grounded, that it is the activities surrounding the production, circulation, and consumption of life's necessities that are determinant. Marx therefore stands Hegel on his head precisely because Hegel begins with a general abstraction rather than the concrete, real world. In "The Holy Family," Marx and Engels criticize Hegel's idealism. They write,

> If from real apples, pears, strawberries, and almonds I form the general idea "Fruit," if I go further and imagine that my abstract idea "Fruit," derived from real fruit, is an entity existing outside me, is indeed the true essence of the pear, the apple, etc.; then, in the language of speculative philosophy I am declaring that "Fruit" is the substance of the pear, the apple, the almond, etc. I am saying, therefore, that to be a pear is not essential to the pear, that to be an apple is not essential to the apple; that what is essential to these things is not their real being, perceptible to the senses, but the essence that I have extracted from them and then foisted on them, the essence of my idea—"Fruit."[43]

In contemporary phrasing, "fruit" is a discourse, and while discourses create the objects of which they speak, they are also not external to those objects. Hence, the discourse of "fruit" brings into existence the concept "fruit," but it does so from a historically and geographically specific standpoint. Note also that it is possible to have the material existence of things we identify as apples, pears, and almonds *without* the concept of fruit. Simply stated, (material) existence precedes (idealistic) essence. Essence, in this sense, is derived conceptually—abstractly—from the existence of very specific, very real *things*.

The concept "violence" is similarly derived—abstracted—from the existence of specific practices. However, it should be clear that different abstractions from specific practices will lead to different, perhaps contradictory, concepts of violence. Thus, for clarity's sake, let us rewrite Marx and Engels's passage on fruit and substitute violence:

> If from rape, murder, and torture I form the general idea "violence," if I go further and imagine that my abstract idea "violence," derived from real acts, is an entity existing outside me [i.e. external to society], is indeed the true essence of the specific actions; then, in the language of speculative philosophy [or criminology] I am declaring that "violence" is the substance of the actions. I am saying, therefore, that to commit a particular action is not essential to that action, that murder is not essential to the taking of life; that what is essential to these practices is not their real occurrence, perceptible to the senses, but the essence that I have extracted from them and then foisted on them, the essence of my idea—"violence."

Thus, what is constituted as violence is derived from my preconceived idea of violence—divorced from any particular action. Heretofore the study of violence has suffered from a similar idealism. Rather than beginning with the concrete, scholars and theorists have started with the most general abstraction (i.e., violence) and subsequently attempted to move to the level of the concrete. Very little discussion has therefore centered on the development of violence as a materially grounded concept; to refuse to contemplate the abstraction of violence is to introduce an element of mysticism into our studies.

Marx and Engels elaborate on the difficulties of working downward from the level of abstraction to that of concreteness. They explain that,

> having reduced the different real fruits to the one fruit of abstraction— "Fruit," speculation must, in order to attain some appearance of real content, try somehow to find its way back from "Fruit," from Substance to the different profane real fruits, the pear, the apple, the almond, etc. It is as hard to produce real fruits from the abstract idea "Fruit" as it is easy to produce this abstract idea from real fruits. Indeed it is impossible to arrive at the opposite of an abstraction without relinquishing the abstraction.[44]

It is this tendency—to begin with abstractions—that bears much of Marx's critique. Hegel's fundamental error sprang from his appreciation of a real problem, namely, that it is impossible simply to stare at the world as it immediately presents itself to our eyes and hope to understand it.[45] To begin with violence in the abstract is therefore to privilege an idealist account, which is akin to having to explain *why* "fruit" appears as apples, pears, and so on. It is rather more appropriate to provide an ascending analysis, to question why some actions (or inactions) are conceived as violent while others are not. This explains why the killing of Jessica Williams is readily viewed as violent whereas the letting die of Mark Price—through a lack of medical care—is not viewed as violent. Our a priori abstractions of violence mask certain actions—and most inactions—as violent. In turn, our inability to see (certain) actions and inactions will affect our ensuing constitution of criminal behavior. As elaborated in subsequent chapters, the key question becomes: why are some actions and inactions abstracted as violence while others are not?

DIALECTICS AND THE PROCESS OF ABSTRACTION

Within the social sciences there is a long-standing empiricist tradition of focusing on measurable, mappable concrete acts. We may, for example, map the distribution of shootings. From these observable, recordable patterns we then abstract certain understandings and interpretations, such as the concept of gun violence. To this end, various government agencies, such as the Federal Bureau of Investigation, routinely collapse a range of specific, real, concrete acts into the concept of violence: homicide, assault, rape, and so forth. Ironically, these are compiled in such compendiums as the FBI's uniform crime reports—a material manifestation of the transformation of qualitatively different acts into quantitatively equal units.

It is necessary to understand, however, that secondary concepts—such as gun violence—are not concrete acts. Gun violence is also an abstraction; it is a quantitative representation of specific, qualitatively different actions. For example, is the accidental discharge of a firearm—an unintentional action that results in the death of a young child—considered a type of gun violence? Or is it simply a tragic mishap? Does it constitute a case of criminal negligence?

Although many scholars of violence acknowledge the different concrete forms or modalities" in which violence appears, there remains an element of mysticism to these studies. Alex Alvarez and Ronet Bachman, for example, argue that "our understanding [of violence] is highly situational and contingent." They further argue that "context is . . . extremely important in helping shape our understanding of and reaction to violent acts and actors." What is less appreciated in this proposition is that contingency and contextuality should not be viewed as being external to any given social formation. Alvarez and Bachman indicate that the context of violence is shaped, in part, by several factors, including the victim, the offender, the specific nature of the violence, the location of the violence, and the rationale for the violence. These contextual factors *appear* to be immutable but are in fact conditioned by the conditioning of the broader relations of society. Thus, the assessment of how the concept of "victim" is related to forms of violence is internally mediated by the specific forms in which a "victim" is conceived (abstracted) for any particular society. To this end, Alvarez and Bachman note that "if the victim is someone with whom we can identify . . . we are more likely to condemn the violence."[46] Following this logic we may surmise that in slave societies, the brutality of enslavement might not be viewed as violent from the vantage point of the slave owner. This calls into question any attempt to empirically measure levels of violence throughout history or, for that matter, across geographic areas.

It is also not appropriate to adopt a historical evolutionist approach such as that found in evolutionary psychology. Here, the mistake is to begin with historically defined specification and then trace that understanding over time and space. As Stuart Hall asks, "Do we . . . assume that there is a common, universal practice . . . which has always existed, which has then been subject to an evolutionary historical development which can be steadily traced through: a practice which, therefore, we can reduce to its common-sense content and employ as the obvious, uncontested starting-point for analysis?"[47] I agree with Hall in answering with a definitive "no."

Take, for example, the apparently precise definitional understanding of poverty. The U.S. Census Bureau uses a calculation based on the ratio of family income and poverty threshold. This latter concept is a dollar amount that is statistically derived but not a complete description of what people and families need to survive; this is an important caveat, as we will see in chapter 2. To illustrate, in 2011 the poverty threshold for a family of five (two children, their mother, father, and great-aunt) was $27,517. If that family's total income was above the threshold, the family was considered to be not living in poverty (a situation of "income surplus"); if annual income was below that level (a situation of "income deficit"), the family was considered to be living in poverty.[48] What is significant here is that poverty is defined according to income level or, stated differently, the amount of money available to satisfy (a statistically derived abstraction of) familial needs. But notice that—by this definition—poverty cannot be said to exist in nonmonetary societies. In subsistence-based economies, where family members produce for their own needs or, to take an extreme example, in a society where there is no established trading system, the notion of income is nonsensical. Poverty, in other words, cannot be considered a transhistorical or transgeographical concept. To ask if poverty existed in hunting-gathering societies twenty thousand years ago or in feudal England in 1300 and then try to compare "levels of poverty" across time and over space is a non sequitur. I argue that just as this example shows for poverty, the same situation exists when considering concepts such as violence, crime, and value.

Any attempt to identify those elements that remain common to all epochs and all types of social formation will by necessity impart a particular ideology that is more indicative of that elemental foundation than it is of a general understanding of violence. In other words, the assertion of particular contextual features of violence defined in an era of neoliberalism will identify those elements unique to neoliberalism; conversely, those contextual features identified in an era of feudalism, for example, would reflect those elements associated with feudal relations. The development of different forms of murder (e.g., homicide, manslaughter) testifies against the use of static, transhistorical, and transgeographical categories. So too does the concept of theft. Much like violence as an abstraction, the act of thievery seems self-evident. And yet, the notion of theft assumes decidedly different forms depending on how property is conceived. Indeed, we may surmise that in propertyless societies theft by definition cannot exist. Such an understanding negates the belief that the idea of theft is universal. Theft can exist only in those societies that exhibit some form of personal or private ownership.

It would seem that we are at an impasse. If our empirical senses are unable to penetrate the mystification of violence, if we cannot begin with the existence of a stable, "real" object of inquiry, where then are we to begin? How are we to proceed? Here, I argue that a dialectics informed by historical-geographical materialism offers one promising route.

Geographers and other social scientists have in recent years largely turned away from abstraction as a methodology. As Derek McCormack writes, "Abstraction has tended to be cast as a malign process of generalization and simplification through which the complexity of the world is reduced at the expense of the experience of those who live in the concrete reality of this world."[49] Ironically, such a simplification of abstraction downplays the epistemological understandings afforded by such a method and fails to recognize that a dialectical approach to abstraction highlights both the complexity and contingency of the real, objective world.

Marx's methodology of abstraction provides a material grounding to a retheorized and dialectical understanding of violence. Following Marx, we recognize that "even the most abstract categories, despite their validity in all epochs—precisely because they are abstractions—are equally a product of historical conditions even in the specific form of abstractions, and they retain their full validity only for and within the framework of these conditions."[50] In other words, we *assume* that violence has a transhistorical essence *because* it is an abstraction, and, as an abstraction, in its most generalized form, it *appears* to exist as an equivalency across time and space. In actuality, however, concrete actions and inactions we count as violence differ according to the dominant mode of production.

Dialectics, similar to empirical approaches, begins with the "real" concrete—the world as it presents itself to us, the world as it is sensed.

However, whereas more conventional and pervasive epistemologies—of which empiricism is exemplary—disaggregate the world into discrete and unrelated entities, a dialectic approach proceeds to abstract from the "real" concrete (an intellectual activity that disaggregates the whole into mental units from which we think about the sensed world) to the "thought" concrete (the reconstituted and now understood whole that is present in the mind).[51] In other words, the "real" concrete is the world in which we live, that reality we perceive; by disaggregating the world into its constitutive parts through a process of abstraction and then reconstituting the world back to a whole, it is possible theorize the underlying social relations that give rise to the phenomenon in the first place.[52] Dialectics, therefore, is a way of thinking that brings into focus the full range of changes and interactions that occur in the world. It challenges empirically based epistemologies that limit analyses to the surface appearance of objects and thereby opens space for a deeper and more profound analysis. Reality, from a dialectical vantage point, consists not simply of disparate things but of processes and relations. In other words, material reality is more than the epiphenomena that can be counted, classified, and mapped; it is more than the observation that strikes us immediately and directly, that masks the underlying structures and social relations. As David Harvey writes, "Dialectics forces us to ask the question of every 'thing' or 'event' that we encounter: by what process was it constituted and how is it sustained?"[53] To counter the premise of violence as epiphenomena it is therefore necessary to think through violence dialectically, as both abstract and concrete.

To better illustrate the dialectics of abstraction, it is helpful to follow the lead of Paul Paolucci. In his elaboration of Marx's method, Paolucci proposes an assemblage of "conceptual doublets" that are derived from four relationships: general relations, specific relations, abstract frameworks, and concrete facts.[54] For Paolucci, the physical, sensuous, observable reality is the concrete, whereas the abstract refers to the interpretive frameworks erected in our minds to think about the concrete.[55] To this, one may add a distinction between the general and the specific, whereby the former "contains the essential elements found across all social formations of interest" and the latter "is a form of a general category but one whose unique traits mark it as a special case."[56] For example, we may posit family (or poverty, or crime, or violence) as a general category that is purported to be constant in all societies. As it should be clear by this point, however, these categories are not static, and while on the surface we may conceive of these concepts as being timeless (and spaceless), they are anything but. Indeed, as detailed below, the term "family" is a general abstraction and an epiphenomenal category.

Combined, the abstract and the concrete, coupled with the general and the specific, allow for four different heuristic categories: general abstract, general concrete, specific abstract, and specific concrete. These are graphically illustrated in the following:

	ABSTRACT	CONCRETE
GENERAL	General abstract	General concrete
SPECIFIC	Specific abstract	Specific concrete

General abstractions are posited at the broadest level; these abstractions attempt to fix a range of determinants across all social formations captured by the concept.[57] Hence, family, violence, crime, poverty, and so on are presumed to be general abstractions.

For Marx, it is inappropriate to begin with general abstractions. Instead, Marx begins with the specific concrete. These are observable, empirical actions (and inactions); it is here, as Paolucci explains, where empirical data are gathered, for the "specific concrete" are the actual data, events, people, and places that can be observed, counted, and measured.[58] And it is from these observations that Marx developed (and examined) the interrelations between specific abstract models and general concrete cases. By way of illustration, let's continue with the example of the family. "Family" is a general abstraction; we can posit it as a collective unit composed of variously related individuals. To speak of the family devoid of context, however, is inappropriate, given that specific, concrete case studies document that the composition of (and obligations within) the family vary from society to society. However, from materially grounded, specific concrete case studies it is possible to forward both specific abstractions and general concrete examples. We may, for instance, examine the specific concrete family forms in the United States of the twenty-first century. From this examination we might consider the specific abstract forms of family as "monogamous" and "nuclear." Similarly, we may consider the form of the family as a *general* concrete form particular to democratic, capitalist societies—of which the United States is a specific concrete example.

Paolucci provides another useful example. Imagine that you desire to study antebellum cotton plantations in the United States—a specific, concrete category. The cotton plantation is particular type of economic system or, conceived as a general abstraction, a mode of production. The mode of production, however, includes various inner-related components, such as the means, forces, and relations of production. In this situation, let us suppose that we are most interested in understanding something about owner-slave relations. Accordingly, we would want to conceptualize the plantation as a form of a specific abstract category, such as "class relations," which is a particular characteristic of capitalism (as a concrete general category of economic systems, or mode of production) that exhibits distinctive class relations.[59]

The advantage of such a conceptualization of abstractions is that one may re-abstract. Indeed, Marx routinely abstracts from a particular vantage point—hence the misplaced criticism that Marx is contradictory and imprecise in his writings. As Ollman writes, the apparently contradictory positions taken by Marx are the result of different abstractions, that is, the same relations viewed from different sides.[60] Hence, following Paolucci, we may re-abstract "U.S. slavery" as a specific concrete category—distinct from slavery in ancient Greece or Rome. Slavery in the United States is thus a specific, concrete form of class system, conceived as a general abstraction. Slavery itself becomes a specific abstraction. General concrete categories could include forms of slavery under agrarian societies, for example.

How then might violence be abstracted? I begin with Robert Muchembled's informative, historically grounded study on the history of violence in western Europe. My intent is less to critique Muchembled's thesis than it is to highlight how particular abstractions in his argument lead to particular (and debatable) conclusions. Muchembled opens his narrative with the following statement: "From the thirteenth to the twenty-first century, physical violence and brutality in human relationships were on a downward trajectory all over Western Europe."[61] This is a bold declaration, one that carries with it bold implications. What is the source of Muchembled's argument?

Having asserted a downward trajectory of violence, Muchembled explains that the number of homicides documented in judicial archives declined by half from 1600 to 1650 and dropped spectacularly over the next three centuries. And while the number of homicide cases since the 1960s increased slightly, the overall trend—for Muchembled—is unavoidable: Western society has undergone a "civilizing process" since the Middle Ages, reaching a point where violence has become anathema. To make such a claim, however, Muchembled abstracts violence in a very particular, very limited way. War, for example, is considered only insofar as it is a *deterrent* to violence; thus, the killings associated with war contributed to an aversion to homicide. The irony that widespread violence—including the twenty million killed and sixty million wounded in declared wars, civil wars, and other major conflicts of the twentieth century—has created a "powerful blood taboo" seems to be lost on Muchembled.[62]

In his history of violence Muchembled excludes war and other forms of mass violence, limiting his analysis to direct, interpersonal violence. This is graphically illustrated in the following:

	ABSTRACT	CONCRETE
GENERAL	Violence	Interpersonal violence
SPECIFIC	Direct violence	Homicide

The object of study is violence; however, in this case Muchembled descends from a general abstraction (violence) to a specific, concrete category: homicide. This category, in turn, constitutes a more specific version of violence, namely, direct violence. As such, other abstract forms of violence (e.g., structural violence, institutional violence, and so on) are excluded. Likewise, homicide appears as but one form of the more general concrete abstraction of interpersonal violence. Rape could have been included under interpersonal violence but is not. Likewise, war as a form of interpersonal violence—albeit on a grand scale—is excluded. In short, by positing violence as a general abstraction, levels of violence appear to have decreased over seven centuries. I suspect that had Muchembled begun from the specific concrete, as opposed to an ethereal abstraction of violence, his conclusions would have been significantly different.

My point is not to dispute the empirical record that homicide in western Europe has declined over the past seven centuries. Rather, I use this record to illustrate how the process of abstraction frames particular studies in limiting ways. Muchembled begins his study with an abstraction of violence. He then descends in analysis to a limiting concrete action of homicide. However, to suggest that violence has declined based on decreased incidences of (recorded) homicides is spurious, for it masks other, perhaps more prevalent, concrete actions (e.g., war, rape, and assault), as well as all inactions (those omissions that constitute structural violence).

What if we abstract the act of killing differently? We may for the moment, following Muchembled, define the act of killing as the taking of life—homicide. However, when we introduce the concept of "letting die"—a topic to which I return in greater detail in chapter 3—we find an internal contradiction. To kill and to let die result in the same outcome: a person is dead. And from the standpoint of the deceased individual, the cause may or may not matter, for in either case the dead person may have wanted to live. However, abstractly, a difference is posited between killing and letting die, namely, that the former consists of an action whereas the latter (usually) is considered a nonaction. Furthermore, in the first instance (killing) there is presumably a victim whereas in the second there is potentially no victim, given that the act of letting die is not considered a crime. Not only do these distinctions significantly inform contemporary debates on abortion and euthanasia but they also greatly influence how we interpret, say, the denial of health care to impoverished individuals who, in turn, die from lack of access to medicine. This distinction has obvious implications for the aforementioned *contextuality* of violence, as identified by Alvarez and Bachman. Depending on one's position—legal or moral—on letting die, violence does or does not happen and may or may not be counted. With Muchembled's account—and his assertion that violence has precipitously declined over the past four centuries—it is a safe bet to conclude that Muchembled did not include the thousands, if not millions, of people who have over the past few centuries died prematurely due to insufficient medical care.

Different abstractions of violence highlight other potential problems for scholarly accounts. Rape, for example, is in the abstract a violent act. However, as legal histories of both rape and domestic violence detail, the meanings (and hence criminal prosecution) of this form of violence have varied tremendously over time and space. This variability is seen most clearly in discussions of marital rape. As a specific concrete act, marital rape appears similar to other forms of rape; the difference lies in the fact that marital rape constitutes a concrete form of a more specific abstraction, namely, domestic violence. In addition, marital rape occurs within the context of the general concrete category of marital relations.

These forms of abstraction are significant because, historically, similar and specific concrete actions (e.g., a male forcibly penetrating a woman against her will) have been considered different simply because the perpetrator and victim were married to each other. Hence, one action may be considered criminal (and from the standpoint of the legal system, violent) because it occurs between, say, two strangers, whereas another action may not be considered illegal (and, presumably, from the standpoint of the legal system, *not* violent). To the extent that histories of violence are constructed through the use of legal, recorded acts, untold numbers of violent actions simply go missing.

Different abstractions may also highlight (or downplay) other potentially violent actions. Child abuse, for example, constitutes a particular form of the specific abstraction of domestic violence. In this case, however, child abuse is seen as a form of the general concrete relationship between parents and children. It should be obvious at this point that to the extent that the parent-child relation is transformed, so too will our understanding of child abuse. At what age, for example, does one cease being a child and become an adult? We saw earlier that categories such as infant, toddler, adolescent, and adult may be considered as either phase sortals or substance sortals. How these transitory concepts are legally and morally defined will greatly inform subsequent interpretations of violence.

These few examples indicate that there is no singular process, no "correct" way, to abstract. Rather, the process of abstraction *as method* enables one to draw attention to particular *relations*. From the above examples, both marital rape and child abuse are concrete forms of the specific abstraction of domestic violence. The manifestation of these actions, however, is related to different general concrete categories, which is important in that one may want to focus more explicitly on how these general categories differ—both historically and geographically. This calls into question, therefore, the positing of long-term (and universal) trends in violence. Both marriage and parenthood as institutions are not static; both are intimately associated with the material (re)production of society, and, as the dominant mode of production has been transformed, so too have these institutions. It follows that legal and moral understandings (and recognition) of violence have also been transformed.

The process of abstraction, furthermore, provides a more flexible method for highlighting other relationships. One might, for example, consider domestic violence as a general abstraction. Here, we might derive the following set of structural relations:

	ABSTRACT	CONCRETE
GENERAL	Domestic violence	Elder abuse
SPECIFIC	Murder	Parricide

In this abstraction, domestic violence is conceptualized as a general abstraction, with murder (homicide) assuming the role of a specific abstraction—as a specific form of domestic violence. Parricide—the murder of a parent by a child—is a specific concrete action, a form of the more general concrete category of elder abuse.

Academically, therefore, the practice of abstraction may be repeated. In this way it is possible to facilitate an increased level of precision—to refine our analyses, both theoretically and empirically, to determine how relational concepts are historically and geographically situated. Of equal if not greater importance, however, is that an understanding of abstraction as method provides insight into the *politics of violence*, namely, how violence is articulated and debated within the political process.

As stated earlier, within the social sciences there is a long-standing tradition of focusing on measurable, mappable, real concrete acts and identities. We may, for example, map the distribution of shootings. From these patterns, subsequently, we abstract certain understandings, such as the concept of gun violence. However, it is important to realize that the concept of gun violence is not a concrete act; it is a representation of a specific, concrete action—a specific abstraction. And yet, public discourse and political practice attempt to redress gun violence as opposed to specific, concrete events. Following the specific, concrete shootings at Sandy Hook Elementary School in Newtown, Connecticut, for example, much discussion focused on school shootings (a general concrete category) or gun violence (a specific abstraction of the more general abstraction, violence); in turn, specific policies were proposed, including the arming of teachers or the placement of armed police officers on school grounds. Neither of these policies, however, would have prevented the mass shooting at the movie theater in Aurora, Colorado, or the killings associated with the attempted assassination of Rep. Gabby Giffords of Arizona. This indicates how one particular concrete event—a shooting at a school—is abstracted to the level of a general (or specific) abstraction and then stands in as a universal descriptor for all other forms of (gun-related) violence. Furthermore, it highlights how public discourses on violence and subsequent policies are initiated, debated, and yet too often remain at the level of general abstractions of violence; these conversations are not necessarily (for political or economic reasons) brought down to the level of the thought concrete. We therefore risk the mistake of conflating specific concrete actions instead of seeing such acts for what they are—acts that are historically and geographically contingent and dialectically related to the society from which they emerge.

Consider, finally, two other events—both of which occurred just days apart in the United States. On April 15, 2013, two bombs exploded along the course of the Boston Marathon. Three people died and nearly 200 were wounded. On April 17, 2013, a fertilizer plant exploded in the town of West, Texas; 14 people died and approximately 160 were wounded. Both events, in the abstract, are considered violent. From that point, however, meaning and interpretation have varied considerably. The former was represented as an act of terrorism—itself an abstraction. And when two suspects were identified as being Muslim, the "terrorist" acts were represented as stemming from Islamic extremism—itself an abstraction. The latter event, conversely, was presented as an unfortunate accident; the blast, while tragic, was portrayed (at least initially) as unintentional, and therefore no deeper meaning was assigned.

Whereas the Boston Marathon bombing is a specifically abstracted form of terrorism, there is no *conceptual* place for considering the explosion in West. While both are considered violent and both satisfy the general concrete form of "explosion," the two events are not considered equivalent. Here, again, this differentiation indicates that public discourses and subsequent policies are *initiated* at the level of the concrete but *debated* at the level of a predetermined abstraction; conversations are rarely if ever brought down to the level of the thought concrete. To ignore this differentiation is to conflate "real" concrete acts (and, in the process, to imbue them within an ontological status) instead of seeing such acts for what they are—acts that are historically and geographically contingent and dialectically related to the society from which they emerge.

CONCLUSIONS

Violence has an outwardly enduring quality; it is presumed to both exist and have an existence that transcends time and space. As Don Mitchell writes, "On the surface, violence appears to be a simple concept: it is the act of doing harm, injury, or desecration through physical force."[63] Thus, if an individual is stabbed by a knife, for example, it seemingly matters little whether the act was perpetrated in fifteenth-century England or nineteenth-century China; in either case, violence is said to have *happened*.

Following scholarly efforts, by Johan Galtung in particular, the theoretical understanding of violence has been extended. Galtung distinguished between physical or direct violence—as illustrated by the above example—and structural violence. Subsequent work has identified many other forms of violence, including but not limited to symbolic violence, cultural violence, slow violence, subjective violence, objective violence, systemic violence, and institutional violence. And while many of these reworkings of violence have highlighted the contingency and contextuality of the appearance of violence, there remains an underlying tendency to treat violence as a universal abstraction.

As David Harvey writes, "Concepts and categories cannot be viewed as having an independent existence, as being universal abstractions true for all time."[64] Indeed, following Marx, "even the most abstract categories, despite their validity—precisely because of their abstractness—for all epochs, are nevertheless, in the specific character of this abstraction, themselves likewise a product of historic relations, and possess their full validity only for and within these relations."[65] Violence is no different; conceptually, violence must be understood as not having a universal quality—an a priori ontological existence.

At a visceral level we understand beatings and shootings as violent acts. We may not agree that these are legal or criminal, but we sense that the actions are most assuredly violent. Other actions—and especially inactions—do not readily appear as violent. The discrepancy between that which is visible and that which is not forms the crux of my argument.

2

Materialism and Mode of Production

Capitalism intrinsically negates individual and collective capacity for equal political representation, social rights, and quality of life, given that its base assumption is that the value of life is determined by its success in individually accumulating and trading wealth.

—J. D. TAYLOR, *Negative Capitalism: Cynicism in the Neoliberal Era*

Violence has no materiality in and of itself. By making this statement I do not imply that people are not hit, slapped, stabbed, shot, or left to die. But these are particular concrete actions (or inactions) that may or may not be considered violent. Therefore, in order to theorize the broader salience of violence in society one must abstract violence from dominant modes of production that give rise to—or contextualize—particular actions and inactions. Such a process of abstraction must always be materially grounded, however, for as John Rees observes, "Even the most abstract theoretical concept ultimately has its roots in real existence. If we are ever to refine our theoretical concepts . . . then we must begin with the real world from which these ideas arise, not with the ideas and then seek to find our way back to their real precondition."[1] It is inappropriate, in other words, to begin with the abstract concept of violence (or even crime) and to then attempt to map it onto some empirical reality. Instead, through dialectic materialism, it is apposite to move from the real concrete, through abstraction, to the thought concrete.

Thus, violence and crime are abstractions, and how they are abstracted is grounded in a particular, dominant mode of production. All modes of production, though, including capitalism, are themselves abstractions, derived from material social relations and practices in existence at any given time and place. Capitalism, in this sense, appears as a system whereby a person's capacity to work becomes a commodity that can be bought and sold on the market—a topic I develop at greater length in the next chapter. For now, suffice it to say that the *commodification* of labor will have a tremendous bearing on our understanding of violence as an abstraction. Just as each mode of production is structured according to its class relations, for which there are appropriate corresponding categories of analysis, so too will each mode of production structure the abstraction of violence in particular concrete forms. First, however, is it necessary to provide a broad sketch of the origins of capitalism and how this particular mode of production—in an ideal form—is determinant of a range of abstractions, including not only violence and crime but also "bodies" and "populations" as the target of criminal justice.[2]

THE MATERIAL CONDITIONS OF PRODUCTION

A materialist conception of violence begins "with real individuals, their activity and the material conditions of their life."[3] Such a beginning is not arbitrary but is instead predicated on what Marx and Engels termed the "first premise" of all human history, namely, "the existence of living human individuals."[4] At a bare minimum, the obtainment of food, water, shelter, and clothing are the conditions for a living existence, for both individual and collective survivability.[5] Accordingly, it is imperative to understand how humans satisfy these needs, whether produced individually or (more commonly) through social relations.

Any given society will have its own way of satisfying (producing) these material needs, for example, through self-production, trade, barter, exchange, and even theft. It is important to always keep in mind, therefore, how violence or crime or even punishment is abstracted from these practices, for they must be viewed as historically and geographically specific phenomena that appear in particular, concrete forms.[6] As Bernard Harcourt cautions, "What is most important to remember is that the categories we use to organize, understand, discuss, categorize, and compare the different organization principles are just that—labels. . . . And they have the unfortunate effect of obscuring rather than enlightening. They obscure by making one set of objects seem natural and necessary, and the other naturally unnecessary."[7]

There is, in other words, no ontological reality of crime; crime and criminal behavior do not exist a priori to systems of criminal justice, for it is the institutions and social relations constituting systems of criminal justice that define what counts (or does not count) as crime. If this appears tautological it is because the relationship between crime and criminal justice is just that. As John Lea writes, we have crime because we have criminal justice systems.[8] A simple scenario will illustrate. Consider the proverbial deserted island. On this particular island there are two men; they are, not surprisingly, confronted with the immediacy of life or death. They can either obtain adequate supplies of food and water or die. One man decides to cultivate a small garden; he also builds traps to catch small animals. For all intents and purposes, this man is engaging in a productive activity known as subsistence production. The other man, however, does not cultivate a garden or learn to catch animals, but his survival is still determinant on his ability to gain access to food and water. Two options are readily available. He can attempt to trade (cooperate) with the first man, or he can steal.[9] In this simplistic scenario, we can readily see how the attainment of the basic necessities of life is foundational to subsequent social practices and relations. What we call theft, for example, may be seen as a means of satisfying the conditions of existence without directly producing those conditions. Consequently, forms of behavior that we might consider responsible, criminal, or even violent must emanate from these activities. Aesop's fable of the ant and the grasshopper springs to mind, suggesting also how forms of socialization impart these material conditions of life.

A historical and geographical materialist account therefore must begin with consideration of how individuals, rooted in time and place, obtain the basic necessities of life: food, water, clothing, shelter. From this, everything else follows, for as Marx and Engels explain, "By producing their means of subsistence men are indirectly producing their material life."[10] To this end, both Marx and Engels forward the proposition that cultural practices and social institutions emanate from satisfaction of the basic necessities of life. Religion, marriage, and inheritance rights, on the other hand, do not precede survivability nor do they emerge apart from the attainment of the conditions of existence. As Marx explains, "Neither legal relations nor political forms could be comprehended whether by themselves or on the basis of a so-called general development of the human mind." Instead, "they originate in the material conditions of life."[11] This is not to suggest that production *determines* all facets of social reality; this is a myth forwarded primarily by postmodernists and other critics who have failed to appreciate (or understand) Marx's usage of the word *determinant*. For Marx, determinism is neither teleological inevitability nor a variant of fatalism.[12]

Marx did argue, of course, that the primary contingency was how any given society satisfied its attainment of the basic conditions of existence (food, water, shelter, and clothing). Over time, as societies were transformed, specific institutional practices, including marriage, as well as divisions of labor, property rights, and criminal justice, emerged vis-à-vis the necessities of life; some of these practices became entrenched and assumed an existence beyond the immediate production process, while others fell into disfavor or were replaced by other practices.

For further clarification, consider the abstraction "division of labor." Following a historical-geographical materialist account, divisions of labor emerge as different individuals allocate different tasks to obtain the basic necessities of life. Women, for example, may assume responsibility for the gathering of fruits and vegetables, while men may assume the task of hunting, and children may be assigned the responsibility of collecting water. Note that these divisions of labor are not inevitable; women do not naturally have to gather while men hunt. Nor, for that matter, is the division of labor a seamless, conflict-free process. My point is, following Marx, that divisions of labor are social relations that emerge to satisfy the provision (production) of food, water, shelter, and clothing. Over time, the satisfaction of these needs is transformed. As Marx and Engels explain, "Each new productive force, insofar as it is not merely a quantitative extension of productive forces already known (for instance, the bringing into cultivation of fresh land), causes a further development of the division of labor."[13] It is for this reason that there is no "natural" or "essential" division of labor (or, for that matter, marriage, crime, or violence). As the conditions of existence are transformed, for example, by the extension of trade or the development of tributary systems, other social relations and social institutions will (most likely) be transformed.

Let's return to the island scenario developed earlier. Now, however, suppose that ten (or twenty, or a hundred) people were stranded on the island. Over time, divisions of labor (may, and probably will) emerge to satisfy the collective survival of this embryonic society. How these social divisions develop is not predetermined. What if there were no women—and sidestepping the truism that, without the possibility for procreation, the entire society would at some point die off—how then would tasks be allocated? Perhaps the men assign tasks by age or strength, or some combination thereof. My point, again, is to illustrate that a materialist account holds that there is no essential, natural, or inevitable development of social relations, but neither is the development random or arbitrary. For Marx, therefore, production was *determinant* only insofar as to say that groups of people will establish (initially at least) particular institutions and productive relations that are reflective of the immediate conditions of existence. These institutions and relations may, and most likely will, change; in future generations "marriage" or "violence" will acquire different meanings that might bear no resemblance to contemporary productive activities. In the United States of the twenty-first century, for example, many people argue that current marriage laws (defined primarily for heterosexual, monogamous couples) are antiquated. We must recognize therefore that marriage as an abstraction has its own history and that this history is grounded in the material reality of survivability.

For Marx, the production of material life was paramount. Accordingly, Marx employs the abstraction "mode of production." Here, "production" is used very broadly to indicate how the basic conditions of existence—the ability to survive and reproduce—are satisfied. By "mode of production" Marx meant relations of production *in their totality*.[14] This is, in other words, an expansive concept, one that is not reducible to a genealogy of self-contained epochs (e.g., feudalism, mercantilism, capitalism, and communism), as is generally thought.[15]

Early on, Marx and Engels explain that any particular mode of production "must not be considered simply as being the reproduction of the physical existence of individuals. Rather it is a definite form of activity of these individuals, a definite form of expressing their life, a definite *mode of life* on their part. As individuals express their life, so they are. What they are, therefore, coincides with their production, both with *what* they produce and with *how* they produce. Hence what individuals are depends on the material conditions of their production."[16]

Marx's clearest definition of the mode of production appears in his *Contribution to the Critique of Political Economy*, wherein he states,

> In the social production of their existence, men inevitably enter into definite relations, which are independent of their will, namely *relations of production* appropriate to a given stage in the development of their material *forces of production*. The totality of these relations of production constitutes the *economic structure* of society, the real foundation, on which arises a legal and political *superstructure* and to which correspond definite forms of social consciousness. The mode of production of material life conditions the general process of social, political and intellectual life.[17]

As this passage indicates, the mode of production, on the one hand, is composed of two inner-related components: the relations of production and the forces of production. This latter component, however, is itself composed of the *means of production* (i.e., raw materials, tools, technology) and the direct "producers," whether these be peasants, serfs, slaves, or wage workers. The *relations of production* consequently encompass the direct producers plus nonproducers (e.g., chieftains, lords, owners). The entire *mode of production* (or "base") is thus the combination of the means, forces, and relations of production. The *superstructure*, on the other hand, is composed of those institutions, relations, and practices that encompass, say, politics, law, education, and religion. These are not mere reflections of the mode of production, but they are (as discussed later) inner-related.[18] In sum, "the totality of human society is thus represented by the preceding elements and relations. These comprise, for Marxist scientists, tools with which we can begin to isolate a part of the social whole for analysis without having to sever it from its defining place within the complete system."[19]

Common to both the relations of production and the forces of production is human labor; indeed, as discussed in subsequent chapters, labor (broadly conceived as those conscious activities that transform nature into use values, that is, things that may be used for consumption, such as food, or for trade and exchange) is a central concept of historical materialism. Originally, according to Marx, human labor was not unlike that of other animals: humans scavenged, gathered food, and hunted. The first transformative moment occurred when humans put consciousness and deliberation into effect; in other words, they made tools—*instruments of production.*[20] Marx explains that "the use and construction of instruments of labor, although present in germ among certain species of animals, is characteristic of the specifically human labor process."[21] Consequently, as Richard Peet summarizes, "shaping natural materials into tools and instruments which shorten necessary labor time ('necessary' in terms of providing the essentials of life) is the economic key to social evolution."[22]

This is a point that bears repeating. In Marx's account, the labor process is *purposeful* activity aimed at the production of use values, that is, those things necessary for life itself.[23] In a famous passage, Marx explains how this process, when undertaken by humans, differs from that of other animals:

A spider conducts operations which resemble those of the weaver, and a bee would put many a human architect to shame by the construction of its honeycomb cells. But what distinguishes the worst architect from the best of bees is that the architect builds the cell in his mind before he constructs it in wax. At the end of every labor process, a result emerges which had already been conceived by the worker at the beginning, hence it already existed ideally. Man not only effects a change of form in the materials of nature; he also realizes his own purpose in those materials.[24]

The implications of such an understanding are far-reaching, for not only did humans begin to create instruments of labor but they also in time developed instruments of warfare. Just as consciousness and deliberation enter into the labor process, so too do consciousness and deliberation enter into the practice of individual behaviors we might term "violent," such as murder and rape, as well as of group behaviors, such as warfare.

For Marx, a second transformative moment occurs when the means of production come to be controlled by a ruling elite, thereby creating a fundamental cleavage between those who control the productive forces and those who perform the work.[25] How these social relations are arranged, between those who labor (the nonproducers) and those who own the means of production (the indirect producers) can and does assume many different forms. Marx clarifies that

> it is in each case the direct relationship of the owners of the conditions of production to the immediate producers—a relationship whose particular form naturally corresponds always to a certain level of development of the type and manner of labor, and hence to its social productive power—in which we find the innermost secret, the hidden basis of the entire social edifice, and hence also the political form of the relationship and dependence, in short, the specific form of state in each case. This does not prevent the same economic basis—the same in its major conditions—from displaying endless variations and gradations in its appearance, as the result of innumerable different empirical circumstances, natural conditions, racial relations, historical influences acting from outside, etc., and these can only be understood by analyzing these empirically given conditions.[26]

The specific—and unique—arrangements of the social relations of production are the pivot to understanding any given mode of production. These arrangements, moreover, exhibit tremendous variation—albeit variability within limits. Similar conditions thus may give rise to very different political-economic structures. Capitalism in the United States, for example, is different from (but similar to) capitalism in Japan or capitalism in Germany. Accordingly, those practices that are characteristic of capitalism, such as private property, manifest differently (but similarly) in the United States, Japan, and Germany. And, by extension, criminal and civil law—as they relate to property relations—will also exhibit differences and similarities. In all three locations, however, it would be possible to empirically document the inner-relations of the capitalist mode of production.

This returns us to the superstructure—those elements of the social formation that include, for example, legal systems, politics, religion, and so on. The relations between any given mode of production (or "base") and its superstructure have often been oversimplified into a fixed, deterministic hierarchy.[27] Such a myopic, reductionist interpretation not only does a disservice to Marx's own complex understanding of the relations but also obfuscates our own understanding of the nonessentialism of any given social institution or cultural practice. Marx writes, for example, that "social relations are closely bound up with productive forces. In acquiring new productive forces men change their mode of production; and in changing their mode of production, in changing the way of earning their living, they change all their social relations. The hand-mill gives you society with the feudal lord; the steam-mill, society with the industrial capitalist."[28]

In my ongoing scenario of the island society, we can readily see how subsequent divisions of labor—social relations—emerge as the inhabitants attempt to survive. This is what Marx means by declaring that men and women enter into relations independent of their will. Certainly, any given individual has the freedom to refuse to participate; in this situation, of course, individuals do so at their own peril. A person may elect to steal rather than cooperate; in turn, the other inhabitants may develop a criminal justice system replete with jails and police officers. Those individuals who serve as enforcement officers may not directly produce their own food but are provided fruits and meats in exchange for their services. Over the years other forms of relations develop, perhaps giving rise to political officials, lawyers, and bankers. And from these conditions arise particular (and specific) moral concepts, including distinctions between legal and illegal, criminal and noncriminal, and even violence and nonviolence. As Marx writes, "These ideas, these categories, are as little eternal as the relations they express. They are historical and transitory products."[29]

Broadly, then, we surmise that the earliest humans most likely gathered foods, foraged, and scavenged, and we may designate these activities as forming a particular mode of production. At some point our ancestors began to hunt and fish. Particular social systems among members of society then emerged, accounting for, say, religion and other rules and responsibilities that emanated from the specific mode of production. It would be quite nonsensical to argue the obverse—that religion precedes the ability to gather food and find shelter. Over time alterations of the rules (located within the superstructure) might lead to transformations of the mode of production; likewise, alterations of the mode of production might lead to transformations of the superstructure. Throughout human history, therefore, a dialectic transformation of social formations is evident—although not predictable in any vulgar, deterministic manner. Academics of course have since abstracted (at very high, universal levels) particular epochal social formations (e.g., feudalism, capitalism) and have often presented these as static, linear stages of development; both approaches actually run counter to Marx's ontology. However, there are no clear breaks or necessarily identifiable irruptions between one mode of production and another. Accordingly, certain elements exhibit continuity; marriage, for example, assumes different concrete forms in different social formations, although the abstraction "marriage" continues. Historians have documented, for example, how dominant conceptions of marriage as an institution defined by monogamous, heterosexual relations have transcended different social formations (e.g., from feudalism to capitalism) and within variants of dominant social formations (e.g., from industrial capitalism to advanced capitalism). In short, once established, any institution (e.g., criminal law, marriage, government) will develop a "life" of its own—albeit a life contingent upon the totality of the social formation. Paul Paolucci explains that superstructural elements may survive over time, especially if they are compatible with a transformed mode of production. Consequently, "if they survive, they are likely to take on the normative and metaphysical appearance of tradition, especially as knowledge of their origins recedes into the past (e.g., religion). This is why tracing human relations historically and materialistically tends to demystify traditional knowledge and poses a threat to received wisdom."[30]

To argue that the superstructure emanates (rises) from the base is not to unduly privilege the latter over the former. It does not follow that emanation equates with domination. Consider, for example, the statement that steam emanates from boiling water. Here, energy combines with water to produce steam; steam emanates from water. This does not privilege water over steam or steam over water. It is recognition that, absent energy or water, steam is not possible. As corollary, is it possible to have law or education, for example, without an underlying mode of production? I would argue no, because the mode of production accounts for the processes by which the materiality of day-to-day life is experienced: the provision of food, water, clothing, and shelter. Does law or education influence how the materiality of social reproduction takes place? Yes, and this brings home the point that the *relation* between base and superstructure is dialectic, that the base and superstructure constitute a totality—a social formation.

Return to our deserted island. Let's imagine a scenario in which the island is populated by, say, fifty men and fifty women. Initially, all inhabitants are able to raise fruits and vegetables and to hunt and fish; the island, in other words, is considered a commons. However, in this scenario a group of five men begins to cordon off areas of the island; they claim *private* ownership of these lands and are able to do so through brute force. Perhaps these men are the biggest and strongest, or perhaps they develop more effective farming and hunting tools, which are transformed into weapons. Over time these men gain control over the entire island.

The remaining ninety-five inhabitants—if they are to survive—have no recourse but to work for the five men.

How this process materializes may assume many different, concrete forms. In the abstract, however, the process is quite clear. Through a process of enclosure—maintained by violence or the threat of violence—a minority of inhabitants are able to transform the social relations of the islands through the introduction of a new form of production. Thus denied access to the means of production, those dispossessed inhabitants, to simply survive, must conform to the dictates of the dominant "class." It is possible, moreover, to see how these transformed relations—in time—may acquire the *appearance* of free choice. One who is denied access to the means of production—because, for example, there is no opportunity to farm or forage because there is no commons—is seemingly confronted with a "free" choice: he or she can choose whether or not to enter into an economic relation with those who control (own) the means of production (i.e., ownership of the once-common land). In such a simplified scenario, however, it should be obvious that there really is no choice, for the simple reason that there is no alternative means of survival.

This last sentence requires some qualification. Any one or all of the ninety-five inhabitants denied access to the means of production may steal from the dominant class. Here, though, we see the beginnings of both criminal "justice" and enforcement. To counter the possibility of theft, for example, the five "landowners" may decide to hire ten men to serve as police officers. These law enforcers are paid through the surplus foods produced by those who "choose" to enter into economic relations with the dominant class. At this point, therefore, we have a small group of elites who own the means of production—an enforcement class, a laboring class, and potentially a class of thieves. Prior to the enclosure process, there was no need for theft; crime in this sense, as well as violence, emerged as a result of a process of accumulation by dispossession. We may posit that any attempt by the dispossessed inhabitants to forcefully reclaim the commons is marked as violent and thus criminal, to be rebuffed by the law enforcers—who are of course paid by the dominant class. Theft of property likewise is criminalized.

In short, the "base" is understood as being *determinant* (but not *determining*) of the superstructure.

It is necessary therefore to understand the internal relations between the structure (base) and superstructure in terms of dialectical determination and to appreciate the relative autonomy of the superstructure.[31] To be sure, critics of Marxist philosophy have challenged the presumption of totality and internal relations, arguing instead that we must focus on the concepts of contingency and contextuality. However, these concepts—contingency, contextuality, and even causality—must be seen as internally related. To argue against the totality of objective reality is to introduce an element of mysticism.

THE VIOLENT TRANSITION TO CAPITALISM

Capitalism is a particular mode of production in which all participants—producers and consumers—depend on the market for their basic needs.[32] Waged labor is a defining characteristic, as is private ownership of the means of production. As a form of economic organization, therefore, capitalism is fundamentally the social (class) separation of direct producers (waged workers) from the (privately owned) means of production. It is because of this relation that workers—although formally free—are forced by material circumstances to sell their labor power to capitalists, who own the means of production.[33]

How, though, did capitalism materialize, and, in particular, how did laborers become dispossessed from the means of production? Why, in other words, are there some men and women who have money (capital) and are able to set up businesses, while other men and women must sell their labor? All too often, answers to these questions appear tautological, as expressed in the old adage, "It takes money to make money." Great. But where does the initial money—what Marx termed "primitive accumulation"—come from?

Various political philosophers and political economists, including both John Locke and Adam Smith, located the source of original capital in frugal behavior, thereby grounding capitalism in a particular valuation of resourceful, industrious individuals in contrast to others who—to put it politely—were somewhat less practical or prudent. Marx disagreed. For Marx, such an account, while intuitively appealing—especially to those who had money—is analogous to the role that original sin performs in theology. Marx writes,

> Adam bit the apple, and thereupon sin fell on the human race. Its origin is supposed to be explained when it is told as an anecdote about the past. Long, long ago there were two sorts of people; one, the diligent, intelligent and above all frugal elite; the other, lazy rascals, spending their substance, and more, in riotous living. . . . Thus it came to pass that the former sort accumulated wealth, and the latter sort finally had nothing to sell except their own skins. And from this original sin dates the poverty of the great majority who, despite all their labor, have up to now nothing to sell but themselves, and the wealth of the few that increases constantly, although they have long ceased to work.[34]

The origins of capitalism, as expressed by Locke and Smith, are premised on a very conservative and individualistic understanding of society. It follows, from this reasoning, that the ability to succeed is rooted from within, that external factors play a minimal role in one's ability to succeed. Moreover, there is an implicit morality associated with the accumulation of wealth: people who act responsibly are rewarded, while those who do not act responsibly are not necessarily punished but are certainly deserving of whatever fate may befall them. We see here how poverty ultimately is portrayed as a sign of personal failure. Marx challenges this position, contending that "it is a notorious fact that conquest, enslavement, robbery, murder, in short, force, play the greatest part" in the process of primitive accumulation.[35] In other words, violence and crime are inseparable from capitalism's birth, but both violence and crime remain hidden behind the morally conservative story of parsimonious behavior.

For Marx, capitalism is predicated on two key conditions that exist beyond the level of the individual. The first is that "labor-power can appear on the market as a commodity only if, and in so far as, its possessor . . . offers it for sale or sells it as a commodity."[36] In other words, capitalism—as a market-defined system—requires workers to obtain waged employment.

Capitalism is predicated upon some women and men (waged workers) laboring for other women and men (owners). Given a choice, though, why would someone labor for another? According to the narrative advanced by Locke and Smith, a simple explanation might be that some individuals do not have the initiative or the desire; they just don't have what it takes. Marx, not surprisingly, takes a different tack, for he proposes (as a second condition of capitalism) that "the possessor of labor-power . . . [must] be compelled to offer for sale as a commodity that very labor-power which exists only in his living body."[37]

Marx's reference to a person being "compelled" is significant. In slave societies, some men, women, and children are—through direct force or the threat of force—compelled to work for another. Likewise, in feudal societies, men, women, and children are required to work because of particular obligations. Within the "free" market of capitalism, how can it be reasoned that workers are compelled (i.e., forced) to participate? Indeed, the phrase "free market" suggests that workers are free to get a job if they want and they are free to leave their job if they want. The market *appears* to be purely voluntary and thus free of any extra-economic condition (force).

Here, it is worth considering Jeffrey Reiman's distinction between subjective illusions and objective illusions.[38] The former refers to individuals' erroneous perceptions of their material conditions. If, in the course of reading a bank statement, someone misreads the numeral 3 for the numeral 8, it would be a subjective illusion. Rereading the original statement will clarify—correct—the mistaken perception. Objective illusions, however, consist of accurate perceptions but mistakes in interpretation or conclusion. Reiman provides the example of the sun and the earth. If we simply observe the relationship between the sun and the earth, it appears as if the sun journeys across the sky; hence, we perceive the rising and the setting of the sun. Such an objective illusion has long been a feature in human societies, with many myths and legends associated with this observation. In the sixteenth century, however, Nicolaus Copernicus advanced the idea that all planets—including Earth—revolve around the sun. Appearances, in other words, are truly deceiving, and no amount of closer inspection or observation will reveal the actual movements.

According to Reiman, "the illusion that capitalism is uncoercive is a mistake of the same type as the illusion that the sun goes around the earth. What corresponds in capitalism to the movement of the sun seen from the earth is the free exchange of wages and labor-power between capitalists and workers."[39] Workers, in other words, do not freely participate in the market, and the market is anything but free of compulsion and force. Of particular significance is that the illusion of freedom hides a particular social relationship that is (outside of a Marxist critique) considered neither violent nor criminal. The illusion of freedom and related concepts (e.g., liberty) is thus fundamental to the subsequent abstraction of both violence and crime within capitalism.

How then are workers compelled to participate, and how does this relate more broadly, therefore, to violence and crime? For Marx, workers appear free in a double sense: as legally free individuals who are free to enter into the waged labor market and as individuals who are free from the means of production. This presumed freedom results from a series of practices that would, over time, become codified in systems of criminal justice. Drawing on the example of England, Marx details how the "process . . . which creates the capital-relation can be nothing other than the process which divorces the worker from the ownership of the conditions of his own labor; it is a process which operates two transformations, whereby the social means of subsistence and production are turned into capital, and the immediate producers are turned into wage-laborers."[40] Marx terms this process "primitive accumulation" in reference to "the historical process of divorcing the producer from the means of production." Consequently, the transformation of feudalism to mercantilism to capitalism—the dispossession of masses of women and men from the means of production—is, according to Marx, "written in the annals of mankind in letters of blood and fire."[41]

Capitalism did not materialize fully formed; rather, as Marx explains, the "economic structure of capitalist society has grown out of the economic structure of feudal society. The dissolution of the latter set free the elements of the former."[42] As a dominant mode of production, feudalism is characterized by being almost wholly agricultural, with the majority of men, women, and children engaged in some form of mixed arable or pastoral farming; other laborers provide necessary and basic goods such as farming implements. More production was predicated on use value, as very little trade occurred beyond the limits of the immediate feudal estate, which consisted of lands owned by lay or ecclesiastical lords, who delegated parcels of land to others in return for allegiance and economic obligations.[43] These lords, in turn, owed allegiance to others, who occupied higher positions of authority. Medieval Europe, in short, was socially, politically, and economically composed of innumerable patron-client ties: king and baron, bishop and priest, lord and knight, master and servant. These ties, moreover, were based on personal obligations as opposed to territorial allegiances.[44]

The key to feudalism's mode of production, according to Paul Knox and John Agnew, was the peasantry.[45] The labor power that ran the estates consisted of both serfs and tenants; both, in their own unique way, had significant limitations on their freedom and both were to contribute to the accumulation of wealth: labor services, rents in kind, taxes, seigneurial dues, and payments for the use of essential services—milling, baking, olive pressing, and so on—that were monopolized by the lords. However, as Silvia Federici explains, it was serfdom that assumed primacy throughout feudal Europe. As a class, serfs were bonded to their landlords, and while not slaves, their persons and possessions were their master's property and their lives were ruled in every respect by the law of the manor.[46] Nevertheless, serfs had direct access to their reproduction; in exchange for the work they were required to perform on the lords' land, serfs received plots of land that they could farm for themselves. It was also not uncommon that these lands could be inherited by their children. In effect, serfs had access to the means of production and had a relatively high degree of autonomy. Moreover, serfs (and other tenants) had access to the use of commons—meadows, forests, lakes, wild pastures—that provided important resources for the peasant economy: wood for fuel, timber for building, wild game to eat, lands for grazing, and so on.[47]

Unlike feudalism, mercantilism (or merchant capitalism) was premised on the idea that a nation's wealth is determined by the amount of precious metals (e.g., gold and silver) it had in its treasury. Profits were obtained in part from the differences between the price paid for goods and the price at which the product or commodity was sold and, more broadly, through favorable balances of trade. Indeed, mercantilism could be a self-propelling economic system only with the continued expansion of trade: without trade, neither merchants nor those dependent upon the successful growth of trade—producers, consumers, financiers, and so on—could maintain their economic standing, let alone amass private wealth. As such, a series of innovations in business and technology contributed to the consolidation of mercantilism; these developments include the emergence of banks, loan systems, credit transfers, shares in stock, and insurance.[48] Equally if not more important were advances made in shipbuilding, navigation, and naval ordnance, for, as Knox and Agnew argue, "these advances made it possible for the merchants of Europe to establish the basis of a world-wide economy in the space of less than one hundred years."[49] Marx notes that "the discovery of gold and silver in America, the extirpation, enslavement and entombment in mines of the indigenous population of that continent, the beginnings of the conquest and plunder of India, and the conversion of Africa into a preserve for the commercial hunting of blackskins, are all things which characterize the dawn of the era of capitalist production. These idyllic proceedings are the chief moments of primitive accumulation."[50]

Monetary wealth, derived in large part from colonialism, slavery, and expanded trade systems, paralleled—and indeed facilitated—the dissolution of feudalism throughout Europe. These externally derived sources of wealth ended up in the hands of merchants and bankers and contributed to the ongoing privatization of land that was occurring throughout much of Europe. This privatization assumed many forms, including the forcible taking of communal property, enclosures, evictions of tenants, rent increases, and increased state taxation that led to debt and the sale of land.[51] These forms of land expropriation undermined both feudal relations and other, traditional forms of subsistence.

Enclosure, for example, was a sixteenth-century technical term applied to a set of strategies used to eliminate communal land property and expand personal holdings; various practices included the abolition of open-field systems, the fencing off of commons, and the establishment of private "deer parks" and other hunting preserves. The conversion of arable land into pasture, likewise, spurred the dispossession of workers from their land and the livelihood it had provided. Similarly, changes in manufacturing led to the decline of artisanal and craft production, further facilitating the conversion self-employed workers into waged workers. Federici explains that merchant capitalists took advantage of the cheap—and landless—labor that was made available following dispossession; in this way, it was possible to break the power of the urban guilds and destroy the artisans' independence.[52]

The advent of capitalism throughout Europe from the fourteenth and fifteenth centuries onward also affected both the spatial practice and gendered meanings and expectations of work. Prior to capitalism the rhythms of work were regulated by need (use values), and the amount of labor used in production was equivalent to the amount of labor needed for reproduction.[53] In most precapitalist societies, for example, work arrangements were based mostly on satisfying immediate needs—as opposed to the profit-driven production typified by capitalism. There would have been a customary division of labor, with women largely responsible for so-called reproductive tasks. Considerable variation existed, however, and social relations—and the attendant divisions of labor—did not necessarily imply a rigid hierarchy.

The widespread introduction of money and waged work, however, provided the catalyst for a reconfigured, gendered division of labor. Three key transformations stand out: the separation of producers from their means of production and subsistence, the formation of a social class that has a monopoly on the means of production, and the transformation of human labor power into a commodity.[54] Combined, these changes would have a profound effect on the household as a unit of production and consumption. As productive tasks were shifted from the needs of the household to those of the market, the household per se no longer had access to the means of production. Familial needs, including the provision of food-stuffs and clothing, were provided through an exchange of labor power for wages. In the process, work for wages became distinct from work in the household.[55] As Lea concludes, unlike in noncapitalist societies, the modern capitalist family largely ceased to play a role as a productive unit; rather, the household is reconfigured as a site of reproduction—of labor power and of the respect for authority and hierarchy that are central in putting labor power to work for capital.[56] The family became a microcosm of capitalism and a key locus in the (re)production of values.

With the ongoing separation between "work" spaces and "living" spaces, men and women, children and adults, experienced different capaci-ties for work and encountered different constraints on their actions.[57] Women, for example, continued to work in the home, engaged in such activities as child care and food preparation. However, these jobs came to be seen as being qualitatively different from men's work.[58] Women's work, in practice, became both invisible and naturalized; it became separated, materially and ideologically, from productive work.[59] These transformations, in short, "redefined women's position in society and in relation to men. The sexual division of labor that emerged from it not only fixed women to reproductive work, but increased their dependence on men, enabling the state and employers to use the male wage as a means to command women's labor. In this way, the separation of commodity production from the reproduction of labor-power also made possible the development of a specifically capitalist use of the wage and of the markets as a means for the accumulation of unpaid labor."[60]

Over time, the gendered division of family labor assumed a new spa-tial dimension, one in which (most) women and children were confined to the domestic sphere, separated from men's activities in the public sphere.[61] How male labor capacity was incorporated into the waged labor market while female labor capacity was excluded from waged work is a complex historical process, one that is intimately associated with the legal prescriptions of private property. These reconfigured geographies were neither natural nor inevitable but instead were the manifestation of particular social practices and relations that constituted a form of "primitive accumulation."[62] However, as Federici indicates, primitive accumulation reconfigured the sexual division of labor, subjugating women's labor and women's reproductive function to the reproduction of the work force; constructed a new patriarchal order based upon the exclusion of women from waged work and their subordination to men; and mechanized the proletarian body, transforming it, in the case of women, into a machine for the production of new workers.[63] Leopoldina Fortunati likewise documents how, under capitalism, "the new mode of production formally established a different production relation with men from that which it established with women."[64] She goes on to state that "the sexual division of labor developed to such a degree that the work subject of reproduction was separated off from that of production; the two processes became separated by value. The man—as the primary work-subject within production, was obliged to enter the *waged-work* relation. The woman—as the primary work-subject within reproduction, was obliged to enter the *non-waged-work* relation."[65]

The development of separate, gendered spheres of daily life served very particular purposes, among which was the reproduction of capitalism itself.[66] As more and more components of social reproductive tasks, including education, health care, and manufacturing, were transferred away from the household, the home became recognized as a separate place in which society could be socialized with appropriate values and attitudes of discipline and service.[67] These values centered on masculinist notions of the male as both provider and protector. Concomitantly, the economic importance of the reproduction of labor power carried out in the home, and its function in the accumulation of capital, became invisible, being mystified as a natural vocation and denigrated as simply women's work. In short, the separation of production from reproduction created a class of proletarian women who were as dispossessed as men but, unlike their male relatives, had almost no access to wages in a society that was becoming increasingly monetarized. Women were thus being forced into a condition of chronic poverty, economic dependence, and invisibility as workers—features of the gendered division of labor that continue to haunt most capitalist societies.[68]

CRIME AND CAPITALISM

The increased dispossession of peasants and serfs was supposedly justified by changing attitudes and practices of crime and punishment. Conventionally, the decline of feudalism is understood as a period of moral progress, with society becoming more civilized. The move from spectacular forms of torture, for example, is often held as reflective of a broader desire to respect the human rights of prisoners. Conversely, as argued by Georg Rusche and Otto Kirchheimer, Evgeny Pashukanis, and Michel Foucault, among others, penal reforms are to be found in changing material conditions. It was the transformation of Europe's political economy rather than some abstract, idealized notion of humanitarian concern that facilitated a change in criminal justice practice. Rather, political-economic transformations contributed to different ways of abstracting crime and violence.

The forcible dispossession of people from land, for example, was not (from the vantage point of the dispossessors) considered criminal; resistance to dispossession was. Likewise, the destruction of guild-based production was not considered criminal; being unemployed was. The increased dispossession of women and men, for example—those who could not be absorbed into the embryonic capitalist industries—contributed to a massive increase in a landless class of beggars, vagabonds, and paupers. The existence of these "free and rights-less" people became, in Federici's words, the "social problem of the day."[69] As Marx points out, "At the end of the fifteenth and during the whole of the sixteenth centuries, a bloody legislation against vagabondage was enforced throughout Western Europe.... Legislation treated them as 'voluntary' criminals and assumed that it was entirely within their powers to go on working under the old conditions which in fact no longer existed."[70] In 1530, for example, under the reign of Henry VIII, beggars who were "old and incapable of working" were to receive a beggar's license. For those caught begging with a license, the punishment for a first offense was whipping and imprisonment; for a second offense, the penalty was repeated, with the added punishment of half an ear being sliced off. Those found guilty of a third offense were to be executed. Similarly, in 1572, unlicensed beggars above the age of fourteen were to be severely flogged and branded on the left ear unless someone took the offending party into service for two years; repeat violators, if over the age of eighteen, were to be executed.[71]

Consider also the existence of "illegalities." For any given society, there exist certain actions that are technically illegal but are commonly overlooked. In a modern example, many office workers take home pens, paper, and other supplies. These actions are illegal, but it is not uncommon for office managers to look the other way—given that the net loss incurred is not too substantial. Likewise, not paying taxes on certain activities that operate in the informal economy, such as teenagers mowing lawns or babysitting, is an illegality that is generally not prosecuted.

Throughout feudalistic Europe there existed many illegalities, such as collecting firewood from hedgerows or farming land not owned. As Foucault indicates, illegality was so deeply rooted and so necessary to the life of each social stratum that it had in a sense its own coherence and economy.[72] To an extent, the nascent capitalist class supported certain illegalities (or at least looked the other way). Smuggling and armed resistance to tax collectors, for example, were viewed as actions that diminished the power and authority of the monarch while simultaneously contributing to the smugglers' and tax protesters' own accumulation of wealth. However, as society became increasingly commercialized and landed property became absolute property, laws against those actions that cut into profits were more vigorously—and violently—enforced. As Keith Wrightson explains, "Certain ambivalent but customarily tolerated practices, such as the retention of a portion of grain by threshers, pulling wool off sheep's backs, gathering kindling, or gleaning, were beginning, in some places, to be redefined and prosecuted as theft."[73] Foucault agrees, noting that all the tolerated rights that the peasantry had acquired or preserved (e.g., the abandonment of old obligations or the consolidation of irregular practices such as the right of free pasture, wood collecting, etc.) were now rejected by the new owners, who regarded them quite simply as theft. The new illegality of these traditional rights, which had often been critical to the survival of the most deprived, tended, with the new status of property, to become an illegality of property.[74]

Shifting abstractions of crime and violence were thus reflective of deeper transformations leading toward the abstraction of property. As Nicholas Blomley explains, "When we talk about land and property, we are not simply talking about technical questions of land use, but engaging some deeply moral questions about social order."[75] Thus, *the privatization of land was not simply a transformation in how goods were produced; it was determinant of how crime was defined and life was valued.* As Foucault writes, "Offences had to be properly defined and more surely punished.... With the new forms of capital accumulation, new relations of production and the new legal status of property, all the popular practices that belonged, either in a silent, everyday, tolerated form, or in a violent form, to the illegality of rights were reduced by force to an illegality of property."[76] This separation of the illegality of rights from those of property—a separation that was restructured with the development of capitalist society—is significant. Simply stated, those actions that were most accessible (and necessary) to the increasingly landless class were defined more and more as theft. Other illegalities—those committed most often by the capitalist class—were considered less severe. This distinction would, in time, be manifest in the establishment of two different types of courts: criminal courts and civil courts.

We see also the subsumption of market logics into the abstraction of crime. Indeed, it is possible to posit the emergence of "abstract" crime, for, as Lea explains, what becomes crucial is "no longer the sanctity of the property of this or that landowner but property in general; no longer violence against this or that person but violence in general."[77] This parallels the broader "ascendancy of capitalist market relations in which individuals related increasingly as abstract legal persons, citizens, buyers and sellers of commodities, bearers of rights and obligations irrespective of other differences and characteristics."[78] The consequences were profound. As David Garland explains, "Precisely because the law deems all individuals to be free and equal and because it protects the rights of property without distinction, it silences the real inequalities of power, status, and freedom which separate the rich from the poor and the owners of the means of production from those groups whose real property is minuscule."[79]

Criminal justice as it metastasized dialectically with the growth of capitalism was predicated on the belief that it was necessary not to punish less, or to punish less brutally, but instead to punish more effectively. Foucault, to this end, identifies three paradigmatic forms of criminal justice practices in modern society: torture, punishment, and discipline. The precise periodization need not detain us; as Foucault understood, these three "periods" are ideal-types—abstractions. The onset of either form, for example, would differ according to the dominant mode of production, and its appearance would be reflective of specific continuities and discontinuities. The important point here is that the mode of production—how society is organized vis-à-vis production, circulation, and consumption—is determinant of the *dominant* criminal justice system. Here, "dominant" suggests that other institutional forms of justice may be (and often are) present; however, one form is hegemonic. Vigilantism, for example, often rests uneasily with other, sovereign forms of justice. This is readily seen, for example, in the existence of various self-proclaimed vigilante or militia groups found in the United States today. Many of these groups operate with the acquiescence, if not support, of the federal government—although they are simultaneously outside of formal law.

In his genealogy of penal reform Foucault provides a critique of the bourgeois narrative that a move from torture to punishment to discipline is derived from humanitarian concerns. During feudalism, for example, criminality was conceived as an offense against the social body; however, the social body was constituted not by the people but rather by the sovereign. Punishment, consequently, was held to be an attempt to reestablish the sovereignty of the regal body; it was a means to restore the balance of power.[80] The torture of prisoners, therefore, was a technique; it was not an extreme expression of lawless rage but instead a calculated practice of maintaining law. Of particular importance is Foucault's assertion that torture forms part of a ritual, one that includes two components: a marking of the victim (often physically) and a spectacular, visible administration. The violence of law enforcement was to serve as an obvious reminder of sovereignty.

As Todd May explains, there were at least two potential problems with visible displays of public punishment. On the one hand the asymmetric display of power not only invoked fear and awe of the sovereign; it could also generate resentment. In other words, the viewing audience might begin to identify with the person being punished. On the other hand, torture and related forms of punishment began to appear arbitrary and capricious. Such concerns paralleled the institution of private property; a system was needed that would afford protection to all individuals in possession of property. Thus, as Foucault writes, the "true objective of the reform movement . . . was not so much to establish a new right to punish based on more equitable principles, as to set up a new 'economy' of the power to punish, to assure its better distribution, so that it should be neither too concentrated at certain privileged points, nor too divided between opposing authorities; so that it should be distributed in homogeneous circuits capable of operating everywhere, in a continuous way, down to the finest grain of the social body."[81]

The definition and control of crime, accordingly, mutated into a means of governance aimed at securing both the conditions for the profitable accumulation of capital and the assured sovereignty of the territorial state.[82] Foucault elaborates that "the reform of criminal law must be read as a strategy for the rearrangement of the power to punish, according to modalities that render it more regular, more effective, more constant and more detailed in its effects; in short, which increase its effects while diminishing its economic cost (that is to say, by dissociating it from the system of property, of buying and selling, of corruption in obtaining not only offices, but the decisions themselves) and its political costs (by dissociating it from the arbitrariness of monarchical power)."[83] Penal reform, consequently, was "to make of the punishment and repression of illegalities a regular function, coextensive with society; not to punish less, but to punish better."[84]

Discipline and punishment were not simply about criminal behavior; they were (and are) also about organizing society. As Lea explains, the aim was the encouragement of good habits of conduct, restraint, self-control, and respect for (especially) bourgeois property in order to facilitate and strengthen that which was already developing under its own laws and dynamics: the accumulation of capital.[85] Foucault writes,

> If the economic take-off of the West began with the techniques that made possible the accumulation of capital, it might perhaps be said that the method for administering the accumulation of men made possible a political take-off in relation to the traditional, ritual, costly, violent forms of power, which soon fell into disuse and were superseded by a subtle, calculated technology of subjection. In fact, the two processes, the accumulation of men and the accumulation of capital—cannot be separated; it would not have been possible to solve the problem of the accumulation of men without the growth of an apparatus of production capable of both sustaining them and using them; conversely, the techniques that made the cumulative multiplicity of men useful accelerated the accumulation of capital.[86]

Dialectically, criminal justice supported and augmented the dispossession of the peasantry and the compulsion to participate "freely" in the waged labor market. Marx captures this process when he declares, "Thus were the agricultural folk first forcibly expropriated from the soil, driven from their homes, turned into vagabonds, and then whipped, branded and tortured by grotesquely terroristic laws into accepting the discipline necessary for the system of wage-labor." He continues by stating that once "freed" from the land, the surplus population was given little or no choice but to participate in waged labor. At that point direct force—violent acts—became less necessary, for the advance of capitalist production developed "a working class which by education, tradition and habit looks upon the requirements of that mode of production as self-evident natural laws."[87]

The penal reform movement and the establishment of new forms of discipline—the prison, almshouse, or factory—was thus marked by the moment when governance was directed not only at the growth of the skills of any particular body or the intensification of subjection but also the "formation of a relation that in the mechanism itself makes [the body] more obedient as it becomes more useful."[88] As Foucault notes,

Discipline produces subjected and practiced bodies, "docile" bodies. Discipline increases the forces of the body (in economic terms of utility) and diminishes these same forces (in political terms of obedience). In short, it dissociates power from the body; on the one hand, it turns it into an "aptitude," a "capacity," which it seeks to increase; on the other hand, it reverses the course of the energy, the power that might result from it, and turns it into a relation of strict subjection. If economic exploitation separates the force and the product of labor, let us say that disciplinary coercion establishes in the body the constricting link between an increased aptitude and an increased domination.[89]

The new system of punishment, in other words, was instantiated within a particular political economy of the body—a process Foucault terms "anatomo-politics," in reference to the observation that "it is always the body that is at issue—the body and its forces, their utility and their docility, their distribution and their submission."[90] And yet, as Foucault elaborates, it was never *just* the body but the body politic as well—the population—that warranted attention. As Lea explains, "Society is no longer seen as consisting simply of subjects to be ruled by the sovereign as patriarch but as a population to be considered as the object of policy interventions to achieve certain ends."[91]

The general abstraction of "population" is explicitly tied to the development of the modern capitalist state, in that population emerged as a factor of state strength, to be considered and calculated alongside other state characteristics (e.g., finances, trade relations, resources, and territorial size). The timing was not happenstance. The elaboration of a concept of population was a gradual process that was both technical and theoretical, relying on the development of statistics and census taking, as well as the techniques of epidemiology, demography, and political philosophy.[92] This has significant implications for our understanding of state intervention in matters of violence, value, and crime, in that the political meaning of "population" as a concept was fundamentally transformed. As Thomas Lemke writes, "Population constitutes the combination and aggregation of individualized patterns of existence to a new political form."[93] With the emergence of the territorial state, populations were no longer conceived as the simple sum of individuals inhabiting a territory; instead, populations were conceived as a technical-political object of management and governance. The relationship between the sovereign and the population is therefore not simply one of obedience or the refusal of obedience. Rather, populations become *productive* through state interventions—through a series of techniques, practices, and calculations.[94] From this moment onward, according to Foucault, government "has as its purpose not the act of government itself, but the welfare of the population, the improvement of its condition, the increase of its wealth, longevity, health, etc.; and the means that the government uses to attain these ends are themselves all in some sense immanent to the population; it is the population itself on which government will act either directly . . . or indirectly."[95]

The modern concept of population, accordingly, became dependent on the establishment of practical equivalences among political subjects— the people within a state.[96] The concept of population, in other words, hinged on aggregates and regularities. Adrian Bailey notes that "essentialist approaches to populations as groups not only infer group meaning from component characteristics, but regard these components as fixed, naturalized and stable elements."[97] According to Bruce Curtis,

> As an object of knowledge, population is primarily a statistical artifact. The establishment of practical equivalences means that population is connected to the law of large numbers, which causes individual variation to disappear in favor of regularity. In its developed forms, population is bound up with the calculus of probabilities. Population makes it possible to identify regularities . . . and such things may be both analytic tools and objects of intervention, such as birth, death, or marriage rates.[98]

What is most remarkable is how the concept of population would inform political practice. Again, turning to Curtis, we see that from the eighteenth century onward, the consolidation of population as a *component* of the state "depends on the establishment of equivalences among the subjects within a particular territory"; consequently, political-scientific knowledge "depends on the discipline of potential objects of knowledge. It is only on the grounds of constructed and enforced equivalences that one body comes to equal another, that each death, birth, marriage, divorce and so on, comes to be the equivalent of any other." Curtis concludes that "it is only on the grounds of such constructed equivalences that it is possible for statistical objects to emerge in the form of regularities and to become the objects of political practice. Population is coincident with the effective capacity of sovereign authority to discipline social relations."[99] From this point forward, it became possible to speak of a state's population as if that population had a transcendental existence and experience above and beyond the government. Furthermore, it is here that we can locate the construction of populations into subgroups that are postulated to contribute to or retard the general welfare and life of the population as a whole.[100] For Mitchell Dean, it is this proclivity that led to the so-called discovery of, for example, criminal classes among the population writ large or the feebleminded and the imbeciles, the inverts and the degenerates, the unemployable and the abnormal.[101] As detailed in chapter 3, this proclivity has had a significant effect on subsequent abstractions of violence and crime.

THE MARKET, NEOLIBERALISM, AND NEOCONSERVATISM

The emergence of the market is neither natural nor inevitable; rather, it arises through specific social relations rooted in the contradictions embedded in past economic systems. Marx writes, "Nature does not produce on the one hand owners of money or commodities, and on the other hand men possessing nothing but their labor-power. This relation has no basis in natural history, nor does it have a social basis common to all periods of human history. It is clearly the result of a past historical development, the product of many economic revolutions, of the extinction of a whole series of older formations of social production."[102] In other words, capitalism, as an abstraction, constitutes a metamorphosis of previous modes of production. However, the particular form that capitalism assumes is not predetermined or fixed. Instead, the concrete peculiarities of capitalism in any given place, at any given time, will reveal variability within the overall contours of capitalism's basic features. In this penultimate section I sketch the contours of three important abstractions: the market, neoliberalism, and neoconservatism. The first abstraction, that of the market, forms the bedrock of capitalism writ large; as I elaborate in chapter 3, it provides the touchstone for the ways in which values are given meaning and promoted in contemporary American society. Neoliberalism and neoconservatism, conversely, are two interrelated abstractions that have been produced by but continue to (re)produce particular configurations of market-derived values.

The Market

Adam Smith (1723–90), a professor of logic and moral philosophy at Glasgow University, developed the ideas that are today understood to be the rudiments of capitalism. In his rejection of mercantilism, Smith forwarded the idea that a nation's wealth was not determined by the amount of gold in its treasury but instead by that state's productivity.[103] According to Smith, "That wealth consists in money, or in gold and silver, is a popular notion which naturally arises from the double function of money, as the instrument of commerce, and as the measure of value." He then explained that "a rich country, in the same manner as a rich man, is supposed to be a country abounding in money; and to heap up gold and silver in any country is supposed to be the readiest way to enrich it."[104] However, Smith countered that "the annual labour of every nation is the fund which originally supplies it with all the necessaries and conveniences of life which it annually consumes, and which consists always either in the immediate produce of that labour, or in what is purchased with that produce from other nations."[105]

Economic growth, for Smith, was based on capital accumulation, which, in turn, was based on a division of labor.[106] Indeed, Smith opened his influential *Wealth of Nations* with an extended discussion of the division of labor: "The greatest improvement in the productive powers of labour, and the greater part of the skill, dexterity, and judgment with which it is any where directed, or applied, seem to have been the effects of the division of labour." For Smith, the "division of labour . . . so far as it can be introduced, occasions, in every art, a proportionate increase in the productive powers of labour."[107] Such reasoning would profoundly influence subsequent developments in European industry. As Peet explains, "By specializing the various tasks involved in production, dexterity could be increased, time saved, and labor-saving machinery invented by persons familiar with minute tasks. The products so made were exchanged through trade. And the division of labor was limited only by the extent of the market. With improvements in transport, the market increased in size, labor became more specialized, money replaced barter, and productivity increased."[108]

For Smith, the market was the ultimate arbiter of economic exchange. In his chapter "Of the Natural and Market Price of Commodities," for example, Smith developed the now-familiar principle of supply and demand. He explained that "when the price of any commodity is neither more nor less than what is sufficient to pay the rent of the land, the wages of the labour, and the profits of the stock employed in raising, preparing, and bringing it to market, according to their natural rates, the commodity is then sold for what may be called its natural price." However, he then observed that the "actual price at which any commodity is commonly sold is called its market price. It may either be above, or below, or exactly the same with its natural price."[109] Such variations in market price were supposedly determined by the relationship of consumer demand and productive supply.

The implications of Smith's reasoning on the workings of the market had a profound influence on the nature of governance. In prioritizing the market, Smith forwarded a principle of laissez-faire capitalism, which suggested that governments should remain—to a certain degree—separate from economic activities. He presumed that the resources of a nation would be best managed when individuals were allowed to pursue economic activities according to market principles. In particular, Smith reasoned that the "invisible hand" of supply and demand would ensure the most beneficial functioning of production and consumption activities.[110]

Smith's notion of the invisible hand warrants additional attention in that it impinges on our broader questions of crime, violence, and state intervention. Unlike feudalism or communally based societies, capitalism assumes that society's best interest is maximized when individuals are free to do what they think is best for themselves individually.[111] Only with the self-determination of people freely operating within markets could society as a whole benefit. Consequently, Smith stressed the "unseen" work of the markets, which not only capitalized on individual freedoms and organized for the provision of mass needs but did so in such a way that the overall interests of the commonwealth were supposedly safeguarded and advanced.[112] The market came to be seen as a self-regulating mechanism tending toward equilibrium of supply and demand, thus securing the most efficient allocation of resources.[113] Neil Smith summarizes that "a society of individual property owners, free and independent before the law and with equal recourse to it, who met in the competitive marketplace, and who enjoyed the right to a democratic vote and voted unashamedly in their own self-interest—such a society, the Enlightenment promised, would produce the best outcome for everyone."[114]

Curiously, Adam Smith mentions the "invisible hand" only once in the entire text—and its mention is considerably more qualified than current proponents acknowledge. His comment arises in a discussion of the promotion of domestic production as opposed to the importation of foreign goods. Although it is lengthy, the passage is important enough to quote in its entirety:

> As every individual, therefore, endeavors as much as he can both to employ his capital in the support of domestic industry, and so to direct that industry that its produce may be of the greatest value; every individual necessarily labors to render the annual revenue of the society as great as he can. He generally, indeed, neither intends to promote the public interest, nor knows how much he is promoting it. By preferring the support of domestic to that of foreign industry, he intends only his own security; and by directing that industry in such a manner as its produce may be of the greatest value, he intends only his own gain, and he is in this, as in many other cases, led by an invisible hand to promote an end which was no part of his intention. Nor is it always

the worse for the society that it was no part of it. By pursuing his own interests he frequently promotes that of the society more effectually than when he really intends to promote it.[115]

In other words, Smith is arguing that individual self-interest (greed?) *may* benefit society as a whole. The invisible hand was not simply a metaphor to help readers understand the relationship between supply and demand but rather a means by which individuals and society could prosper. However, such decisions of individual capitalists were to be based *not simply on the market* but on other principles and concepts, such as that of comparative advantage.[116] Indeed, he reasoned that those who offered quality goods at reasonable prices would prosper, while those who did not would find themselves forced out of the market.[117]

Did Adam Smith, then, champion a minimalist government that rarely, if ever, would intervene? In a word, no. It is true that Smith advocated the greatest possible individual liberty.[118] However, he did so with some important qualifications, writing that "every man, *as long as he does not violate the laws of justice*, is left perfectly free to pursue his own interest his own way, and to bring both his industry and capital into competition with those of any other man, or order of men." In other words, on the assumption that individuals did not intentionally subvert the activities of others, the state should not intervene. Smith is in fact clear on this: given that individuals are not in violation of the laws of justice, the "sovereign is completely discharged from . . . the duty of superintending the industry of private people, and of directing it towards the employments most suitable to the interests of the society."[119] However, the state did retain, in Smith's view, three sovereign duties: the protection of society from foreign invasion (i.e., maintaining territorial integrity), the protection of every member of society from the injustice or oppression of all members, and the creation and maintenance of public works and public institutions.[120] The first of these duties need not concern us at this point. It is the second and third duties that need to be addressed now.

Despite rhetoric to the contrary, Smith did not forward a situation of "anything goes"; he acknowledged that individuals, while rational, were not above moral failings. Accordingly, it was incumbent upon the state to intervene in the name of social justice. Smith wrote that it was the duty of the sovereign—the state—to protect "as far as possible, every member of the society from the injustice or oppression of every other member of it."[121] Smith likewise argued that it was the duty of the sovereign to erect and maintain "those public institutions and those public works, which, though they may be in the highest degree advantageous to a great society, are, however, of such a nature, that the profit could never repay the expense to any individual or small number of individuals, and which it therefore cannot be expected that any individual or small number of individuals should erect or maintain."[122] Stated differently, there are certain public works, institutions, and projects that should not be privatized; rather, the sovereign state should provide—on the condition that citizens pay for these beneficial works through taxation—these elements. Such works included both the building and the maintenance of highways, bridges, canals, and harbors, as well as the establishment of public institutions (i.e., schools). Taxes, in turn, were necessary and based in part on usage. The building and maintenance of highways, for example, would be provided by "a small toll upon the carriages which make use of them," and thus taxation "works exactly in proportion to the wear and tear which they occasion of them."[123] Smith anticipated that these costs ultimately would be borne by the consumer.

Of note, also, is that Smith advocated that tolls be proportionate to wealth; in other words, it was expected that the rich would pay a disproportionate share because they had benefited so much more from the state. Smith explained that "when the toll upon carriages of luxury . . . is made somewhat higher in proportion to their weight, than upon carriages of necessary use, such as carts, wagons . . . the indolence and vanity of the rich is made to contribute in a very easy manner to the relief of the poor, by rendering cheaper the transportation of heavy goods to all the different parts of the country."[124]

Elsewhere, Smith reinforced his notion that the expenses of the state, in pursuit of its duties, be proportional. Thus, expenses "should be defrayed by the general contribution of the whole society, all the different members contributing, as nearly as possible, in proportion to their respective abilities," and the "subjects of every state ought to contribute towards the support of the government, as nearly as possible, in proportion to their respective abilities; that is, *in proportion to the revenue which they respectively enjoy under the protection of the state.*"[125] In sum, Smith recognized that individuals could only benefit—could only accumulate capital—because of the state. It was the state that ensured the territorial integrity that allowed capitalists to conduct business without fear of foreign invasion; it was the state that initiated favorable treaties with foreign nations; it was the state that provided and maintained the infrastructure upon which trade could flourish. It was thus only proper that those who benefited the most provide the most in return. In doing so, the state was obligated to ensure—through regulations—that all participants in society had equal access (i.e., members of society did not violate the laws of justice) and were protected from injustices and oppression.[126]

These caveats and qualifications of Smith, however, are all too often conveniently ignored by those who promote an extreme laissez-faire attitude toward the market. As Bernard Harcourt explains, the doctrine of laissez-faire from the mid-nineteenth century onward essentially allowed three functions for the government: maintaining the external defense of the country, providing for the internal order and security of persons, and providing for minimal public amenities. This last principle has been tenuous at best.[127] As detailed below, these functions have metamorphosed into the abstractions of neoliberalism and neoconservatism.

Neoliberalism

An extreme variant of laissez-faire capitalism is currently found in the promotion of the doctrine of neoliberalism. Rooted in the classical liberal ideals of British philosophers, neoliberalism premises that states should play a minimal role in the day-to-day working of markets. Liberalism, as a critique of feudalism, emphasized the priority of the individual and thereby privileged concepts such as reason, equality, and competition. This view contrasted, as we have seen, with that of earlier feudalistic societies, which were defined by community, authority, and hierarchy.

Liberty was especially promoted, although in this sense the term meant the relative absence of external impediments to rational behavior.

Neoliberalism traces its lineage to classical liberal thinkers such as Smith but also to David Ricardo and Herbert Spencer. Smith, as indicated earlier, argued that governmental interference should be minimal—but not absent—from the workings of the market. He presumed that the resources of a nation would be best managed when individuals were allowed to pursue economic activities according to market principles. It was through his writings in particular that the market came to be seen as a self-regulating mechanism tending toward equilibrium of supply and demand.

The ideas of Smith were adopted and modified by a generation of economists and political philosophers—often to the detriment of the worker and to the benefit of the capitalist. Indeed, subsequent itera-tions of Smith's invisible hand and the primacy of the market resulted in a growing disparity between the wealthy and the poor. David Ricardo (1772–1823), for example, suggested that it was appropriate for capitalists to force labor to surrender a large part of the value created; this exploi-tation was necessary to ensure the continued existence of the private capital that would be needed for future investment.[128] This view formed the backbone of Ricardo's theory of the "iron law of wages," wherein the capitalist should pay workers only enough to keep them on the job—a topic I explore in greater detail in chapter 3. Crucial to this idea, moreover, is that capitalism so conceived required an environment whereby other nonwage modes of existence were removed. In short, capitalism, to be fully profitable, required the participation of everyone—willing or not.

Ricardo further developed the idea of comparative advantage, which was used also as an argument against governmental interference in free trade. First specified by Robert Torrens in 1815, the law of comparative advantage states that a country will benefit by exporting a good that it produces at a lower cost relative to that of other countries; conversely, a country will benefit by importing a good that it could produce at a higher relative cost. Consequently, all countries would eventually (in theory) specialize only in the production of those commodities for which they had a comparative advantage. Implicit in this theory is the necessity that all countries participate in systems of capitalist exchange.

Competition among numerous small buyers and sellers was viewed as the engine of economic growth. This idea was elaborated in the social Darwinist writings of Herbert Spencer. Spencer's liberalism was concerned with the welfare of society—but from an economically competitive orientation. Modifying the evolutionary ideas of Charles Darwin, Spencer argued that welfare programs were tampering with the "invisible hand" of evolution. Spencer suggested that free-market economies constituted the most civilized form of human competition, one in which the "fittest" would "naturally" rise to the top and succeed. Consequently, he denounced socialism, trade unions, and social regulation insofar as these, in his view, would inhibit rational progress and individual freedom.[129] Spencer's theory was immensely popular in the United States, resonating strongly with the notion of rugged individualism that was promoted during the late nineteenth and early twentieth centuries.

Given this ancestry of neoliberalism, its central features—as currently expressed in the United States and elsewhere—include the primacy (indeed, necessity) of continued, expansive economic growth; the importance of free trade; the existence of an unrestricted free market; individual choice; unrestricted privatization; and the reduction of government regulation.[130] For David Harvey, neoliberalism is first a theory of political-economic practices proposing that human well-being can best be advanced by liberating individual entrepreneurial freedoms and skills within an institutional framework characterized by strong private property rights, free markets, and free trade. Furthermore, if markets do not exist, then they must be created—paradoxically, by state action if necessary.[131]

Two neoliberal commitments stand out in particular as being foundational to the promotion of values and the abstraction of violence under capitalism. The first is the claim that the efficiency of the market is a superior allocative mechanism for the distribution of scarce public resources.[132] This claim, we will see, is especially important for understanding the violence attendant to debates over health care. It is also apparent in the role of the state's security apparatus. Governmental intervention in the market is abstracted as oppressive and detrimental to the self-regulating market. However, with respect to the role of crime and punishment, given that the market is presumably best left alone, it is necessary for the state to ensure that citizens abide by the market logic of capitalism. Workers must be "free" to participate in the labor market, private property must be protected at all times, and the police should be related to a realm outside the market—not policing corporate transactions but directing attention toward those who do not comply with the natural order.[133]

A second, and related, commitment of neoliberalism is that the market is a morally superior form of political economy. This claim has profound implications given that individual exchanges *appear* to be privileged under capitalism. Workers are ostensibly free to enter the formal labor market at will, and if they do not like their present job—as the adage goes—they can always get another job. For Michael Peters, neoliberalism signifies a primitive form of individualism, one that is "competitive," "possessive," and constructed often in terms of the doctrine of "consumer sovereignty." He further notes that this "involves an emphasis on freedom over equality, where freedom is construed in negative and individualistic terms. Negative freedom is freedom from state interference, which implies an acceptance of inequalities generated by the market."[134] I return to this point in the following chapter.

That the free market is anything but free and equal is beside the point. Capitalism thrives on the illusion of freedom and choice; indeed, it is this illusory component that helps maintain order and stability. Because we *want* to believe that markets operate on their own and thus are realms of equality and freedom, we fail to properly scrutinize how the workings of the market actually concentrate wealth in the hands of a few.[135] We fail to see that the appearance of the so-called free market—a particular abstraction—is manifest in concrete conditions that significantly alter one's exposure to harm, injury, suffering, and premature death.

Neoconservatism

The doctrine of neoliberalism is often coupled with another doctrine, that of neoconservatism. In certain respects, these two doctrines are variations on the same liberal themes: the importance of free markets and free trade. However, neoconservatives are more apt to combine a hands-off approach to economic regulation with intrusive—but highly selective—government action for the regulation of "ordinary" citizens in the name of public security and traditional values.[136] In other words, governmental interference in social and cultural spheres is acceptable, presuming that this interference promotes a particular morality and value system and that it does not alter the free-market system. Neoconservatives, accordingly, do not favor social welfare programs; instead, Spencerian ideas of private responsibility and individualism are promoted.

According to Andrew Bacevich, neoconservatism originated within the context of America's defeat in Vietnam. Various intellectuals believed that the lessons of Vietnam did not revolve around the overextension of American power or around a moral irresponsibility. Rather, the consequences of defeat in Vietnam demonstrated the *absence* of American power and will. Such weaknesses endangered the security and prosperity of the United States and its allies.[137]

The neoconservative movement in the United States, as it emerged during the 1970s and into the 1980s, viewed state power not as a necessary evil but as a positive good to be cultivated and deployed for moral purposes. It was, in essence, a transformative endeavor to remake American society and, by extension, a global environment ripe for capital accumulation. Bacevich identifies six propositions that summarize the embedded value system of neoconservatism. First, there is a fundamental understanding—an abstraction—of history that is built upon supposed truths. The first is that evil is real; the second is that, for evil to prevail, it requires only one thing: for those confronted by evil to flinch from duty. This abstraction of history arises from a particular reading of the Great Depression of the 1930s and the ascension of Adolf Hitler and Nazi Germany.[138] In the realm of foreign policy, therefore, a proactive, aggressive course of action is required when confronted with evil dictators and regimes. This proposition finds its counterpart in domestic policy, whereby neoconservative politicians promote the idea that some people are naturally evil. Throughout the 1980s, for example, such politicians emphasized street crime in their efforts to steer state policy toward social control and away from social welfare.[139] Portraying their Democratic opponents as "soft on crime," Republican Party members critiqued rehabilitation measures and instead promoted increasingly draconian punitive practices (e.g., zero-tolerance and three-strikes policies). Underlying these efforts was a particular abstraction of criminal behavior as being inherent in "evil" people, that these men, women, and even children were beyond the hope of rehabilitation and thus had to be dealt with severely.[140]

A second proposition with recourse to supposed historical fact was that diplomacy and accommodation do not work. Hence, just as appeasement failed to stem Hitler's evil, so too are "peaceable" means insufficient to confront the evil facing society. At the international level, this view means that there is no substitute for military power. Closer to home, a similar reasoning applies. Such a position, for example, is regularly heard in debates surrounding gun regulations, conceal-and-carry laws, and stand-your-ground laws. Simply stated, for neoconservatives the combination of the civil rights movement, women's movement, gay rights movement, and even the environmental movement has had a catastrophic effect on the moral fiber of American society and—by extension—on the U.S. economy. Those holding extremely conservative views thus fear that an increasing tolerance of divorce, abortion, homosexuality, drugs, and sexual promiscuity—to name but a few—will lead to the downfall of society. Marijuana use was labeled a gateway to heroin and crack cocaine, same-sex marriage would lead to bestiality, and divorce would contribute to the decline of traditional moral values that were the glue holding society together. Such attitudes have contributed to support for the militarization of U.S. borders, the emergence of vigilante patrols, the growth of gated communities, the privatization of the penal system, and the dramatic expansion of the U.S. prison population. Such attitudes likewise have contributed to the continued support of capital punishment.

A third proposition relates to the perception of America's presumed mission. Reworking the idea of manifest destiny, neoconservatives maintain that alternatives to, or substitutes for, American global leadership simply do not exist. As Andrew Bacevich writes, according to neoconservatives, "history [has] singled out the United States to play a unique role as the chief instrument for securing the advance of freedom, which found its highest expression in democratic capitalism. American ideals defined America's purpose, to be achieved through the exercise of superior American power."[141] Here we see clearly the confluence of neoliberal economic ideals and the moral justification for American empire building. The neoconservative movement thus recaptures many of the claims to legitimacy that were used in support of earlier American military interventions, including the forcible acquisition of the Philippines, which came, in the words of Marx, "dripping from head to toe, from every pore, with blood and dirt."[142]

Vietnam provided another lesson for neoconservatives, namely, that foreign policy must not be subsumed by domestic policies. The fourth proposition, therefore, concerns the relationship between cultural politics and the United States' purpose abroad. Simply put, neoconservatives promote "traditional" values; these include, but are not limited to, marriage and the nuclear family, the advocacy of law and order, and respect for organized (Christian) religion. Only by supporting these beleaguered institutions, it is argued, can the United States promote a powerful and transformative foreign policy. Consequently, appeals to traditional family values, opposition to same-sex marriages, and even antipathy toward welfare are couched in a particular abstraction of "legitimate" forms of law-making and law-preserving violence. A fifth proposition, also drawing on Vietnam, suggests that, absent decisive action to resolve a crisis, unspeakable consequences await. And for neoconservatives, this is a permanent condition. Reflecting a heightened form of *realpolitik*, neoconservatives view the world (and, frankly, American society) as being in a state of total and unending risk. Within such an environment, as indicated earlier, a powerful military and police presence is required, as is an armed citizenry. Lastly, neoconservatives maintain that strong leadership is needed to guide America to its global destiny and to promote a particular morality at home. As Bacevich concludes, neoconservatives seek leaders who demonstrate unflinching determination, moral clarity, and inspiration: in short, they advocate for "heroic" leadership, even at the risk of losing individual freedoms and democratic practice. Such is the cost of security and salvation.

CONCLUSIONS

In *Violence in Capitalism* I begin with the premise that every society produces its own space and that this socio-spatial production is, in large part, derived from the existing, dominant mode of production. Simply put, a mode of production includes both means of production and relations of production. The means of production include those elements that constitute the productive capacity of the economy—the instruments of labor—including, for example, land and machinery. Relations of production, conversely, include the social relations among economic actors. Within capitalism, the most basic social relation is that between those who own the means of production (capitalists) and those who are denied access to the means of production (laborers). Other relations exist between and among those, for example, who are denied access to the means of production (the unemployed who work in the informal economy).

Beginning with the mode of production directs attention to the fundamental social (and spatial) relations of society—a necessary step given that violence, whether considered direct or structural, is ultimately relational. However, to begin from the standpoint of the mode of production also highlights the complex relationship between violence and crime. Too often, these concepts are conflated and used interchangeably or the former stands as a proxy for the latter, that is, violence stands as a proxy for crime. This is evident, for example, when crime is mapped and then, by extension, levels of violence are inferred. However, not all acts of violence are considered criminal and thus are not necessarily included in crime statistics. An obvious—but important example—is the gap between the incidence of intimate partner violence and the reporting of such acts. In short, what constitutes a criminal act is intimately associated with the reigning judicial system—itself an intricate component that originates in the overall political-economic system.

In principle, capitalism differs from other modes of production because the class relation can be reduced without reliance on extra-economic force when commodification is complete.[143] For example, unlike slave-based societies, capitalism does not rely upon direct violence to compel individuals to participate; rather, capitalism *appears* as an all-pervasive system to which there is no (legal) alternative. Furthermore, the confluence of neoliberal and neoconservative attitudes—both grounded in a particular understanding of the capitalist market—has significantly shaped both the understanding of violence (broadly) and the criminal justice system (more narrowly). Whether any specific concrete action or inaction is considered violent or criminal is predicated upon, and abstracted from, a particular market logic.

Within capitalism—and especially as articulated through neoliberalism and neoconservatism—the free market, supposedly free of governmental interference, is posited as a utopian space of individual liberty and societal equality. This holds because of the dominant narrative that force and violence are absent from capitalism as mode of production. However, as Marx explains, "wherever a part of society possesses the monopoly of the means of production, the worker, free or unfree, must add to the labor-time necessary for his own maintenance an extra quantity of labor-time in order to produce the means of subsistence for the owner of the means of production, whether this proprietor be an ... Etruscan theocrat, a civis romanus, a Norman baron, an American slave-owner, a Wallachian boyar, a modern landlord or a capitalist."[144] In other words, in slave societies or "free" societies, where one class owns the means of production and another is denied, members of the laboring class must work to support both their own subsistence as well as that of the owning class. The difference between slave societies and capitalism is simply that force is apparent in the former and illusory in the latter. Paul D'Amato elaborates:

> Under slavery and feudalism, the way in which a surplus was extracted was completely transparent. Anything produced over and above the costs of purchasing the slave and maintaining him (which varied depending on whether the owner profited more from working the slave to death or stretching his service out longer) was taken by the slaveowner as surplus product. The feudal peasant or serf was required

either to hand over a portion of his crop to the lord and/or the state in rent, tithes, or taxes, or to perform unpaid labor (called "corvee") for the lord. . . . Whereas serf and slave labor was to varying degrees forced or bonded labor, modern capitalism is dependent on "free labor." This sweet-sounding term, however, disguises a bitter truth.[145]

The bitter truth is that many concrete actions and inactions that unevenly subject individuals to harm, injury, and even death are not viewed as violent. It is for this reason that Marx is able to make his sardonic conclusion about the market:

[It appears] a very Eden of the innate rights of man. It is the exclusive realm of Freedom, Equality, Property and Bentham. Freedom, because both buyer and seller of a commodity are . . . determined only by their own free will. They contract as free persons, who are equal before the law. Their contract is the final result in which their joint will finds a common legal expression. Equality, because each enters into relation with the other, as with a simple owner of commodities, and they exchange equivalent for equivalent. Property, because each disposes only of what is his own. And Bentham, because each looks only to his own advantage.[146]

3

The Market Logics of Letting Die

The capitalist can live longer without the worker than can the worker without the capitalist.

—KARL MARX, *Economic and Philosophic Manuscripts of 1844*

Thus far I have argued my first proposition, that violence is a general abstraction, and my second proposition, that abstractions of violence must be materially grounded within concrete modes of production. In this chapter I develop my third and most specific proposition, that, under capitalism, violence is abstracted according to a particular assemblage of market logics, a specific valuation of—and indifference to—life. As Robert Albritton writes, it is the subsumption of production to the commodity form that ultimately places the entirety of the earth—all living beings, all inanimate objects—at the service of short-term profits, no matter what the long-term consequences.[1]

More specifically, this chapter also provides a critique of the moral distinction between "killing" and "letting die" from the standpoint of Marx's critique of capitalism. The commodity, that which personifies the metamorphosis of living labor into dead labor, fetishizes the structural violence that is intrinsic to capitalism. What appears as an equal exchange within the supposedly free market is simply that: an appearance. In critiquing the distinction between the two views of death, I recast our understanding of structural violence as something that is historically and morally conditioned by capitalism itself: violence is not transhistorical or transgeographical but, as a general abstraction, conditioned by dominant economic relations, and our current conception of positive and negative rights and duties is conditioned specifically by our acceptance, and promotion, of the capitalist wage relation as something that is presumably free and equal. First, though, I revisit my earlier discussion of anatomo-politics and biopolitics, introduced in the previous chapter. Here, I introduce Giorgio Agamben's corrective to Michel Foucault's conceptualization. This theoretical intervention is necessary in that Agamben directs attention to the governance of death, to the political-economic practices associated with the taking and disallowing of life, and, more narrowly, to the moral distinction between killing and letting die.

TO LIVE, KILL, OR LET DIE

Beginning generally in the seventeenth century, the sovereign power over life developed along two competing but complementary poles. On the one hand, there emerged an anatomo-politics of the human body. As explained by Foucault, "It is always the body that is at issue—the body and its forces, their utility and their docility, their distribution and their submission."[2] Accordingly, part and parcel of the emergence of governmentality is a motivation to maximize the forces of the body and to integrate these into the nascent capitalist mode of production. This political investment of the body, consequently, is bound up in accordance with complex reciprocal relations: it is largely as a force of production that the body is invested with relations of power and domination. On the other hand, its constitution as labor power is possible only if it is caught up in a system of subjection (in which need is also a political instrument meticulously prepared, calculated, and used); the body becomes a useful force only if it is both a productive body and a subjected body.[3] The individual body becomes not only the object and effect of various techniques and practices but also, as Mitchell Dean writes, a collection of "resources to be fostered, to be used and to be optimized."[4] There thus emerged a suite of regulatory controls articulated at the level of the population. With the emergence of the capitalist state, populations were no longer conceived as the simple sum of individuals inhabiting a territory; instead, populations were conceived as a technical-political object of management and governance.

The distinction between these two techniques of biopower—anatomo-politics and biopolitics—has a tremendous bearing on our understanding of capitalism. As Foucault explains, the instantiation of biopower was an "indispensable element in the development of capitalism" and, by extension, the modern state. Indeed, capitalism would not have been possible were it not for the assemblage of practices and techniques associated with both anatomo-politics and biopolitics; required was the controlled insertion of bodies (at one level) into the machinery of production and (at a second level) the adjustment of the phenomena of population to economic processes.[5] In short, one technique, anatomo-politics, is disciplinary and centers on the body. This exercise of power produces individualizing effects and manipulates the body as a source of forces that have to be rendered both useful and docile. The second set of techniques brings together the mass effects characteristic of a population and then attempts to control the series of random events that can occur in a living mass (for example, births, deaths, and illnesses).[6] Biopolitics therefore does not exclude considerations of the anatomo-politics of the human body. Rather, the two forms of power are seen as complementary; they exist on different levels: one directed toward the body, the other toward the population. It is the combination of the two that contributes to a particular era of "biopower," one that is marked by an explosion of numerous and diverse techniques for achieving the subjugation of bodies and the control of populations.

What the modern state reveals therefore is a decidedly more nuanced management of life and death in that anatomo-political and biopolitical practice greatly altered political sovereignty. In the classic conception of sovereignty, the right of life and death was one of the sovereign's basic attributes. In other words, to say that "the sovereign has a right of life and death means that he can . . . either have people put to death or let them live." Foucault suggests, also, that sovereigns cannot grant life in the same way that they can inflict death. The right of life and death, therefore, "is always exercised in an unbalanced way: the balance is always tipped in favor of death." Consequently, the "very essence of the right of life and death is actually the right to kill: it is at the moment when the sovereign can kill that he exercises his right over life."[7] This is most apparent, obviously, in the use of torture and execution as penal practice.

The origination and transformation of the capitalist state, however, coincided with a changed ethic regarding the sovereign's right over life and death. According to Foucault, the ancient right to take life or to let live was gradually supplemented by a power to foster life or to disallow life to the point of death.[8] As David Nally explains, this "does not mean that the 'power of death' is completely abandoned, but rather that violence must be rationalized by appealing to *future improvements*."[9] This shift, which paralleled the rise of modern medicine and its attendant body of medical ethics, entailed a repositioning of the population vis-à-vis the state. As Adam Thurschwell questions, how could the sovereign power exercise its highest prerogatives by putting people to death when its main role was to ensure, sustain, and multiply life, to put this life in order?[10]

Biopolitics signaled a move toward the calculation of both life and death decisions at the level of the population. As such, the birth and death of an individual was no longer the limit point of governance but rather its site of mediation and operation.[11] Certainly the modern state's right to "foster life or to disallow it to the point of death" never completely erased the classical right to kill. Sovereignty was still exercised over the life and death of individual bodies. This is seen most immediately in the form of capital punishment; it appears also in matters of torture, political assassinations, and war. As Austin Sarat and Jennifer Culbert explain, "In a regime dedicated to putting and keeping life in order and safe, the state may still exercise the right to death associated with the classic sovereign. To do so, however, it has to describe those who will be put to death as incorrigible monsters or as biological hazards so that their demise and final disposal can be represented as an unpleasant but necessary task that the state reluctantly but decisively undertakes for the well-being of its citizens."[12]

At this point, however it is appropriate to consider the extension of Foucault's work as developed by Giorgio Agamben. In presenting a corrective to Foucault, Agamben argues that thanatopolitics—a politics of death—is actually the first principle of biopolitics. Agamben makes his argument through a focus on *homo sacer*, an archaic figure of Roman law.[13] Homo sacer constitutes "bare life," a threshold position between zoē and bios. The former term designated "the simple fact of living common to all living things" whereas bios represented a collective and qualified life; it is that which emerges when life enters the polis, or political space.[14] One who was reduced to bare life, however, occupied a liminal position. Bare life remains included in politics in the form of the exception, that is, as someone who is included solely through an exclusion.[15] For homo sacer, however, the operative principle was that those excluded could be killed with impunity, for such deaths constituted neither homicide nor sacrifice. Returning to our understanding of sovereignty, what is conceived within the sovereign ban is a human who may be killed but not sacrificed.[16] *Homini sacri*, consequently, are situated outside both human and divine law; they are included in politics only through their exclusion; they constitute, in short, "bare life."

A thanatopolitics, Nikolas Rose explains, is predicated on the understanding that "life itself is subject to a judgment of worth, a judgment that can be made by oneself (suicide) but also by others (doctors, relatives) but is ultimately guaranteed by a sovereign authority (the state)."[17] As such, decisions to kill, to foster life, or to disallow life to the point of death are made within a context of valuation: matters of life and death are understood within the domain of bioethics. As Agamben writes, for example, "In modern biopolitics, sovereign is he who decides on the value or the nonvalue of life as such."[18] This theme is developed more fully by Stuart Murray, who argues that life is now the rubric through which death must be understood; life is no longer presumed as given but instead becomes constituted in relation to political power. Consequently, "living individuals cannot be said to 'exist' de facto . . . they must be made to live." These lives, moreover, "are perpetually manufactured," and "livingness" itself is "indexed by regulation, control, normativization, and state administration."[19]

But who, under capitalism, is reduced to bare life?

In a well-worn and rather unfortunate quote, Agamben suggests that "if today there is no longer any one clear figure of the sacred man, it is perhaps because we are all virtually *homines sacri*."[20] His assertion is problematic because it presumes a homogeneity of society that simply does not exist. *Not everyone is equally susceptible to becoming reduced to bare life.* This in fact provides the foundation for the gross disparities in life expectancy. We are *not* all virtually homines sacri, nor are we all exposed to the same risks. The structural violence that permeates—indeed, constitutes—capitalism is unevenly experienced, for the calculated valuation and management of life and death ensure that survival operates on an uneven playing field. What is most crucial is that an ever-increasing number of people are in fact being abandoned, and it is this abandonment that needs addressing. Within the twenty-first century, bare life is given form through the production of structural violence in that an ever-increasing number of lives are being abandoned through political, economic, and social decisions. In essence, more and more people are being left to die, and their deaths not only carry no meaning but also are morally and legally permitted.

In the United States, for example, violent criminal activities did not increase appreciatively during the 1980s and, based on nationwide surveys, neither did the public's awareness or fear of violence and crime noticeably increase during the period. What did change, however, was the use of the language of "public violence" (a general abstraction) by both the political community and the mass media as a resource or (particularly for the media) as means to generate wealth. As a case in point, Pres. Ronald Reagan solidified the abstraction of crime as a central component of the national political agenda in the United States. His approach was to reject the idea that crime and social ills have socioeconomic causes, preferring instead to find criminal causality—and the potential for violence—in the body of the homogenous "criminal." According to Reagan—and the approach of social conservatives more generally—the social welfare programs of the 1960s, exemplified by the "war on poverty," simply created a cycle of dependency (and a related "culture of poverty") in which not only did the poor get poorer but the poor also became more violent. That studies indicated the opposite, namely, that increased welfare spending did in fact reduce criminal activity, was of little consequence.[21]

Since the 1980s political leaders (on both ends of the spectrum) have emphasized the problem of street crime in their efforts to steer state policy toward social control and away from social welfare.[22] Portraying opponents as "soft on crime," these politicians would critique rehabilitation measures and instead promote increasingly punitive practices. Underlying these efforts was a recurrent theme that criminal behavior was essentialized within people who were evil and therefore beyond the hope or scope of rehabilitation.[23]

In other words, the political narrative of crime and violence since the 1980s is indicative of a particular abstraction that is continually reproduced as political discourse. As Jeffrey Reiman and Paul Leighton explain, systems of criminal justice are not simply reflections of an objective reality; they are not neutral systems that prohibit and punish essential behaviors deemed harmful. Rather, for Reiman and Leighton, the criminal justice system acts as a carnival mirror that distorts reality by magnifying the threat of street crime—dominated by young men and persons of color— while minimizing other harmful behaviors.[24] Thus, the reality of crime and violence is not an objective reality; it simply cannot be construed based on empirically observable criminal acts, arrests, convictions, or incarceration rates, for these accountings are themselves reflective of innumerable decisions about which behaviors are considered (or pursued) as criminal and which are not. Judges and juries, prosecutors and legislators: all of these parties play a role in determining what is counted and what is not counted. It is for this reason that the intentional, planned killing of one person constitutes murder whereas the intentional, planned decision to cut costs through a reduction in health and safety measures by the CEO of an industry that results in substantial loss of life is often not considered criminal. Noting that each year in the United States upwards of fifty thousand deaths result from occupational disease (workplace exposure to cancer-causing chemicals), Reiman and Leighton ask rhetorically: Is a person who kills another in a bar brawl a greater threat to society than are business executives who refuse to cut into their profits to make their plants safe places to work?[25]

That neither Foucault nor Agamben satisfactorily addresses the interconnections of violence, values, crime, and capitalism should come as no surprise. Missing from both Foucault's and Agamben's accounts of biosovereignty is any sustained engagement with the question of why some governing authorities would elect *not* to intervene when they could or, conversely, why they would select one subset of the population for life enhancement while abandoning another.[26] In other words, insufficient attention has been directed toward the market logics that underpin the practice of letting die. Required is a more theoretically nuanced understanding of the moral and political distinction between "making live," "killing," and "letting die," an understanding predicated upon hegemonic discourses of, but not limited to, race, gender, and sexual orientation as manifest in the contemporary, formal labor market. Accordingly, I propose a corrective to both Foucault and Agamben, namely, that it is necessary to articulate more clearly the distinction between making live, killing, and letting die within the context of the intersectionality of racialized, gendered, and classed market relations. Simply put, within society we witness, on a day-to-day basis, that the right to live continues to be unequal, that while some efforts are made—by the state—to ensure survivability (i.e., making live), for others, for those populations deemed superfluous to society, there are no such assurances.

KILLING VERSUS LETTING DIE

What is our obligation—either legally or ethically—to help? If I see a person in need, I may choose to intervene, or not. For example, if I come across a man who is seemingly lying comatose on the ground, I might stop and offer assistance. The degree of my intervention is, of course, predicated in part on my own abilities. If I can determine that cardiopulmonary resuscitation is required and I am able to perform this action, then I can do so. Otherwise, I might attempt to attract the attention of some other person who can perform CPR. I might also, if I have a phone, call for emergency responders. It goes without saying that these are not mutually exclusive actions.

Most people would probably agree that my actions—to the extent that I offered assistance—were laudable, perhaps even heroic. But did I have an obligation or responsibility to offer assistance? Perhaps not—at least, not legally—but again, most people would find inaction on my part to be callous and unconscionable. After all, we live in a civilized society, and it is simply the right thing to do—to help one who is in need of assistance.

Let's continue the example. Suppose the man, through my actions, survived—but suffered brain damage not because of any negligence on my part but only because he had already endured oxygen deprivation for too many minutes before I was able to help. Do I—or does society—have an obligation to help with the man's long-term medical costs? Does it matter if the man had medical insurance? Does it matter if the man was old or young, black or white? Does it matter if the man collapsed because he was a habitual drug user or morbidly obese? Expand the example. Rather than confronting a comatose man lying on the ground, we now encounter a family living in poverty. Do we intervene? How? We can ask similar questions of the state: Does the state have an obligation to help those in need? Is assistance proffered only on the condition that need is determined not as a result of individual inaction? In other words, do we help the unemployed or the poor only if their present condition was caused by events beyond their control, such as a factory closing? We recognize that shooting or stabbing someone constitutes a direct action that is generally abstracted as violence. Accordingly, these actions have been criminalized. Do (or should?) inactions also constitute a moment of violence or, more specifically, a criminal offense? Such questions are far from simple and call attention to a long-standing debate—widely engaged in by scholars of philosophy but less so in other social sciences—this being the moral division (and distinction) between "negative" and "positive" duties. On the one hand, we—at least from a Western perspective—have duties not to harm others. These duties, which require restraint, are termed negative duties. On the other hand, we also have positive duties, those being duties (some might say, obligations) to help others. All else being equal, the obligation to not harm people is considered to be more stringent than the obligation to benefit (or even to help) people.[27] In law, religion, and medicine, for example, negative duties to not harm often outweigh positive duties.[28] Indeed, we are neither expected nor always encouraged to engage in charitable or philanthropic activities. If one does pursue these goals, fine, but no one is punished for not pursuing positive duties.

Criminal law, at a basic level, exists to make society possible. Composed of various rules, regulations, and punishments, criminal law in general assumes three forms: protection from harm caused by others, protection from harm caused by ourselves, and protection of societal morals.[29] The form these protections assume, however, is neither universal, transhistorical, nor transgeographical. Rather, criminal law is contextual and contingent; it is dialectically related to the dominant mode of production. Such a position challenges those claims that presume law to exist independent of a material reality, that law and justice, broadly conceived, are derived from universal morals. In the United States, for example, criminal law coexists with the capitalist mode of production. This is not to argue that crime and criminal law are mimetic to capitalist production, circulation, and exchange; rather, it is to argue that the particular shape that criminal justice assumes is governed according to certain principles that together constitute capitalism.

From a legal standpoint, a criminal act in the United States consists of a perpetrator (usually a person but, in limited situations, a corporation), a criminal act (*actus reus*), intentionality (*mens rea*), causation, and concurrence.[30] Stated more directly, for a criminal act to occur, it must be perpetrated by some*one* against some*one* or some*thing*. We may readily see that such a banal statement belies a deeper racialized, gendered, and sexed history of what constitutes a prohibited or criminal act. In the seventeenth century, for example, the jurist Matthew Hale formulated the legal position that a woman could not be raped by her husband. Hale argued that by "their mutual matrimonial consent and contract the wife hath given of herself in this kind unto her husband, which she cannot retract."[31] In other words, it was legally impossible for a man to rape his wife. This "marital exemption" or "marital immunity," which was codified in the United States as early as 1857, remained in place until well into the twentieth century. Indeed, as recently as 1984 about forty states retained some form of marital exemption.[32]

That marital rape was not considered criminal does not suggest that the act was not violent or, even more broadly, that it did not occur. Clearly, we have a real, concrete act that most people (though not all) would recognize as being violent. And yet, in many histories of violence, such acts—because they were not conceived as criminal—went unrecorded and thus unacknowledged. One wonders, therefore, about the claims (introduced in chapter 1) that violence has decreased over the last few centuries.

The point is that our understanding—and indeed acknowledgment—of violence is intricately associated with our criminal justice system. This is seen especially in the distinction between crimes of commission and crimes of omission. According to U.S. criminal law, although an affirmative act is usually required for criminal culpability, in some instances liability may result from the failure to act.[33] Various statutes have identified four types of duty that may create liability if there is an omission: statutory duties, relationship duties, contractual duties, and failure to continue care duties. Statutory duties, for example, are those whereupon an individual is required by law to do something (e.g., file a tax return) but fails to do so. Relationship and contractual duties, conversely, impose an obligation on a person because of particular relational obligations. Parents, for example, have certain relationship duties and thus may be found criminally liable if they fail to act on behalf of their children. Doctors, nurses, and lifeguards, likewise, have contractual duties to act; if they fail to act, they may, accordingly, be held liable. Lastly, failure to continue care duties arise when a person who has no legal obligation to render aid assumes this obligation and then leaves the victim. Apart from these relational obligations, U.S. criminal law does not prosecute individuals for failure to help. Unlike many governments in Europe, most states in the United States do not have "Good Samaritan" laws that create a duty to render assistance when one citizen sees another in distress.[34]

The legal concept of *actus reus* and the distinction between crimes of omission and crimes of commission have a significant bearing on our abstraction of violence within American society. As mentioned earlier, we have negative duties, or obligations, to refrain from doing others harm. Also, we have positive duties; these are predicated on the notion that we have an obligation to help others. The promotion—and practice—of positive and negative duties in American society is not equal, and this in fact is reflected in the legal concept of *actus reus*, whereby crimes of omission—the failure to act—are decidedly more narrow and restrictive than crimes of commission. Moreover, negative duties are premised to involve less sacrifice and are thus easier to fulfill. To help a person in need might necessitate an expenditure of time or money whereas to refrain from directly harming requires no such effort. A society that promotes negative duties over positive duties may, from this vantage point, be seen as an exceptionally conservative society; with no legal and quite possibly no moral guidance to affect positive change, we necessarily reproduce the status quo.

The separation and unequal promotion of positive and negative duties also finds its counterpart in the philosophical distinction between killing and letting die. This distinction, widely discussed and debated within philosophy, has received surprisingly little attention in the social sciences, particularly in studies of violence.[35] Intuitively, it is presumed that the act of killing is morally worse than letting die. Such a presumption hinges partially on our understanding of agency: to kill is considered an action, whereas letting die is perceived as an omission, or lack of action. A related factor hinges on the question of intentionality, or *mens rea*, a key component in the definition of crime. Here, actions that *intentionally* injure or kill are considered more serious than failures to act—bearing in mind the aforementioned relational obligations. Philippa Foot argues, for example, that those who maintain that there is no morally relevant distinction between killing someone and allowing one to die are mistaken.[36] To make her case, she introduces two scenarios that purportedly negate the contention that both killing and letting die should hold the same moral plane. In the first scenario, Foot imagines that we are hurrying in our jeep down a narrow road to save five people who, without our assistance, will certainly drown. However, we hear also of another woman who is drowning and, without our help, will die. It is not possible to save both the group of five people and the woman; consequently, most people will choose to save the greater number. In the second scenario, Foot again begins with five people drowning. Now, however, in order to save those people, we are confronted with a man who is trapped on the narrow road that we must traverse. If we stop, the man will eventually free himself, but, because of the lost time, the five people we are attempting to rescue will perish. Our other option is to run over the one man and thus save the five. This latter scenario, of course, seems particularly unpleasant, in that it entails our killing of one person (as opposed to letting one person die, i.e., scenario one) to save the greater number. For Foot, the end result is the same: either five people are saved and one dies, or five people die and one lives. Foot's argument therefore is that "it makes all the difference whether those who are going to die if we act in a certain way will die as a result of a sequence that we originate or one that we allow to continue."[37]

The rescue scenario, according to Foot, is intended to demonstrate that there is a moral distinction between killing and letting die. She reasons that "what matters is that the fatal sequence resulting in death is not initiated but is rather allowed to take its course."[38] In scenario one, the lone woman will die, but her death is not the result of any action on our part. In scenario two, it is not acceptable to deliberately run over the man, killing him, in order to save the other five people. Foot concludes that this is "what we find in circumstances that allow a positive but not a negative duty to be overridden."[39] Our negative duty to not do harm to the man (in scenario two) is more compelling than our positive duty to provide aid to the sole woman (in scenario one). This "Doctrine of Doing and Allowing," according to Warren Quinn, is "meant to capture and explain pairs of cases like these in which consequential considerations are apparently held constant (for example, five lives versus one) but in which we are inclined to sharply divergent moral verdicts."[40] We are left with the moral position that if we (apparently) did not bring about the dismal conditions confronting other members of society, that is, if we did not initiate the fatal course of events, then we are neither morally nor legally obligated to rectify those conditions; it is simply easier to blame the victim or to rely on charitable actions—actions that are, in this sense, treated as elective options. This will resonate loudly with subsequent arguments over individual responsibility, whereupon society bears no obligation to help those less fortunate on the presumption that their misfortunes result from individual failings and personal irresponsibility, or what Rose Galvin describes as "behavioral culpability."[41]

What I find problematic in Foot's scenario, however, is that in practice our quotidian experiences are not based on having to choose between saving five people or just one. Rather, our choices are considerably more mundane, yet equally grave. We can, for example, refrain from buying yet another cup of Starbucks coffee in order to provide aid to starving children. And while it is true that we (perhaps) did not initiate the sequence that led to a child starving (wherever that child may be in the world), I fail to see why consumer spending trumps our positive duties to help those in need.

That said, it is worth pausing to consider the arguments of those who do prioritize consumer spending over humanitarian contributions. Richard Trammell, following Foot, contends also that a person has a greater obligation to refrain from killing someone (a negative duty) than to save someone (a positive duty).[42] In support of his position, he posits three principles, the first of which he deems the "Dischargeability of Duty" principle. According to Trammell, "The negative duty of not killing can be discharged completely," whereas "the positive duty of saving can never be discharged completely." In other words, it is eminently possible to not kill another person, while it is not possible to save everyone who is in need. Furthermore, negative duties involve less sacrifice and are therefore easier to fulfill; to help others might necessitate an expenditure of resources (e.g., time or money), whereas to refrain from directly harming requires no such efforts. We may readily see this as an exceptionally conservative position, whereby, with no moral guidance to affect positive change, we necessarily reproduce the status quo. For Trammell, however, "denial of the distinction between negative and positive duties leads straight to an ethic so strenuous that it might give pause even to a philosophical

John the Baptist."[43] He likewise constructs two scenarios to drive home his point. In scenario one Mr. Smith, by spending a dollar—to make a minor but essential repair on his car—can avoid harming a person in the future; in scenario two, Mr. Smith can help a person avoid harm by giving a dollar to charity. Trammell maintains that in both scenarios Mr. Smith's motivation is the same, and the effort is minimal and identical in amount. In playing out these scenarios, Trammell writes, "But the poor are always with Smith. Before he has a chance to fix his car, Smith notes that another dollar to this charity would have the same beneficial effect. . . . Bit by bit, Smith gives away all his resources." We are left with the prospect that Mr. Smith, having no money left to fix his car, may in fact harm someone while trying to help others. This in fact is what Trammell argues in his privileging negative duties over positive duties: "If one maintains as a general principle that we have equal duty not to kill as to save, then either one must uphold an ethic so strenuous that asceticism is the only morally defensible way of life; or else one must be willing to allow Smith to harm someone with his car for lack of a simple repair."[44]

It is curious, first off, that Trammell can so blithely state that "the poor are always with [us]" and, second, that we should guard against a strenuous ethic of asceticism. My point is not that we should live a life of asceticism and donate all our worldly possessions to charity. Rather, my point is one of priorities. In our daily lives it is more likely a choice not between charity and a necessary car repair but between charity and some form of conspicuous consumption. Do we really need a new toaster when the old one works just fine? My point, which will be picked up later in my discussion of capitalism, is that our priorities are misplaced, that we place material needs ahead of social justice, that our consumer-oriented society works against an ethics of care. Our inability to help everyone should not be used as an excuse to help no one; positive duties should be as stringent as one's duty to not inflict physical injury.

What of Trammell's other two principles? He argues that the "optionality" principle is crucial in distinguishing between negative and positive duties. For Trammell, a "negative duty is a duty not to do an action that closes all options," whereas a "positive duty is the duty to do an action to bring about a certain good, which someone else might also have the option to bring about."[45] In other words, if I kill Mr. Smith, it is certain that Mr. Smith will not live. However, if I fail to save Mr. Smith, there is always the option that someone else may save him. This again is a very conservative argument, one that bypasses the obligation to do good to someone else. Are we to take solace in the thought that even though we neglect to save someone in need, there *might* be another charitable person? This optionality principle will, likewise, be revisited in later sections.

Lastly, Trammell promotes the principle of responsibility. Simply put, Trammell maintains that "a person is not necessarily responsible for someone else's needing to be saved; but he is responsible for the life of anyone he kills."[46] This last principle brings us full circle to Foot's argument and, in fact, is the keystone to our current legal system: it is criminal to harm someone, but, unless one is legally responsible for the life another, it is not criminal to not save someone. We may better understand at this point why "letting die" constitutes neither homicide nor sacrifice. If bodies reduced to bare life may be killed with impunity, so too may they be disallowed life. Consequently, we must recognize also that the disallowance of life to the point of death constitutes an act of sovereign violence. It is, in Agamben's words, a violence that is "founded not on a pact but on the exclusive inclusion of bare life in the state."[47]

In the following sections I argue that such an attitude is intrinsic to capitalism, that it is in fact the promotion of the labor contract as a free exchange and individual choice between capital and workers that calculates the determination of worth in capitalist society, that ultimately the answer to who lives and who dies in our present age is found in the waged labor market. My starting point, therefore, is to follow Marx into the labor process, to unpack the principal social relation of capitalism, namely, the distinction between the owners of the means of production and those who are compelled to sell their labor in order to live. My initial vantage point is orthodox Marxism; such a perspective, however, is woefully incomplete. It is necessary, as I argue in the following section, to critically work through Marxism from the standpoint of feminism and antiracism. Here, I concur with Julie Matthaei, who writes that the "theoretical merging of Marxism, feminism, and anti-racism allows the development of a more inclusive, and more liberatory, understanding of the economy."[48] By extension, it becomes possible to more clearly articulate the intersectional workings of class, sex, and race (among other axes of difference) within capitalism. Lastly, I assemble the pieces, so to speak, to situate the moral distinction between killing and letting die within capitalism.

THE COMMODIFICATION OF SOCIETY

I begin, as does Marx, with the concept of the commodity. I do so not because I want to forward an overly simplistic argument that life has become commodified within capitalism. It is well established that, within capitalism, human bodies are considered commodities, that men, women, and children—as commodities—are to be inserted, indeed subordinated, into the labor market. The canons of neoclassical economics maintain that labor is impersonally regulated by the market; these beliefs have only deepened under neoliberalism.[49] Instead, I focus on the commodity because, as Moishe Postone indicates, "this category refers not only to a product but also to the most fundamental structuring social form of capitalist society, a form constituted by a historically determinate mode of social practice."[50] In short, as Melissa Wright explains, to begin with the commodity is "to demonstrate that the things of capital cannot be understood without seeing their intimate relationship to the people who make them."[51] A focus on the commodity, therefore, directs attention first to the particular socio-spatial relations that constitute capitalism and, second, to the *economic* distinction between use value and exchange value. It is this latter distinction, I argue, that is especially salient with respect to the moral distinction between killing and letting die.

According to Marx, commodities have a dual character, being composed of both use values and exchange values. On the one hand, commodities, as products of human labor, possess some useful quality for people, and, on the other hand, commodities have exchange values, in that one commodity may be exchanged for another commodity. The use value of a commodity, therefore, stems from the qualitative properties that make it useful, while exchange value stems entirely from the social homogeneity of commodities, whereby they differ only quantitatively.[52] Marx explains, however, that within capitalism (unlike, say, a barter system), commodities are not simply exchanged (e.g., a shirt is exchanged for a bushel of corn). As Marx writes, these "are only commodities because they have a dual nature, because they are at the same time objects of utility and bearers of value."[53] Furthermore, "the volume of the mass of commodities brought into being by capitalist production," Marx elaborates, "is determined by the scale of this production and its needs for constant expansion, and not by a predestined ambit of supply and demand, of needs to be satisfied."[54] Stated differently, under capitalism the rationale for production is profit—not need or use in the abstract. There are many people in dire need of food, water, shelter, and medicine, but products that satisfy these vital needs are produced only to the degree that profits may be realized.

The profit motive of capitalism has profound implications for the abstraction of violence, for given that "the commodity form reifies and objectifies social relations by subsuming them to a commodity-economic logic," it follows that the accumulation of wealth for its own sake will be determinant of a particular market logic.[55] This logic, I maintain, is characterized by a value system predicated on indifference. In other words, rather than focusing on difference as the basis of societal inequalities, it is necessary to engage in the capitalist logic of indifference.

It matters little if the capitalist produces bicycles or binoculars; whichever offers the best opportunity for capital accumulation will, in principle, be produced. Marx refers to this tendency as "indifference to use-value." Faced with a seemingly indifferent choice, how then are decisions made? Within capitalism, all else being equal, the choice is actually straightforward. Capitalists *prefer* to produce those commodities that will generate profits. Marx explains that "capital withdraws from a sphere with a low rate of profit and wends its way to others that yield higher profit."[56] If it becomes too costly (because of, say, declining profits) to produce bicycles, the capitalist may direct his or her attention to the production of, perhaps, binoculars. Albritton concludes that exchange value must always be connected to a use value wanted by someone, but value as capital strives to be indifferent to use value in the sense that it would always prefer to focus single-mindedly on maximizing quantity in the form of profit. In order to behave according to the imperatives of capitalist rationality (i.e., market logics), capital must always be opportunistic (i.e., indifferent to use values).[57]

What is most important in this trade-off of products is that the concept of indifference to use value contains within it its own inner contradictions, namely, a unity of opposites between "indifference" and "preference." Restated, systemic to the concept of indifference is the concept of preference. To be indifferent to something is, at one level, to exhibit a nonpreference. I may be indifferent to having apple pie or pumpkin pie for dessert; a capitalist may be indifferent to producing bicycles or binoculars. Indeed, a Good Samaritan may be indifferent to saving one person or five people. Such indifference is commonly understood as being neutral and, by extension, objective. However, when faced with a choice—to which one may be initially indifferent—one must still make a decision. Unless I don't care about the added calories, I must choose either the apple or pumpkin pie; likewise, the capitalist (in the abstract) must produce either bicycles or binoculars—but (generally) not both.[58] And our Good Samaritan, as the aforementioned thought experiments demonstrate, must also choose.

As society becomes ever more subsumed to the market logics of capital, societal values exhibit a general preference toward those practices that generate surplus value; a commodified society therefore is one that expresses the dominant value of indifference and a corresponding preference based on those elements that are deemed most valuable. Production under capitalism is first and foremost a profit-driven activity; it is not needs based. This does not deny that any given capitalist may altruistically manufacture certain commodities and provide selected services that "do good." Recall, however, that Marx's critique was at a very abstract level; capitalism as a pure mode of production is predicated on the valorization of capital: the accumulation of wealth. Marx went to great lengths to explain that any given capitalist is not necessarily greedy or evil. That being said, the market logics of capitalism, and in particular the existence of competition and the preference for wealth generation, impel capitalists to place profit over welfare. If more profits are to be made in the production of medicines for erectile dysfunction as opposed to malarial treatments, then so be it. To say, therefore, that all the fundamental categories of economic life are fully commodified means that their quantitative or value side is not disrupted by their qualitative or use-value side, with the result that, as quantitative variables, they can all in principle be interrelated through the homogeneity of numbers.[59]

Under capitalism, it is crucial to recognize that societal values are part and parcel of the production, distribution, and consumption of commodities. Marx argued that commodities are not exchanged according to their degree of usefulness; instead, there is in all commodities a quantitative relation that facilitates their exchange. This common denominator, Marx concluded, was not money (itself a representation of value) but instead labor power. Such an argument, which is an extension of the writings of Adam Smith and David Ricardo in particular, is crucial in that it establishes a foundation by which not only work but also life itself is evaluated within capitalism. As Marx indicates, labor power "exists only as a capacity of the living individual. Its production consequently presupposes his existence. Given the existence of the individual, the production of labor-power consists in his reproduction of himself or his maintenance."[60]

Marx writes, "Because all commodities, as values, are objectified human labor, and therefore in themselves commensurable, their values can be communally measured in one and the same specific commodity, and this commodity can be converted into the common measure of their values, that is, into money."[61] Consequently, the "process of exchange is . . . accomplished through two metamorphoses of opposite yet complementary character—the conversion of the commodity into money, and the re-conversion of the money into a commodity."[62] This is illustrated in Marx's well-known form: "commodity-money-commodity," or simply C-M-C. The first transformation, C-M, represents the conversion of a commodity into money (i.e., the act of selling), while the second transformation, M-C, represents the conversion of money into a commodity (i.e., the act of buying). Hence, this single process is two-sided: from one pole, that of the commodity owner, it is a sale; from the other pole, that of the money owner, it is a purchase.[63]

Alongside this form of circulation is another form of circulation: M-C-M, the transformation of money into commodities, and the reconversion of commodities into money. Whereas the first circulation resulted in the exchange of commodities (albeit mediated through money), under the second circulation there is an exchange of money for money via commodities. And here, Marx finds the crucial component of capitalism, in that "the circulatory process of M-C-M would be absurd and empty if the intention were, by using this roundabout route, to exchange two equal sums of money."[64] Marx explains that "in the simple circulation of commodities [C-M-C] the two extremes have the same economic form. They are both commodities, and commodities of equal value. But they are also qualitatively different use-values, as for example corn and clothes."[65] However, within the second circulation, "both extremes have the same economic form. They are both money, and therefore are not qualitatively different use-values, for money is precisely the converted form of commodities." Consequently, the "process M-C-M does not . . . owe its content to any qualitative difference between its extremes, for they are both money, but solely to quantitative changes."[66] As David Harvey writes, "M-C-M only makes sense if it results in an increment of value," this being surplus value.[67] For this reason, it is more proper to rewrite the circuit as M-C-M', with M' designating the added value.

For Marx, commodities are exchanged not according to their usefulness; rather, commodities are exchanged according to how much labor time they take to produce. Stated differently, the value of a commodity—and not its price—is determined by the amount of labor time necessary to produce that commodity. The capitalist labor market, therefore, appears as a system whereby a person's capacity to work becomes a commodity that can be bought and sold on the market. Many of our contemporary values and rights are grounded in the formal, waged labor market. Consider, for example, the promotion of freedom in the United States. It is frequently claimed (usually by those on the far right of the political spectrum) that participation in the labor market or selling one's own labor capacity is a matter of free choice. Recall, however, the distinction made between positive rights and negative rights. Positive rights permit or oblige action, whereas negative rights permit or oblige inaction. In other words, to promote positive rights is to actively intervene: to create those conditions that allow one to participate fully in society. To promote negative rights, conversely, is to ensure that one is not denied the right to participate within society. In the United States, negative rights are promoted to the degree that all citizens and permitted residents are to be allowed to participate in the labor market; this is not the same as a provision of equal participation, because this "right" indicates only that the state will ensure that no one is prohibited from participating. Stated bluntly, the state does not guarantee (full) employment; it only guarantees (in principle) that one is not prohibited from participating in the quest for employment. As Kathi Weeks explains, "From the perspective of the work ethic, governments are seen to protect the welfare of citizens by defending their *right to work*, while employers are not so much extracting surplus value as they are meeting the concrete needs of their employees for work."[68]

In practice, one's access to waged work has been (and often continues to be) determined by racist and sexist structures that permit some to participate while others may be relegated to either the nonpaid and thus insecure "reproductive" sphere or, increasingly, to nonformal means of employment—those activities that, perversely, are classified as criminal. Labor capacity, as well as one's participation in the circulation of capital, therefore, is necessarily precarious. It is for this reason that the sovereign decision to make live or to let die must begin with the supposedly free and equal exchange of work for wages.

Under capitalism, the formal waged labor market became and still largely remains the key to understanding the valuation of life as embodied by workers. Waged work, according to Weeks, "is not only the primary mechanism by which income is distributed, it is also the basic means by which status is allocated, and by which most people gain access to healthcare and retirement."[69] Furthermore, she suggests, making people ready for waged work is the central goal of schools, prisons, and the various "welfare-to-work" programs initiated in recent decades. Simply put, "work produces not just economic goods and services but also social and political subjects. In other words, the wage relation generates not just income and capital, but disciplined individuals, governable subjects, worthy citizens, and responsible family members."[70] In short, it is through the promotion of waged work that values are instilled. Waged work "is not just defended on grounds of economic necessity and social duty; it is widely understood as an individual moral practice and collective ethical obligation."[71] It is also through the pivot between the waged work and unwaged work that gender and other social integuments are produced.

It should be noted that the separation between waged work and unpaid housework has never been as clearly demarcated as conventionally thought.[72] Likewise, the exclusion of women, for example, from so-called productive work has never been complete. Both the labor market and the home continued to be fluid places, sites where different living and working relationships both produced and were produced by different social relations. Feminist scholars have documented that while women—in the abstract—have largely been relegated to selected tasks outside of the formal labor market, including the provision of food, care of the home, child care, and nursing the sick, women did find and continue to find (limited) waged employment—often in the secondary labor market. Unlike the primary (waged) labor market, which offers jobs with relatively high wages, the possibility of benefits, good working conditions, and employment stability, the secondary labor market offers jobs that pay relatively little and come with poorer working conditions, little opportunity for career advancement, frequently harsh and capricious work discipline, and considerable employment instability, characterized by high turnover.[73] Additionally, while women (as a generic category) operate within gender-restricted labor markets (both primary and secondary), racism and discrimination ensure that the position of women of color (and men of color) is even more restricted.[74]

Considerable misunderstanding exists vis-à-vis Marx's discussion of productive and unproductive work; this misunderstanding is crucial for discussions of domestic violence. Marx writes that "since the immediate purpose and the *authentic product* of capitalist production is *surplus-value*, *labor is only productive*, and an exponent of labor-power is only a *productive worker*, if it or he creates *surplus-value* directly, i.e. the only productive labor is that which is directly *consumed* in the course of production for the valorization of capital."[75] What exactly does Marx mean in this passage? For many readers, this sentence is taken as evidence that Marx diminished the role of those activities that take place outside the formal production process; by extension, therefore, work that is performed in other venues, such as the household, that does not generate surplus value because it is not sold on the market, is nonproductive (or, alternatively, unproductive). And given that historically women have been denied access to the (formal) means of production, and given that women, under patriarchal systems of oppression, have been relegated to the home, therefore women's work is marginal and thus not important.

This is not what Marx is saying, and the misinterpretation is very important. Marx continues: "*Looked at from* the simple standpoint of the labor process, labor *seemed* productive if it realized itself in a product, or rather a commodity. *From the standpoint* of capitalist production we may add the qualification that labor is productive if it directly valorizes capital, or creates surplus-value. That is to say, it is productive if it is realized in a surplus-value without any equivalent for the worker, its creator; it must appear in surplus produce, i.e. an additional increment of a commodity on behalf of the monopolizer of the means of labor, the capitalist."[76]

Notice the numerous qualifications, which I have emphasized, that Marx uses in this passage. Marx is explaining that, if we consider production only from the viewpoint of the capitalist, we see that only certain types of labor (i.e., employment or work) are productive, that only those activities that generate exchange value are valuable. This is not Marx's attitude but rather his critique of bourgeois political economists who diminished the contributions of activities outside the formal—and readily observable—circuits of capital. Indeed, Marx continues, writing that "it is only bourgeois obtuseness that encourages the view that capitalist production is production in its absolute form." Moreover, Marx then clarifies that "only the bourgeoisie can confuse the questions: What is productive labor? And what is a productive worker from the standpoint of capitalism? with the question: What is productive labor as such? And they alone could rest content with the tautological answer that all labor is productive if it produces, if it results in a product of some other use-value or in anything at all."[77]

Marx's discussion of productive and nonproductive labor is, in the main, an explication of the commodification of society, of the "real subsumption of labor under . . . the capitalist mode of production."[78] Writing at a very abstract level, Marx forwards the proposition that "an ever increasing number of types of labor are included in the immediate concept of productive labor, and those who perform it are classified as productive workers, workers directly exploited by capital and subordinated to its process of production and expansion."[79] In other words, productive workers, from the vantage point of capital, are those waged laborers who valorize capital, those workers who, through their selling of labor power, generate surplus value. Marx goes on to note, however, that not all wage laborers are productive—again, from the standpoint of capital. He writes that "whenever labor is purchased to be consumed as a use-value, as a service and not to replace the value of variable capital with its own vitality and be incorporated into the capitalist process of production—whenever that happens, labor is not productive and the wage-laborer is no productive worker. His work is consumed for its use-value, not as creating exchange-value; it is consumed unproductively, not productively."[80] To better understand what Marx is saying, consider, for example, a janitor, Pete, working in Joe's factory. Here, Joe hires Pete to keep the factory clean; perhaps Pete even helps with the maintenance of the machines in Joe's factory. From Joe's vantage point, Pete provides an important service; however, given that Pete does not explicitly produce commodities, Joe does not immediately realize surplus value from Pete's labor. For Joe, the work of Pete is not productive; it does not immediately or proximately generate surplus value. The implications of this are far-reaching, for it suggests that even though waged laborers are quantitative equivalents in the (formal) labor market, their positions are qualitatively different. Indeed, it is this difference that is manifest in the unequal precariousness of the formal labor market. Those workers who are viewed as not productive (i.e., nonessential) are in decidedly more vulnerable positions; they are generally paid less and are most likely to be laid off in economic recessions.

Capitalism, as we have seen, is indifferent to use value. It matters little to Joe the factory owner if he (or, more precisely, his workers) produces lightbulbs or linguine. What is important is the valorization of capital—the realization of surplus value through commodity exchange. That being said, Joe prefers to produce commodities that will realize the highest returns. For this reason, Joe must be cognizant of the many inputs that go into production—the factors of production. Following the labor theory of value, the ability to secure necessary labor power is crucial. At the abstract level, capital requires labor that is concurrently use value and exchange value. Here, Marx explains that, under capitalism, productive labor is given a specific use value not from its particular utility but by its ability to generate exchange value.[81] In other words, and as Marx emphasizes, identical activities may be seen as either productive or unproductive; what matters is how these activities are inserted into capitalism. Marx writes that

> labor with the same content can be either productive or unproductive. For instance, Milton, who wrote *Paradise Lost*, was an unproductive worker. On the other hand, a writer who turns out work for his publisher in a factory style is a productive worker. Milton produced *Paradise Lost* as a silkworm produces silk, as the activation of his own nature. He later sold his product for £5 and thus became a merchant. But the literary proletarian of Leipzig who produces books, such as compendia on political economy, at the behest of his publisher is pretty nearly a productive worker since his production is taken over by capital and only occurs in order to increase it. A singer who sings like a bird is an unproductive worker. If she sells her song for money, she is to that extent a wage-laborer or merchant. But if the same singer is engaged by an entrepreneur who makes her sing to make money, then she becomes a productive worker, since she produces capital directly. A schoolmaster who instructs others is not a productive worker. But a

schoolmaster who works for wages in an institution along with others, using his own labor to increase the money of the entrepreneur who owns the knowledge-mongering institution, is a productive worker.[82]

How work is valued under capitalism, in short, is based on particular and specific market logics. Those activities that have been formally subsumed are, by and large, valued more than activities that remain marginal—though not necessarily less integral—to capitalism. Hence, according to the dictates of capitalism, professional musicians and others working in the music industry are productive workers; those engaged in street performances are not. Chefs are considered productive; a mother or father who cooks at home for the family is not. Nannies and domestic workers are waged laborers but not productive; men, women, and children who clean and take care of others at home are neither paid (in wages) nor considered productive.

It is because of these calculations that certain activities historically have or have not been incorporated (abstracted) into neoclassical economic models and, likewise, that certain activities are utilized in the computation of economic measures. Marx recognizes that "types of work that are consumed as services and not in products separable from the worker and hence not capable of existing as commodities independently of him, but which are yet capable of being directly exploited in capitalist terms, are of microscopic significance when compared with the mass of capitalist production."[83] What is more important for my particular argument, however, is that the *valuation* of productive or nonproductive labor significantly informs the valuation of particular populations within capitalism and, by extension, how violence and crime are understood.

Following Marx, the "desire to define productive and unproductive labor in terms of their material content" is related to the "fetishism peculiar to the capitalist mode of production from which it arises." This, for Marx, "consists in regarding economic categories, such as being a commodity or productive labor, as qualities inherent in the material incarnations of these formal determinations or categories."[84] Stated differently, certain economic categories and concepts are seen as natural, essential, ahistorical—including the belief that labor is productive only if it appears in commodity form. From this, according to the logics of capitalism, certain activities are naturally less important. Herein lies the differentiation of worth among populations, for these logics underpin the gendered (and racial) valuation of work.

SOCIALLY NECESSARY LABOR

How, though, does labor capacity exist as a commodity? Following Marx, labor capacity (or labor power) is defined as "the aggregate of those mental and physical capabilities existing in the physical form, the living personality, of a human being, capabilities which he sets in motion whenever he produces a use-value of any kind."[85] However, "labor-power can appear on the market as a commodity only if, and in so far as, its possessor, the individual whose labor-power it is, offers it for sale or sells it as a commodity."[86] Thus, when capitalists purchase labor power—the capacity to work—they do so on two conditions: first, that the laborer works under the control of the capitalist to whom his or her labor belongs and, second, that the product is the property of the capitalist and not that of the worker. In so doing, the capitalist is able to "produce a commodity greater in value than the sum of the values of the commodities used to produce it, namely the means of production and the labor-power he purchased with his good money on the open market."[87] Therein lies the source of surplus value, in that "by incorporating living labor into their lifeless objectivity, the capitalist simultaneously transforms value, i.e., past labor in its objectified and lifeless form, into capital, value which can perform its own valorization process."[88]

To fully appreciate the generation of surplus value, which is one of the defining features of capitalism, it is necessary to "leave this noisy sphere [i.e., the exchange of money for labor], where everything takes place on the surface and in full view of everyone" and to move into "the hidden abode of production," as Marx did.[89] In this "hidden abode" capitalists combine the means of production (machinery and raw materials) with labor power (purchased on the labor market) in order to transform materials into commodities for exchange. The exchange value of the commodity, consequently, is composed of two parts: constant capital and variable capital. Constant capital is past labor already congealed in commodities that are used as means of production in a current labor process; variable capital, conversely, is "living labor."[90] As Marx explains, variable capital is added in the process of production and is thus the source of surplus value (i.e., profit). The increase in value accruing from variable capital occurs in two forms. On the one hand, "dead labor" is passed on into the value of the new commodity, and, on the other hand, laborers add value by congealing socially necessary labor time into the commodity.[91]

Exploitation is intrinsic to capitalism. Marx argues that the value of labor power (wages) is equal not to what a worker can produce (e.g., a shirt) but instead to the labor time necessary to make up what it costs to keep the laborer and his or her family alive. In other words, "the value of labor-power is the value of the means of subsistence necessary for the maintenance of its owner."[92] To clarify this process, Marx distinguishes between "necessary labor time" and "socially necessary labor time." He explains that socially necessary labor time is that amount required to reproduce the laborer and his or her family; this is the "value of labor-power" and is used to determine wages. Workers, for example, may produce enough value in six hours to offset their reproduction. Capitalists, however, purchase labor power for a full day's work, say, ten hours. The remaining four hours, Marx argues, appear as surplus labor time. Stated differently, workers produce enough value to cover the costs of their wages in just a part of the working day; the labor performed for the remainder of the day, therefore, does not have to be paid for—it is "surplus labor," which produces "surplus value."[93]

It bears repeating that "every social process of production is at the same time a process of reproduction."[94] Marx, in his discussion of socially necessary labor time, recognized the need of capital to reproduce its supply of laborers. The worker, Marx writes, "is nothing other than labor-power for the duration of his whole life," while capital, "in its blind and measureless drive, its insatiable appetite for surplus labor[,] . . . oversteps not only the moral but even the merely physical limits of the working day."[95] What becomes clear, therefore, is that the commodity of labor capacity is unlike other commodities. The process of the production of the worker, for instance, itself entails a process of consumption. Marx explains that "in taking in food, for example, which is a form of consumption, the human being produces his own body."[96] And yet, the exploitation of workers under capitalism threatens their very existence. Denied access to the means of production—but likewise denied access to their own means of subsistence—waged workers are compelled to purchase commodities necessary for their own reproduction; this is Marx's concept of "individual consumption." In other words, it is necessary for workers to purchase the material requirements needed to live: food, shelter, and clothing. Confronting, therefore, the very survivability of workers, Marx concludes that "capital asks no questions about the length of life of labor-power. What interests it is purely and simply the maximum of labor-power. . . . It attains this objective by shortening the life of labor-power, in the same way as a greedy farmer snatches more produce from the soil by robbing it of its fertility."[97]

The reference to the soil's fertility in Marx's account is particularly apt, for it is within the household—and specifically in the female body— that capital itself is to be reproduced. Drawing on the work of Mariarosa Dalla Costa, for example, Maria Mies explains that what the housewife produces in the family is not simply use value but the commodity of labor power, which the husband, as a "free" wage laborer, can then sell in the labor market. In effect, "the productivity of the housewife is the precondition for the productivity of the (male) wage laborer. The nuclear family, organized and protected by the state, is the social factory where this commodity 'labor power' is produced. Hence, the housewife and her labor are not outside the process of surplus value production, but constitute the very foundation upon which this process can get started. The housewife and her labor are, in other words, the basis of the process of capital accumulation."[98]

The family became the principal institution by which labor power was to be reproduced; consequently, the family came to be identified almost exclusively in terms of biological reproduction. Heterosexuality likewise became the unquestioned norm. It was widely understood and promoted that the natural—if not exclusive—purpose of sex was for biological reproduction and that sexual identity was inextricably linked to the individual's role in the reproductive family.[99] Marriage as a legal institution—and by extension, the criminalization of divorce—was thus predicated on procreation; the family was to ensure a proper upbringing based on strictly defined gendered (and aged) roles. The husband or father figure came to be identified as primary provider, protector, and disciplinarian; the wife was seen as both subservient and complementary in that she was the fundamental caretaker and spiritual center.[100]

Consequently, the emerging capitalist state apparatus worked to facilitate the hetero-patriarchal foundations of the home and family in order to guarantee the reproduction of capitalism. Thus, "with the help of the state and its legal machinery women have been shut up in the isolated nuclear family, whereby their work there was made socially invisible, and was hence defined ... as 'non-productive.'"[101]

The generation of surplus value through the exploitation of waged work has profound implications for our understanding of the distinction between killing and letting die, in that the commodification of labor is directly associated with the survivability of the laborer. As Marx writes, "Capitalist production ... not only produces a deterioration of human labor-power by robbing it of its normal moral and physical conditions of development and activity, but also produces the premature exhaustion and death of this labor-power itself."[102] Indeed, Marx wrote at length on the direct harm caused to laborers by their being forced to work in injurious conditions and by the failure of employers—or society more generally—to prevent suffering and premature death that could easily, and at little cost, be prevented.[103] Exploitation, however, appears natural and normal; it is not viewed as criminal but simply part of the production process.

LETTING DIE UNDER CAPITALISM

According to Julie Matthaei, "Capitalism's greatest victims are not, as Marx suggested, white working-class men, but rather poor women of color, especially single mothers and their children."[104] Marx argues that "the driving motive and determining purpose of capitalist production is the self-valorization of capital to the greatest possible extent, i.e., the greatest possible production of surplus-value, hence the greatest possible exploitation of labor-power by the capitalist."[105] But just as the "werewolf-like hunger for surplus-labor" was hidden by the fetishizing of the free market, so too is the violence intrinsic to capitalism hidden.[106] This is so because violence under capitalism entails not only the direct, interpersonal force required to appropriate land and the means of production from the many to privilege the few; violence is also systemic and structural, built into the very foundation of capitalist relations. This violence, I argue, is founded in the contradiction that workers are both producers and consumers; this, under capitalism, creates the structural conditions of heightened vulnerability and susceptibility to premature death.

We have seen how the production process establishes a decidedly unequal relationship—masked by the fetish of the "free" market—between employers and employees. Here, we consider more closely the unity of production and consumption. Marx identifies two forms of the "worker's consumption": individual consumption and productive consumption. Marx explains that

> while producing he [the worker] consumes the means of production with his labor, and converts them into products with a higher value than that of the capital advanced. This is his productive consumption. It is at the same time consumption of his labor-power by the capitalist who has bought it. On the other hand, the worker uses the money paid to him for his labor-power to buy the means of subsistence; this is his individual consumption. The worker's productive consumption and his individual consumption are therefore totally distinct. In the former, he acts as the motive power of capital, and belongs to the capitalist. In the latter, he belongs to himself, and performs his necessary vital functions outside the production process. The result of the first kind of consumption is that the capitalist continues to live, of the second, that the worker himself continues to live.[107]

There is a lot of information in this statement. What Marx proposes is to understand both production and consumption as dialectically related and to acknowledge that production and consumption both represent unities of opposites. For example, consider a woman (Annie) who sells her labor power to a factory owner (Joe). During the production process Annie converts existing materials (e.g., cloth and thread)—what Marx terms "dead labor"—into other goods (e.g., shirts); this is what Marx means by "reanimating" past labor. In the process, the capitalist is consuming the labor capacity of Annie; in so doing, the capitalist is then able to realize surplus value when the commodities are sold. It is this *productive consumption* that permits Joe (as an individual capitalist) and capitalism (as a system) to be reproduced. Conversely, Annie—who is denied the means of subsistence—must purchase (consume) goods obtained in the market in order to survive. This is *individual consumption.* Notice also that both forms of consumption are required in capitalism, in that workers (as producers) are simultaneously consumers. To be denied access to the means of production is also to be denied access to the means of subsistence. Not only are workers "free" to sell their labor; they are also "free" to purchase commodities in order to live.

The unity of production and consumption highlights an especially important contradiction inherent in capitalism—a contradiction that is manifest in the tendency to let die. As explained earlier, capital strives to minimize labor costs in order to accumulate greater profits—the so-called minimum wage. Marx explains that the minimum price paid (the wage) is that of "the means of subsistence that is customarily held to be essential in a given state of society to enable the worker to exert his labor-power with the necessary degree of strength, health, vitality, etc. and to perpetuate himself by producing replacements for himself."[108] In other words, concrete wages are determined abstractly, calculated on the basis of market logics that determine the least outlay necessary to keep workers and the next generation of workers alive.

This tendency, however, is hidden within the workings of the formal waged labor market. The wage appears as something that results from an equal exchange between employer and employee. As the saying goes, workers receive a "fair day's wage for a fair day's work." Marx shows that this is anything but the case. In a well-known—but particularly apt—section of *Capital*, Marx writes that "capital has one sole driving force, the drive to valorize itself, to create surplus-value, to make its constant part, the means of production, absorb the greatest possible amount of surplus labor. Capital is dead labor which, vampire-like, lives only by sucking living labor, and lives the more, the more labor it sucks. The time during which the worker works is the time during which the capitalist consumes the labor-power he has bought from him."[109]

Through the generation of both absolute and relative surpluses, workers are necessarily exploited in the production process. Moreover—and this is key—the workers must still purchase their means of subsistence from *other capitalists*. Annie, to continue the above example, must obtain food, shelter, and clothing from the market; she must purchase these commodities from other capitalists. Annie, of course, is able to do so only through the wages she receives from Joe. As Marx explains, "The capital given in return for labor-power is converted into means of subsistence which have to be consumed to reproduce the muscles, nerves, bones and brains of existing workers, and to bring new workers into existence."[110] Annie (along with her family) is dependent upon formal wages in order to survive.

In actuality, workers such as Annie may supplement their income through other means. Annie can, for example, participate in the informal market (e.g., doing odd jobs); she might also grow vegetables in her backyard—if she is fortunate enough to live in a house and to have sufficient yard space. It should be clear, however, that many of these ancillary activities may be (and frequently are) made illegal. While it is true that some nonwaged forms of employment (e.g., babysitting or lawn mowing) are generally not prohibited, other activities—including prostitution—certainly are. Likewise, zoning ordinances restrict where and what types of activities are allowed. In cities, for example, homeowners are generally not permitted to raise livestock; similarly, some residential areas place restrictions on backyard gardens. The existence of prohibitions on these activities, as a whole, is to be understood as means of reining in one's ability to acquire means of subsistence outside of the formal market.

As both producer and consumer, Annie embodies the inherent and vital contradiction of capitalism. Joe the employer wants to pay Annie the least amount possible, and yet, in order for Annie to survive (and to continue working), she must also consume (from Joe or other capitalists). Following Marx, "the individual consumption of the working class is the reconversion of the means of subsistence given by capital in return for labor-power into fresh labor-power which capital is then again able to exploit. It is the production and reproduction of the capitalist's most indispensable means of production: the worker."[111] This is why capitalists (usually) cannot work their laborers to death—unless, of course, there is a ready surplus of workers to take Annie's place. For Marx, therefore, (biological) reproduction is inseparable from class and capitalist reproduction, and reproduction is inseparable from production. There is, in other words, no dichotomy between these processes; all are internally and dialectically related.

Within capitalism, therefore, it is not simply that some are denied access to the means of production; it is also that some are denied access to the means of subsistence. It is this vulnerability, this precariousness, which reproduces capitalism. As Marx explains, "Individual consumption provides, on the one hand, the means for the workers' maintenance and reproduction; on the other hand, by the constant annihilation of the means of subsistence, it provides for their continued re-appearance on the labor-market." Marx then concludes that "the Roman slave was held by chains; the wage-laborer is bound to his owner by invisible threads. The appearance of independence is maintained . . . by the legal fiction of a contract."[112]

"The maintenance and reproduction of the working class," Marx argues, "remains a necessary condition for the reproduction of capital." But, as Marx also indicates, "the capitalist may safely leave this to the worker's drive for self-preservation and propagation. All the capitalist cares for is to reduce the worker's individual consumption to the necessary minimum."[113] Capitalists, in other words, are—in the abstract—indifferent in their hiring of labor. It matters little if Joe the factory owner hires Annie or Cindy; all that is important is that the worker hired is able to perform the necessary assigned tasks and, in so doing, generate profit. That being said, the notion of indifference entails a concomitant preference. If, at the concrete level, Annie is a superior worker—a concept that, it should be noted, can be operationalized in numerous ways—Joe will prefer to hire Annie over Cindy. Now, as to Annie's ability to live from day to day, or to contribute to the next generation of laborers, Joe remains largely indifferent. If Annie is unable to work or fails to provide for her family and future workers, Joe can always hire Cindy or some other worker waiting in the wings.

To summarize the argument thus far: the exchange between labor and capital, in which workers are forced by their very survival needs to seek employment, is readily and routinely portrayed as a fair exchange between two equal partners.[114] Of course, such a portrayal—of a fair exchange of a day's labor for a day's wage—is anything but fair. No surplus value is added to commodities during the process of circulation—c-m-c; it instead originates in the process of production: the difference between necessary labor time and surplus labor time. It is thus incumbent upon capitalists to keep wages as low as possible—an observation made both by Adam Smith and Marx. Marx, for example, explained that the "lowest and the only necessary wage-rate is that providing for the subsistence of the worker for the duration of his work and as much more as is necessary for him to support a family and for the race of laborers not to die out."[115]

That said, capitalists cannot (usually) work their laborers to death or work to prevent their living. Indeed, Marx indicates that the health and fitness of the working class is often a matter of considerable state interest.[116] This is a point clarified by Tania Murray Li: "Make live interventions become urgent when people can no longer sustain their own lives through direct access to the means of production, or access to a living wage."[117] Ironically, it often becomes necessary for both the state and the capitalist to limit the exploitation and degradation of the living worker, if only to facilitate the generation of further surplus value. As Marx recognizes, the "labor-power withdrawn from the market by wear and tear, and by death, must be continually replaced by, at the very least, an equal amount of fresh labor-power. Hence the sum of means of subsistence necessary for the production of labor-power must include the means necessary for the worker's replacements, i.e., his children."[118]

How, though, might this exchange operate if it were truly open and unregulated? Albritton provides a particularly apt summary of life and death in the capitalist labor market: "A completely commodified labour market would be managed completely by the wage rate, which in turn is a result of the supply of and demand for workers. A large supply of workers relative to demand will lead to lower and lower wage rates. If this situation continues, wages will eventually fall below bare physical subsistence and workers will die off, until their supply shrinks enough to once again push wages to a level at or above subsistence."[119] In other words, a pure, completely commodified capitalist labor market would necessarily operate on the basis of letting die a certain proportion of workers. In theory, the inability to survive within the labor market would operate as a biological regulatory mechanism, not unlike ecosystems. Of course, given the vagaries of capitalism, it is not always profitable to have excess labor die off. At times, when capital is rapidly expanding, additional workers are required immediately. Capitalists cannot wait for additional workers to be born, raised, trained, and inserted into the labor market. Consequently, this is one reason (among others) why it is advantageous to capitalism to have a reserve supply of labor waiting in the wings. As Harvey notes, the existence of a surplus population permits capitalists to superexploit their workers without regard for their health or well-being; consequently, a surplus population affects whether the capitalist has to care about the health, well-being, and life expectancy of the labor force.[120] This is also why there exist (selectively) "make live" interventions. However, to make live is to sustain not the life of the laborer as an individual but instead to sustain the capacity of the laboring class as a population. To make live is to make capitalism.

Throughout much of the twentieth century many capitalist societies—including the United States—witnessed attempts to decommodify the labor market. Governmental intervention, in the form of "safety nets" such as welfare, Social Security, and Medicaid, worked to (literally) keep workers alive in economic downturns. Likewise, the formation of unions and other forms of community organizing achieved modest improvements in workers' lives. The pendulum, though, is once again moving. Under neoliberalism we are witnessing a recommodification—and revaluing—of life and death. Such transformed valuations are part and parcel of a revanchist neoconservatism that is thoroughly imbricated within neoliberal policies. Indeed, in many respects, both neoliberalism and neoconservatism are two sides of the same coin. For example, both promote the importance of the self-correcting free market as a solution to societal ills. However, neoconservatives are more apt to combine a hands-off approach to economic regulation with intrusive government interference for the regulation of society in the name of public security and traditional values. The neoconservative movement in the United States, as it emerged through the 1970s but especially in the 1980s under the leadership of President Reagan, viewed state power vis-à-vis social problems and not as a necessary evil but as a positive good to be cultivated and deployed. It was, in effect, a transformative endeavor to remake American society along the lines of traditional values. This is seen, for example, throughout the late twentieth century, as neoconservative politicians used state apparatuses to implement desired reforms, particularly in relation to state-supported religious philanthropy, religious education, and the regulation of sexuality.[121] In other words, governmental interference in *selected* social spheres (e.g., so-called "family values") is acceptable, presuming that this interference promotes a particular morality and value system and does not alter the free-market system. Neoconservatives, as a whole, do not favor social welfare programs for those living generally outside the formal, waged labor market: the elderly, the disabled, and the poor and indigent.

The callous disregard shown by neoconservatives for those less fortunate is exemplified by the statements of Mike Huckabee, former governor of Arkansas and a U.S. presidential candidate in 2008. In late September 2010 Huckabee attended the Values Voters Summit, a political event held in Washington, DC.[122] The list of attendees and speakers included a number of luminaries of the ultraconservative wing of the Republican Party, including Newt Gingrich, Michele Bachmann, Christine O'Donnell, and Sarah Palin. When Huckabee took the stage, he used the opportunity to criticize Pres. Barack Obama's health-care reform legislation. More specifically, however, Huckabee railed against a law that required insurance companies to cover people with preexisting conditions. According to Huckabee, people with preexisting conditions—such as heart disease, diabetes, or Parkinson's disease—are like houses that have already burned down and thus should not be covered by insurance. He explained, "It sounds so good, and it's such a warm message to say we're not gonna deny anyone from a preexisting condition." However, he continued, "I want to ask you something from a common sense perspective. Suppose we applied that principle [to] our property insurance. And you can call your insurance agent and say, 'I'd like to buy some insurance for my house.' He'd say, 'Tell me about your house.' 'Well sir, it burned down yesterday, but I'd like to insure it today.' And he'll say, 'I'm sorry, but we can't insure it after it's already burned.'"[123] For Huckabee, common sense holds that once a person is "damaged" they are no longer worthy of our care. As William Pitt details, in 2010 more than 81 million Americans suffered from one or more forms of cardiovascular disease, more than 11 million people in the United States suffered from some form of cancer, approximately 23.6 million Americans were diagnosed with diabetes, between 50,000 and 60,000 Americans were being treated for Parkinson's disease, and 400,000 individuals were living with multiple sclerosis. According to Huckabee's logic, all of these people, Pitt explains, "are not worthy of health insurance because they had the misfortune of getting sick before they got insurance."[124]

Henry Giroux maintains that "we live at a time when the conflation of private interests, empire building, and evangelical fundamentalism brings into question the very nature, if not the existence, of the democratic process." He argues that the social contract (but not the labor contract) is under attack, with its emphasis on enlarging the public good and expanding social provisions—such as access to adequate health care, housing, employment, public transportation, and education—which have provided a limited though important safety net. In its place has emerged a notion of national security based on fear, surveillance, and control. Indeed, under a neoliberal domestic restructuring, militant foreign policy, and evangelical conservatism, the United States has witnessed the increasing obliteration of those discourses, social forms, public institutions, and noncommercial values that are central to the language of public commitment, democratically charged politics, and the common good.[125] Giroux concludes that, "with its debased belief that profit-making is the essence of democracy, and its definition of citizenship as an energized plunge into consumerism, neoliberalism eliminates government regulation of market forces, celebrates a ruthless competitive individualism, and places the commanding political, cultural, and economic institutions of society in the hands of powerful corporate interests, the privileged, and unrepentant religious bigots."[126]

In bringing this argument full circle, we are left with the unpalatable proposition forwarded by conservatives and proponents of neoliberalism (among others) that people fail in the labor market not because of systemic inequalities or inherent exploitation but rather because of individual limitations, poor decision making, and (possibly) bad luck. And while positive duties (e.g., charity and philanthropy) may be promoted to temper some of these inequalities, there is no obligation on behalf of either capitalists or the state to intervene. This point cannot be overemphasized. Under the myth of the free market, coupled with a long-standing tradition to privilege negative duties over positive duties, we have in place a system that is inherently oppressive with respect to one's survivability.

To a large degree, such inequalities are not readily abstracted as violent because of a misplaced idealism of the capitalist market. In *The Wealth of the Nations* Adam Smith remarked that "as every individual . . . endeavors as much as he can both to employ his capital in the support of domestic industry, and so to direct that industry that its produce may be of the greatest value; every individual necessarily labors to render the annual revenue of the society as great as he can." In so doing, Smith explained, as individuals follow their own self-interests, they "neither [intend] to promote the public interest nor [know] how much he [or she] is promoting it." As noted earlier, Smith argues that, "by directing that industry in such a manner as its produce may be of the greatest value, he intends only his own gain, and he is in this, as in many other cases, led by an

invisible hand to promote an end which was no part of his intention. . . .
By pursuing his own interest he frequently promotes that of the society
more effectually than when he really intends to promote it."[127]

Smith's forwarding of the "invisible hand" has been adopted by (mostly)
right-wing and conservative economists and politicians to promote the
idea that markets, when freed of governmental interference, cannot fail,
that if left to their own devices, markets are self-regulating and beneficial to all. However, as Jared Bernstein succinctly writes in the *Atlantic*,
"We are like travelers who have followed a road map to a destination
that promised bliss but instead delivered stagnation and joblessness to
many and political dysfunction to all. The economic geography behind
that roadmap is a misreading of the original mapmakers—the founders
of free markets—which eventually morphed into the deeply damaging
belief that markets never fail and always self-correct; and therefore, government actions can only distort otherwise self-correcting markets."[128]
Dieter Plehwe, senior fellow at the Social Science Research Center in
Berlin, likewise explains that whereas "social liberals thrived on market
failure, which was very appropriate for the 1930s, '40s, and '50s," they
did not "look carefully at the contradictions of state intervention." Now,
he continues, "neoliberals [have] turned that upside down and suggested
that state failure, not market failure, was the problem and that we had to
address the problems of the state rather than the problems of the market."[129] And the way to address the problems of the state was, in principle,
to reduce its role in the market.

Markets, of course, as Smith well understood, were not self-regulating
entities. Rather, markets are "the product of volitional arrangements
that incentivize particular networks and patterns of exchange"; they are
not, *contra* conservative economists, "objects that can be observed and
studied as something real."[130] As Robin Malloy continues,

Economists often talk about markets as if they are real objects and as
if people simply find themselves placed in naturally existing market
environments in which they respond to stimuli by taking self-interested
actions to maximize their own wealth. This idea of the market as a real

place is, however, a metaphor, as are the many models that economists generate and use to describe markets. The economists' idea of the market is a representation or model of the underlying networks and patterns of human exchange; it is not itself the real to which it refers, just as a map of a given city or of the world is not the real to which it makes reference.[131]

The belief in the existence of markets as real, tangible places—places that must be secured against both internal and external threats—does have profound implications for subsequent discussions of social injustice and particular abstractions of violence. When neoliberals speak of self-correcting markets, they conclude on the one hand that governmental regulation can only distort or destabilize the natural functioning of capitalism. However, on the other hand, neoliberals (and neoconservatives) also argue that market failure occurs because of personal irresponsibility and because too many people refuse to participate (responsibly) as productive citizens in the formal waged labor market. Those who fail in society have failed—according to neoliberal and neoconservative dogma—because of their own moral deficiencies. These men, women, and even children are framed as lacking in those qualities deemed necessary to participate in society, but because their failings are seen as the result of their own negligence and carelessness they are deemed not worthy of our assistance or even (increasingly) our sympathy. Likewise, their susceptibility, their vulnerability to premature death does not constitute violence.

As Joseph Stiglitz writes, the "more divided a society becomes in terms of wealth, the more reluctant the wealthy become to spend money on common needs." The implications, as Stiglitz explains, are as remarkable as they are disturbing:

> The rich don't need to rely on government for parks or education or medical care or personal security—they can buy all these things for themselves. In the process, they become more distant from ordinary people, losing whatever empathy they may once have had. They also worry about strong government—one that could use its powers to adjust the balance, take some of their wealth, and invest it for the common

good. The top 1 percent may complain about the kind of government we have in America, but in truth they like it just fine: too gridlocked to re-distribute, too divided to do anything but lower taxes.[132]

To better illustrate the market logics of letting die, in the following section I provide a case study of the Personal Responsibility and Work Opportunity Reconciliation Act (PRWORA). Signed by President Bill Clinton in 1996, the PRWORA provides a stark example of how violence, values, and crime are juxtaposed in material practice.

THE VIOLENCE OF WELFARE REFORM

The debates leading up to the passage, as well as the technical details, of PRWORA are well established.[133] I will address these in reverse order, beginning with the specifics of the law and then the debates. The 251-page PRWORA addressed eight broad entitlement programs: replacement of Aid for Families with Dependent Children (AFDC) with Temporary Assistance to Needy Families (TANF); restrictions on Supplemental Security Income (SSI, which comprises benefits granted to the indigent or disabled elderly); the enforcement of child support; the exclusion of aliens from public benefits; child protective services; child nutrition programs; food stamps and hunger prevention; and a suite of miscellaneous measures, including the drug testing of recipients, the elimination of assistance to drug offenders, and abstinence education.[134] Overall, however, these programs, according to the work of Loïc Wacquant, may be aligned along four key dimensions. First, PRWORA was predicated on the principle of "welfare to workfare." The intent, simply put, was to facilitate the transition of ostensibly nonworking recipients of welfare into the labor market. This was to be accomplished bureaucratically, through a series of negative conditions for the receipt of welfare. In particular, the law stipulated that recipients—presumed mostly to be single mothers—on assistance must obtain waged work within two years; furthermore, a lifetime cap of five years of support was introduced. Once this personal quota was reached, recipients would be ineligible for any further assistance from the state for the rest of his or her lifetime. As Patricia O'Campo and Lucia

Rojas-Smith explain, for low-income families the five-year cap represented the lifetime elimination of an important albeit meager refuge from the volatility of the low-wage labor market—a safety net that is in any case typically insufficient to meet a family's economic needs and has few if any benefits.[135] The two-year time frame imposed its own hardships on welfare recipients. With such a shortened time period, aid recipients had fewer opportunities to pursue higher education or job training—two necessary conditions that might help people actually move beyond poverty.

In the second move the federal government devolved responsibility for assistance to the state level and, ultimately, to the county level. Consequently, eligibility criteria, payment disbursement, and job search and support programs became highly localized and thus uneven.[136] Furthermore, no state was allowed to establish a welfare program that was either less moralistic or more generous than the federal policy.[137] Indeed, states were encouraged to establish even harsher limitations on welfare. The message was clear: potential welfare recipients were to be punished for their plight. State governments, in turn, were quick to oblige. In response to PRWORA, twenty states adopted time limits shorter than the federal government's lifetime limits, and twenty-three states adopted a "family cap" or "child exclusion" policy that denied additional benefits for children conceived while the parent received welfare payments.[138] Consider, for example, the case of Michigan. Gov. John Engler sought to make his state a "national model for welfare reform." Under the decentralized welfare reform framework, Engler proposed cutting all assistance to poor mothers who would not work within six weeks of giving birth and to reduce benefits by 25 percent for all participants who failed to be gainfully employed within two months of receiving assistance.[139]

Third, welfare budgets were established not as a function of the needs of the populations served but by fixed endowments called block grants. Thus, for example, the amount allotted to TANF for the country as a whole was set at $16.3 billion per year until 2002. As Wacquant explains, if unemployment or poverty levels were to rise suddenly, due to a recession, for instance, states would face rising demand for assistance with stagnant means. Fourth, PRWORA excluded from the welfare rolls entire categories of people: foreign residents who had arrived within the preceding six years (even if they paid taxes and social premiums), persons convicted of narcotics offenses under federal law, poor children suffering from disabilities, and teen mothers who refused to live with their parents. PRWORA also eliminated medical assistance to the indigent.[140]

How are we to understand the bipartisan passage of the Personal Responsibility and Work Opportunity Reconciliation Act of 1996? There has always been a disciplinary dimension built into welfare policies, a dimension that has aimed to transform particular bodies into corrected subjects who will engage in productive roles, whether these are located within the nuclear family or the labor market.[141] As Sharon Hays explains, "Ever since the inception of government-funded programs for the poor, policymakers have believed that the giving of benefits comes with the right to interfere in the family lives of the poor." She continues that this "is a notable exception to [America's] strong cultural and constitutional prohibitions against state interference in private lives."[142] The 1996 act was no exception; indeed, it readily conformed to the long-standing dismissal of those less fortunate in society. Thus, for example, supporters of welfare reform—which included both Democrats and Republicans, liberals and conservatives—advocated that tough rules and regulations were necessary for disciplining the poor and encouraging self-sufficiency.[143] Conservatives in particular held that cutbacks to welfare were required because any form of government assistance carried an intolerable social cost. Welfare, as Melissa Gilbert explains, was believed to foster a culture of dependency, namely, that childbearing fuels a cycle of poverty by producing children who will likewise depend on the government for sustenance.[144] Such a belief was complemented by another mythology, namely, the presumption that people are poor because they lack a work ethic and do not conform to traditional "family values."[145] Debates surrounding welfare, in short, were located within the formal labor market. It was presumed by supporters that *individual* change was necessary, for poverty was conceived as resulting from individual failings: the needy were irresponsible in their lifestyle choices.

But where was the problem? Historically, opposition to welfare has emanated from myriad groups, including social conservatives, low-wage employers, and white working- and middle-class citizens. Employers, in general, oppose welfare because they view such policies as threats to the continued supply of cheap labor; so too do many white voters, who believe that racialized minorities are cheating the system.[146] In the 1990s public opposition to welfare rose in response to widely publicized conservative interpretations of rising welfare caseloads and increasing rates of out-of-wedlock and teen births.[147] There were, consequently, both moral and economic arguments presented in support of welfare reform. On paper, the reform was aimed at "moving people from welfare to work."[148] However, most welfare recipients were in fact already working; indeed, many recipients were working *two jobs* in an attempt to make ends meet. And yet, because of the systemic problems of the American social infrastructure—lack of affordable, reliable, or accessible child care combined with insecure employment, insufficient minimum wages, lack of health insurance, and inadequate public transportation—most recipients were unable to make ends meet. Consequently, welfare assistance, such as AFDC supplements, was used only to stave off the most dire effects of abject poverty. As Dorothy Roberts explains, "Any work disincentive that exists is not caused by overly generous welfare benefits, but by the miserable conditions" confronting those living on the margins of society.[149]

Contrary to both public opinion and the conservative rhetoric used to gain support for the act, the vast majority of welfare recipients were not trapped in a cycle of long-term dependence; indeed, studies showed that up to 80 percent of white mothers and more than two-thirds of African American mothers who received AFDC were off assistance within two years.[150] Likewise, there was and is no sound evidence that welfare is an incentive for women to create single-mother households.[151] The prevalent notion that most children who grow up on welfare land on the assistance rolls as adults is empirically unfounded: only 20 percent of daughters raised in a highly dependent household became reliant on public aid at some point in adulthood, and they did so not because they got habituated to welfare but because, like their parents, they faced a closed opportunity structure.[152] And lastly, rhetoric aside, most welfare recipients were not drug addicts.[153] Nevertheless, welfare reform enshrined a situation whereupon those deemed irresponsible and unproductive were to be denied any form of assistance; they were, in effect, to be disallowed life.

The real intent of the welfare-to-workfare legislation is found in the broader neoliberal and neoconservative trends of American society that differentiate the value of life and facilitate the construction of economically productive and politically docile subjects. On the one hand, PRWORA essentially abolished the right to assistance for the country's most destitute and replaced it with the obligation to undertake unskilled and underpaid wage labor. On the other hand, the act demarcated a distinction between the worthy and the unworthy poor so as to force the latter into the inferior segments of the job market and correct the supposedly deviant and devious behaviors believed to cause persistent poverty in the first place.[154] As Sharon Hays concludes, "At the heart of welfare reform is a debate over whether individual self-sufficiency should be our nation's central goal or whether, for women at least, the maintenance of 'traditional' family values should remain central. The controversy . . . speaks to foundational American ideals of independence and commitment to others, and it underlines just how precarious those ideals have become in the age of fragile families, social mistrust, rising economic inequalities, and an unstable global marketplace."[155]

The proclaimed objective of PRWORA, Loïc Wacquant argues, was to reduce not poverty but the alleged dependency of families on public aid; this was to be accomplished by the slashing of programs devoted to supporting the most vulnerable members of American society: women and children of the working class, the indigent, the elderly, and recent (legal) immigrants.[156] PRWORA focused exclusively on those programs that had been reserved for poor people receiving direct income or in-kind support: Aid to Families with Dependent Children, Supplemental Security Income, and the Supplemental Nutrition Assistance Program (SNAP, sometimes called food stamps). These programs, however, represented a minuscule portion of the federal budget; the act, therefore, affected only a small sector of American social spending—the outlays targeted at dispossessed families, the disabled, and the indigent. In 1996, for example, thirty-nine million Americans lived below the official poverty level, and yet fewer than thirteen million people (including nine million children) received AFDC payments; likewise, in 1992 only 43 percent of the families officially designated as poor received income assistance, 51 percent got food stamps, and only 18 percent benefited from some form of housing assistance.[157]

Perhaps the most telling piece of evidence revealing the real intent of PRWORA is that *the law had absolutely no jobs component*; none of the law's eight titles addressed economic issues and not a single measure in the law was aimed at improving the employment options or conditions faced by welfare recipients.[158] In fact, as Wacquant writes, the new law carefully avoided confronting the more systemic economic causes of poverty: the stagnation of median household income and the uninterrupted decline of the real value of the minimum wage over the previous two decades; the explosive growth of so-called contingent jobs, held by more than one-quarter of the country's labor force; the erosion of social and medical coverage for low-skill workers; the persistence of astronomical unemployment rates in the neighborhoods of relegation in big cities, as well as in remote rural counties; and the pronounced reluctance of employers to hire ghetto residents and deskilled welfare recipients. None of the provisions contained within PRWORA were intended to address the deeper, more widespread systemic barriers that prevent full-time employment, discourage family formation, and keep people poor: the lack of steady, living-wage jobs and the shortage of child care, health care, adequate public transportation, affordable housing, job-training programs, and education.[159] Rather, the Personal Responsibility and Work Opportunity Reconciliation Act placed most of the blame for poverty—and, indeed, for the entire reproduction of poverty—on one presumed category of persons: *sexually irresponsible women.* Single motherhood is effectively depicted in this act as a high-risk activity that exposes women and children to poverty in the immediate term and to the conditions that will ensure the perpetuation of poverty for generations to come.[160] As Wacquant concludes, it was, simply put, "more expedient, and more profitable electorally, to pitch vituperative portrayals of the poor that alternatively feed and tap the resentment of the electorate toward those who receive 'handouts' from the state."[161] Such myths resonate in a culture saturated with rags-to-riches narratives, where all people can pull themselves up by their own bootstraps and succeed in society. In this view, all that is required is a little elbow grease and determination. In fact, PRWORA expresses a remarkable, hybrid discourse: it appropriates both the religious right's moralistic emphasis on patriarchal and heterosexist "family values" as well as the neoliberal emphasis on downsizing government and exposing the poor to the "corrective" rigors of the market.[162]

The objective of PRWORA was not to reduce poverty levels; if that was the intent, then the act would have addressed other conditions. Thus, when Congress restricted welfare and adopted tough welfare-to-workfare policies, it did little to provide single mothers (in particular) with sufficient jobs, wages, education, training, or services; instead, it contributed to added costs that were to be incurred by women already struggling to survive. Forced into dead-end jobs with few or no benefits (e.g., retirement plans or health coverage), many women had to spend their precious few resources in an attempt to obtain child care or to utilize woefully inadequate public transportation systems.[163] Thus, while the government has historically subsidized certain "deserving" mothers to enable them to stay at home, its welfare policy has also ensured the availability of less privileged—less worthy—women to do low-wage work.[164] However, in turn, many welfare recipients, because of the low levels of cash assistance and employment opportunities available to them, are at an even greater risk of long-term poverty.[165] Consequently, the poor are ever more being disallowed life to the point of death.

CONCLUSIONS

I have argued thus far that it is necessary to consider more explicitly the moral distinction between killing and letting die and how this distinction is manifest in the inner workings of the capitalist waged labor market. I suggest that the determination of worth—the decision to make live or to let die—within capitalism is predicated on two overlapping criteria found within the formal labor market: productivity and responsibility. On the one hand, capital values those populations deemed productive, and, under capitalism, productiveness is reduced to the ability to produce surplus value.[166] Consequently, those who are determined based on market logics to be nonproductive—the precariat, the redundant, the surplus populations—are increasingly being disallowed life to the point of death. Indeed, Jamie Peck explains that such an unfettered faith in the market gives rise to the presumption that "the market gives people what they deserve." In other words, those who fail—the impoverished, the homeless, the destitute—do so because of their own decisions; "failure follows from the individual inadequacies of the workers."[167] These presumptions have only deepened within the neoliberal state as its promoters hold that the "market's role in producing inequality is an unfortunate, unforeseen, and unintended consequence" but nevertheless is a condition "that should not be redressed through government intervention."[168]

On the other hand, capital values those populations deemed responsible. And here, responsibility is conceived simultaneously as the ability to participate fully as producers and as consumers in the capitalist system (a form of anatomo-politics) and to not incur a net loss to the system (a form of biopolitics). By extension, capitalism places little or no value on those deemed irresponsible: those who are unable to contribute to the realization of surplus value through either production or consumption. Increasingly, they too are being disallowed life to the point of death. Not everyone is equally susceptible to becoming reduced to bare life; one's life chances, so to speak, are intimately associated with (but not solely determined by) one's position vis-à-vis class struggle and, by extension, their access to (waged) work in either the primary or secondary labor market or, conversely, to nonwaged work in the informal sector. We witness therefore the decision to let die in the repeated attempts to eliminate various governmental safety nets: welfare, health care, Social Security. Both the services provided and the actual monies are being eliminated on the grounds that either these lives are not productive and thus not worthy of assistance or that these lives constitute a net loss to society and hence threaten the ability of the state to accumulate wealth. That these vital inequalities of the precariat are not (normally) seen as violent is itself a feature unique to capitalism, for just as the exploitation of labor is hidden by the myth of the free market so too is violence hidden in the "naturalness" of the market.

4

The Violence of Redundancy

Is the care of the fragile to be an essential practical good, or is medicine to be simply another commodity whose delivery is predicated on the basis of economic efficiency?

—TOM KOCH, *Thieves of Virtue: When Bioethics Stole Medicine*

Zygmunt Bauman writes about "redundancy" in contemporary society. Such a condition, according to Bauman, "whispers permanence and hints at the ordinariness of the condition. It names a condition without offering a ready-to-use antonym. It suggests a new shape of current normality and the shape of things that are imminent and bound to stay as they are." He continues, arguing that "to be 'redundant' means to be supernumerary, unneeded, of no use—whatever the needs and uses are that set the standard of usefulness and indispensability. . . . To be declared redundant means to have been disposed of because of being disposable—just like the empty and non-refundable plastic bottle or once-used syringe."[1]

This is an important distinction—separate from the concept of "surplus populations." Surplus populations—the infamous "reserve army of labor" so crucial for capitalism—are *necessary but contingent*. To be redundant suggests that capitalism no longer has any productive use for those who are labeled as such. Redundancy suggests but is not reducible to "waste." Some waste by-products are converted into productive use values and exchange values—depleted uranium, for example. Other wastes, however, have not been recommodified and are to be disposed of in the least costly manner, such as being deposited in landfills. Within neoliberalism, "wasted lives" are similarly being discarded.

Redundancy is an antiseptic word. It is found in the vocabulary of the bureaucrat, of the administrative bean counter who makes rational calculations to balance the bottom line. And much like beans all appear the same—a homogenous biomass—so too are individuals rendered identical within the bio-arithmetic of capitalism. As Bauman explains, "Routinely, people declared 'redundant' are talked about as mainly a financial problem. They need to be 'provided for'—that is fed, shod and sheltered."[2] They would not, could not, survive on their own, for they seemingly are unable to provide their own means of survival. That such reasoning exists is not the point. In contemporary society no individual is able to live autonomously, completely independent of assistance or input from others. Those who are the wealthiest in society, for example, are entirely dependent on the labor of others: someone must grow, process, and distribute their food; someone must ensure an adequate supply of clean water; someone must build their homes and resorts; someone must provide necessary medical and health care. We are all dependent; we are all entwined in a series of complex social relations.

But in the sterile world of the "free" market the indifference to use value conceals a preference for a narrowly defined, utilitarian productivity. As Lisa Marie Cacho explains, "In the era of American neoliberalism, social value and moral behavior are interpreted through and evaluated on economic terms, and, as a result, capitalist logic and ethics prevail in the social sphere as well as the economic and political realms." She continues her argument by stating that "in neoliberal ways of knowing, the *value of life* is subjected to an economic analysis and assessed accordingly: How has this person contributed to society? What will he or she accomplish in the future?"[3]

In this chapter I trace the penetration of society by the belief in redundancy and disposability with the intent of exposing the administration of violence and the letting die of men, women, and children who are deemed unproductive and wasteful. Through an engagement with eugenics and its recent incarnation in the administration of health care I detail an abstraction of violence that is predicated on the political-economic negotiation of life, for it is my argument that life continues to be subsumed under the domain of market logics, that life—its existence and vitality—is linked to the regulation and contestation of who has priority to live and flourish and who might be left to wither and die. In particular, I am drawn to governmental policies that impinge on the maintenance of life itself—the domains of fertility and mortality, those regulations that impose on the materiality of life and death from the standpoint of a multilayered demographic question: who lives, who dies, and who has the power to decide?[4]

THE MARKET LOGIC OF EUGENICS

The period between the sixteenth and nineteenth centuries marked the apex of European colonialism; this was an era of exploration and observation, classification and conquest. It was an era marked by European discoveries of new lands, new flora, and new fauna.[5] Such explorations would have far-reaching effects on our understanding of humanity. As Londa Schiebinger writes, naturalists of the time "sought to make sense of this mass of often contradictory information by sorting humankind into distinct types."[6]

To place an object (such as a human body) in one class rather than another establishes its central characteristics and creates assumptions about matters that are not seen.[7] This holds particularly true for the scientific construction and promotion of racial categories. Out of the scientific discourses emerged (supposedly) objective criteria that purported to explain the spatial distribution and diffusion of racialized bodies. Classifications were initially constructed according to observed, yet highly selective, physical traits; these, in turn, were used to explain cultural traits and behaviors, including poverty and promiscuity. In actuality, these presumed correlations worked both ways. The presumptive inferiority of "blacks" for example (but, in general, all "nonwhites") was taken as given and subsequently prompted the scientific search for associated morphological and anatomical signs distinguishing the previously labeled races.[8]

While somatic differences were the most common indicator of racial variation, other measurements compared facial angles, cranial capacity, and hair texture. Other, more innovative physical markers were also used. Étienne Serres, for example, compared the distance between a man's navel and penis to establish differences between Europeans and non-Europeans. Even more ambitious was the work of F. G. Crookshank, who attempted to establish the relationship between "Orientals" (also labeled "Mongols"), the "mentally retarded" (also labeled "Mongoloids"), and orangutans. He provided as evidence of these relationships such observations as differences between palm markings and hand gestures, body and limb postures, eyes, noses, teeth, arms, feet, mouths, tongues, varicose veins, brains, stomachs, anuses, and scrotums.[9]

The medicalization of race afforded a significant degree of legitimacy and authority to existent racial (and sexual) beliefs. Racial classifications were ordered hierarchically. Northern and western European "races" were held as the normative yardsticks against which all other races were measured. The most common standard included a tripartite abstraction of the "white" race: Nordics, Alpines, and Mediterraneans. The tall and fair-skinned Nordics (e.g., peoples from northern and western Europe) were thought to represent the highest echelons of humanity; presumed to be lower down the ladder of civilization were the shorter and somewhat darker Alpines (e.g., people from central Europe), followed by the supposedly much shorter and darker Mediterranean peoples (e.g., people from southern and eastern Europe). Trailing behind the "white" races were the various "yellow," "brown," "red," and "black" populations.

When anatomists and naturalists focused on sexual difference, Schiebinger explains, they often (with notable exceptions) limited their studies to male bodies of European origin. She states that "at least since Aristotle natural historians had given preference to the study of male bodies, or more precisely, the bodies of male citizens."[10] The bodies of women, it was believed, were simply deviant forms of male bodies. Thus, when anthropologists of the eighteenth and nineteenth centuries directed their gaze toward women, their interest most often centered on presumed sexual traits: feminine beauty; redness of lips; length and style of hair; size and shape of breasts or clitorises; the shape, size, and position of the pelvis; intensity of sexual desire; and, of course, fertility.[11] During the eighteenth century, for example, a commonly held view among the scientific establishment was that women were responsible for the "shaping" of physical characteristics. It was argued, for instance, that Germans had especially broad heads because German mothers always put babies to sleep on their backs; Belgians, conversely, had oblong heads because Belgian mothers wrapped their infants in swaddling clothes and laid them in bed on their sides.[12]

In general, through the late nineteenth century the physiological mechanisms of heredity were obscure. As Diane Paul explains, it was generally assumed that characteristics acquired by organisms during their lifetimes were transmissible to their progeny; such a belief was put forward in the writings of Jean-Baptiste Lamarck. In what became popularly known as Lamarckism, it was understood that animals, for example, would alter their behaviors in response to changing environmental conditions. One consequence of such changes was that certain, and selected, organs would come into or out of use.[13] When applied to humans, this principle of inheritance of acquired characteristics would have direct policy relevance. Simply put, the environment in which children were born and raised would play a major bearing on subsequent generations.

By the late nineteenth century the scientific study of both heredity and (racialized) populations had undergone a paradigmatic change. Most notably, the publication of Charles Darwin's *On the Origin of Species* (1859) began to undermine ideas of fixed biological categories and the principle of inheritance of acquired characteristics. Darwin's work posited that humans evolved through natural laws of selection and competition. As Noel Castree summarizes, Darwin, from his expeditionary observations and his studies of pigeon breeding, derived the notion of "natural selection"; from his reading of Thomas Malthus's work on population and resources, he derived the idea of the "survival of the fittest"; and from, his understanding of the work of geologists James Hutton and Charles Lyell, he articulated the principle of "deep time"—the idea that change occurs slowly over the *longue durée*. Combined, these elements suggested to Darwin that species interacted with each other and that those species best able to adapt to their conditions of existence were most likely to survive and to produce offspring similarly well adapted.[14]

Although Darwin's theory of natural selection is in many respects counter to that of Lamarck, Darwin's theory of heredity (which he termed "pangenesis") proposed that acquired characteristics were heritable. According to pangenesis, minute particles thrown off by various cells circulate through the body and ultimately concentrate in the "germ cells"; through this process, changes in parents' bodies could be manifest in their children. Opposing the concept of the inheritance of acquired characteristics was Francis Galton (1822–1911), a statistician, naturalist, policy advocate, and cousin of Darwin. Galton postulated that hereditary material was transmitted one from generation to the next.[15] Both specific talents and traits of character and personality were inherited; so too was tuberculosis, longevity, madness, gambling, sexual passion, criminal inclinations, and alcoholism.[16]

The mechanisms for inheritance were most clearly articulated by a German biologist, August Weismann. Throughout his writings, Weismann forwarded his theory of the continuity of the "germ plasm." He argued that there existed two types of cells that constituted the human body: the germ cells—present in the gonads and giving rise to sperm and egg—and somatic cells, which are present in other tissues in the body. For Weismann, the germ cells (or germ plasm) were isolated from somatic cells, and, while the somatic cells could be affected by the environment, the hereditary units of the germ plasm could not. In proposing that the germ plasm was completely independent from the rest of the cell, Weismann argued that it was the germ plasm that was inherited continuously by one generation from another without alteration from outside influences. Of significance, and in contrast to Lamarckism, Weismann's theory of germ plasm posited that environmental conditions were largely inconsequential, that no matter how much parents worked to improve their bodies or minds, their heredity would be unchanged and their children none the stronger or smarter.[17]

By the turn of the twentieth century, scientists and social reformers had already begun to advance the idea that society should recognize the power of heredity in its social laws, in such a way as to favor reproduction of the physically and morally fit.[18] Now, with the sustained assault against the belief in the inheritance of acquired characteristics, there appeared to be clear understanding of the task at hand. Specifically, the emerging science of genetics—buttressed by statistical and biometric studies—indicated that environmental factors played at best a minimal role in affecting the human condition.

Many scientists at the time identified and classified human worth based largely on intelligence, a trait, moreover, that was held to be heritable. To this end, the statistician and colleague of Galton, Karl Pearson, developed a series of analytical methods used to measure and correlate mental ability. The idea of systematically measuring intelligence circulated widely in scientific communities throughout both the United States and Europe at the turn of the twentieth century. In 1904, working at the request of the French government, Alfred Binet developed a series of tests consisting of numerous short problems designed to probe such qualities as memory, ratiocination, and verbal facilities. Subsequently, working with Theodore Simon, he developed a scheme for classifying people according to their supposed mental age. Of significance, however, is that Binet did not consider intelligence to be a genetic trait nor was his test designed to measure some supposedly innate level of intelligence. Rather, Binet envisioned his tests as a diagnostic to identify children in need of remedial education; it was a tool designed to redress structural and institutional factors that benefited some children while harming others through a lack of satisfactory educational opportunities.[19]

In 1908 Henry Goddard, an American psychologist, brought these tests from Europe to the United States. Working at the Training School for Feeble-Minded Boys and Girls, located in Vineland, New Jersey, Goddard employed the Binet-Simon test in an attempt to classify children according to mental acumen.[20] However, his use of the test differed considerably and perversely from Binet's. Previously, individuals who were judged to be mentally deficient were broadly defined as "feebleminded." Following Goddard's research, however, an entirely new vocabulary—and biosecurity threat—came into existence. Specifically, Goddard implemented a three-tiered system: idiots, imbeciles, and morons. According to Goddard, idiots—with a mental age of one or two—occupied the lowest rank. Next were the imbeciles, defined as having a mental age of three to seven; and last were morons, with a mental age between eight and twelve.[21] Within these broad divisions were subgradations, so that one could be classified, for example, as a "high-grade idiot" or a "low-grade imbecile."[22]

Intelligence tests were complemented by the flourishing of "family studies." Beginning in the late nineteenth century, an emergent social science developed that attempted to trace family lineages through the use of public records and field interviews. Reflective of the pressing social issues of the time, these studies focused especially on the continuity of negative traits, such as alcoholism, mental illness, sexual vices, and other criminal activities. Overall, the objective was to understand the hereditary character of social pathologies in the interests of limiting the cost of relief and custodial institutions.[23]

An early and highly influential study that was later co-opted by eugenicists was that conducted by Richard Dugdale. Published in 1877, Dugdale's study traced the ancestry of a dysfunctional family—the "Jukes"—through seven generations. Noting the prevalence of criminals, prostitutes, and other social misfits in the family, Dugdale attributed the Jukes' misfortune in significant part to the degradation of their environment. Dugdale, in fact, was a Lamarckian, and he believed that a change in the environment could lead to changes in behavior. Accordingly, the response to the inheritance of negative characteristics was to improve societal conditions. This element of his study, however, was overlooked by later social scientists. Believing that undesirable traits, such as a proclivity for criminal violence, were embedded within a person's germ plasm, subsequent writers and reformers used Dugdale's study as evidence for the hereditary nature of social pathology. Indeed, in a follow-up study, Arthur Eastbrook published

The Jukes in 1915, which purported to provide evidence of heredity factors. In contrast to Dugdale and his conclusions, these scientists firmly believed that inherited traits were not affected by environmental change. Another individual who made significant contributions to these early family studies was Charles Davenport, a Harvard-trained biologist and mathematician. In 1912 Davenport published *The Trait Book*, a detailed listing of individual characteristics, predispositions, and behavioral tendencies. Davenport also established scientific guidelines for field observations, pedigree charts, and surveys to facilitate the conduct of family studies. Influenced by his understanding of animal husbandry, Davenport approached his scientific studies with a considered pragmatism. Specifically, he sought to identify and isolate the feebleminded, the degenerate, the perverts, morons, imbeciles, epileptics, and paupers from the general population because all of these people were defined as having less worthy lives.[24] Davenport would later write, in 1915, that "apart from migration, there is only one way to get socially desirable traits into our social life, and that is by reproduction; there is only one to get them out, by preventing their reproduction through breeding."[25]

Goddard himself contributed to the science of family studies. Through the Eugenic Records Office (ERO), Goddard sent field workers to carry out systematic studies of local populations. Resulting from these efforts was *The Kallikak Family: A Study in the Heredity of Feeblemindedness*, published in 1912. Although the "Kallikaks" constituted a pseudonymous family— their name was constructed from the Greek words *kalós* (good) and *kakós* (bad)—Goddard's study would have far-reaching consequences. In particular, Goddard warned that mental illness was a threat to the health and well-being of American society; moreover, this threat could potentially pass unnoticed. Goddard cautioned, for example, that morons—although equipped with a mental age of between eight and twelve—could "pass" in public society. As such, there existed the very real possibility that morons could reproduce and thus hasten societal degeneration.[26]

Social reformers of the early twentieth century, influenced by Darwin, Weismann, and Mendel, held little faith that improvements in social conditions would lead to a healthier, more vital population. Rather, it was believed that paupers, prostitutes, and other declared criminals were genetically inferior and that no amount of reform would change these essential traits.[27] The survival of a thriving, prosperous society was at stake. Simply put, if left unchecked, the higher birth rates and artificially reduced death rates among society's least capable—those considered less worthy—would result in the steady degeneration of the population.[28] Galton himself, among others, proposed that boundaries between more and less valuable life could and should be drawn.[29]

Throughout the late nineteenth and early twentieth centuries, concern grew among the academic community that contemporary society—through charity and welfare programs—was tampering with the laws of nature, that unfit people were being allowed to survive and reproduce, that "lives not worth living" constituted an unbearable financial burden on national and local budgets, and that those deemed undesirable constituted a criminal and violent threat. In other words, "positive" duties threatened to harm society at large; what was required was an end to such charitable actions and a concomitant political will to intervene in the management of life.

These political valuations of life identified a grievous and imminent social problem and demanded an immediate solution. Fueled by Darwinian concepts of sexual selection and evolution, competing concepts of genetics, Malthusian perspectives on overpopulation, and environmental determinism, widespread fears of racial and societal degeneration permeated both popular and scientific venues. These fears were augmented by a growing—and scientifically documented—understanding of demographic changes. In the United States, for example, long-established patterns of immigration were drastically changing. Prior to the 1880s immigration was dominated by peoples from northern and western European nations; in the decades around 1900, however, the main source areas shifted to southern and eastern Europe and, increasingly, Asia. Citing these changes, the labor historian and university professor John Commons in 1907 warned that "the change is one that should challenge the attention of every citizen."[30]

Threats to the body politic of the United States were not simply external. Following the abolition of slavery a moral panic ensued over the moral presence and economic position of newly freed black members of American society. Thus, in the wake of the American Civil War, politicians from the South implemented a series of laws to keep the black population in position as docile, landless laborers. Known as the Black Codes, these laws were designed to effect white social control over black occupational, social, and geographic mobility. And while varying by state and by local jurisdictions, the Black Codes generally denied freed slaves the right to marry white persons, bear arms, or assemble after sunset.[31] Unfair labor arrangements were also instituted, and, consequently, African Americans often became debt bound to their former slave-owning masters.

Throughout the late nineteenth century but especially during the early twentieth century the problem of the African American found its most forceful crystallization in the eugenics-inspired fear of unmitigated violence and racialized sexuality. In part, (white) scientists reasoned at the time that slavery had been beneficial—from an evolutionary standpoint—to the black population. Slavery, in fact, was presented as a form of genetic welfare, a viewpoint often reflecting a misappropriation of Darwinian thought and the process of natural selection. For example, George T. Winston, president of the North Carolina College of Agriculture and Mechanic Arts, argued that slavery "transformed the Negro so quickly from a savage to a civilized man."[32] H. E. Belin, writing in the *American Journal of Sociology*, concurred: "Slavery, so far from degrading the Negro, has actually elevated him industrially, mentally, and morally, the term of his involuntary tutelage [slavery] to the white race raising him to a vastly higher level than that ever occupied by his kinsmen in Africa."[33] According to these experts, however, the abolition of slavery threatened to curtail this evolutionary improvement. Members of the black race were, on this account, retrogressing to their "natural" and "uncivilized" violent condition. Belin described this transformation as "frenzied," noting that black persons who "but one brief hour before, were laughing, chattering, peaceable members of the community, are subject at any moment to be converted by some trivial occurrence into fierce, howling, blood-thirsty savages."[34]

In short, academics and other so-called experts maintained that African Americans, now freed from the "beneficence" of slavery, posed direct threats to the well-being of American society. These violent threats, moreover, were often sexual in nature and revealed a starkly gendered component. African American *men* posed a threat to the purity of the white race, through their supposed and unquenchable desire for virginal white women. African American *women*, on the other hand, also posed a threat by way of their supposed hypersexuality and hyperfertility. Combined, these discourses contributed to an overall image of uncivilized and uncontrolled blacks who retained no positive *productive* capability but considerable negative *reproductive* potential.[35]

Ongoing demographic and family studies revealed that immigrants and African Americans exhibited higher fertility rates. If left unchecked, these reproductive trends allegedly would lead to an overall decline in the proportion of the "original" Nordic stock of the United States. Numerous—and widely circulated—texts of the period attest to these fears: Madison Grant's *The Passing of the Great Race* (1916) and *The Conquest of a Continent* (1933), Lothrop Stoddard's *The Rising Tide of Color against White World-Supremacy* (1920), and James Herbert Curle's *Our Testing Time: Will the White Race Win Through?* (1926).

Progress in the natural and social sciences—coupled with a proper political will—was required to understand both the implications of human interference on natural selection and, if possible, to provide viable methods to promote a healthier and safer population. What was required, in practical and legal terms, was biopolitical control over the three fundamental processes of population change: migration, fertility, and mortality. What emerged was the eugenics movement.

As Sheldon Ekland-Olson writes, the eugenic argument was attractively simple: would it not be better to have a society enriched by those who are productive, healthy, emotionally stable, and smart than one stifled by degenerate, feebleminded, disabled, and criminal citizens?[36] Framed as concern over differential worth, the eugenics movement effectively combined sexist, racist, classist, and nationalist sentiments. Indeed, as Saul Dubow writes, eugenics coincided with the rising intensity of imperialist feelings, which also helped augment nationalist fervor and provide a convenient rationale for the colonial subjugation of non-European peoples.[37] Thus, as a globalizing paradigm, eugenics sought not only to identify differences within the human population but also to evaluate and calculate the potential contribution of various groups toward the betterment of society. As explained by the eugenicist L. H. M. Baker, "When we have ascertained . . . the qualities we want to preserve and the characteristics we desire to eliminate we must be courageous in the application of our remedy."[38] From the United States to Germany, from Japan to Mexico, an array of segregation policies, immigration laws, relocation schemes, antimiscegenation laws, and sterilization and euthanasia programs emerged as tangible—and viable—instruments in the practice of statecraft.[39] Indeed, the eugenics movement marks the apex of overt state intervention into the calculation of life and death.

As both an academic field and political agenda, eugenics mandated no singular approach. Rather, individual practitioners segregated themselves according to beliefs and largely formed four main groups: mainline eugenicists, racial anthropologists, reform eugenicists, and socialist eugenicists. Indeed, what is striking about eugenics was that it could be, and was, adopted by people spanning the political spectrum. And while significant differences existed, what is most noteworthy is that all retained a central tenet in that it was possible—in fact, it was necessary—to engage in a calculated management of valued life. These calculations invariably focused on reproductive control and, by extension, the regulation of female sexuality.

The institutionalization of the eugenics movement provided scientific and political clout. As both producers and disseminators of the science of eugenics, myriad associations and organizations emerged: the American Breeders' Association, the American Eugenics Society, the Galton Society, the Race Betterment Foundation, the Battle Creek Human Betterment Foundation, and the Station for the Experimental Study of Evolution (SESE), along with its affiliated Eugenics Record Office (ERO). These institutions were complemented by the rapid expansion of eugenics as an academic field of study. By 1914 courses on eugenics were offered at 44 American colleges and universities; by 1928 the number had increased to 376. Education in eugenics was not limited to the upper echelons;

indeed, eugenics was endorsed in more than 90 percent of high school biology textbooks.[40]

In their widely used textbook *Applied Eugenics*, Paul Popenoe and Roswell Hill Johnson argued that the birth rate of the American stock was too low; consequently, the most desirable seed stock was dying out and being supplanted by immigrants. Citing studies on the fertility rates of female students and alumni of Vassar, Bryn Mawr, Mount Holyoke, and Wellesley, Popenoe and Johnson concluded that the most "fit" women were delaying marriage and thus not contributing substantially to societal reproduction. Such behaviors on the part of these women, they argued, posed a "great harm" to the "white race."[41] Likewise, the sociologist Edward A. Ross warned of "conquest made by childbearing" of African Americans and immigrants.[42] The politics of reproduction, however, were situated within a broader context in which minimum wages, set working hours, public education, public health reforms, and charity were combining to enable inferior peoples to live longer and to reproduce.

In the United States, given its history of slavery, considerable attention was devoted to interracial sexuality. The polemicist Madison Grant, for example, condemned interracial unions, stating that miscegenation should be regarded as "a social and racial crime of the first magnitude."[43] The academics Popenoe and Johnson were even more blunt in their assessment: "If you have mixing, you produce a mongrel.... The blending of the two destroys the purity of the type of both and introduces confusion."[44] Indeed, according to the science of the era, the progeny of interracial couples were genetically defective and thus contributed to two unacceptable societal consequences: a financial and social burden on the dominant (white) society and an overall deterioration of the dominant (white) race and society. Popenoe and Johnson professed that "if the choice of a proper life partner is to be eugenic, random mating must be as nearly as possible eliminated, and assertive and preferential mating for desirable traits must take place."[45] And while eugenicists such as Popenoe and Johnson saw prejudice and racism as nature's way of preventing the union of different races, many also believed that nature alone was not sufficient to prevent these "mongrel" births from occurring. According to Popenoe and Johnson, although Nordics had "long ago reached the instinctive conclusion . . . that [they] must put a ban on intermarriage," the "taboo of public opinion [is] not sufficient and must be supplemented by law."[46] This was a conclusion that Madison Grant readily accepted: "Laws against miscegenation must be greatly extended if the higher races are to be maintained."[47]

Eugenicists differed in their application of science. Whereas some favored "positive" eugenics (i.e., policies to increase the contribution of populations deemed most desirable), others advocated "negative" eugenics (i.e., policies to decrease the biological contribution of inferior or less valuable populations). With respect to the latter, for example, Grant argued that "the most practical and hopeful method of race improvement is through the elimination of the least desirable elements in the nation by depriving them of the power to contribute to future generations."[48] In practice, the forwarding of "positive" or "negative" eugenic practices was itself determined by the calculation of a population's worth. Thus, for example, eugenicists advocated positive techniques to increase the fertility levels of middle- and upper-class white women; negative techniques were promoted and employed to lower the fertility of those deemed inferior, namely, most immigrants, African Americans, the mentally ill, prostitutes, criminals, and the poor. Over time, sterilization became the favored option—in part because of advances in medical techniques— but also, and equally important, because of financial considerations. As Davenport explained in 1911, "It is a reproach to our intelligence that we as a people . . . should have to support about half a million insane, feeble-minded, epileptic, blind and deaf, 80,000 prisoners and 100,000 paupers at a cost of over 100 million dollars per year."[49] A particularly blatant, calculated management of life and death was provided by Harry Laughlin of the Eugenics Record Office. In 1914 Laughlin released a two-hundred-page report on the "best practical means of cutting off the defective germ plasm in the American population." Embedded in this report was a precise schedule, complete with "Rate of Efficiency" graphs, that specified how the total elimination of "the lowest and most degenerate one-tenth of the total population" could be achieved by 1985. In effect, the total number of yearly sterilizations nationwide would need to rise from 92,000 in 1920; to 121,000 by 1930; 158,000 by 1940; 203,000 by 1950; 260,000 by 1960; 330,000 by 1970; and 415,000 by 1980.[50]

Despite their zeal to eliminate those deemed less worthy, many (but not all) eugenicists were concerned with the legality of their methods. In other words, was the harmful (and, one might add, violent) practice of involuntary sterilization considered criminal? Proponents recognized that *success was predicated upon state support*; procedures adopted had to be deemed both just and constitutional. These concerns were made apparent in 1905, when the Pennsylvania legislature passed a bill titled "Act for the Prevention of Idiocy." This act would have permitted involuntary sterilizations to be performed by doctors. However, Gov. Samuel Pennypacker vetoed the bill. In part, he did so because of ambiguities contained within the bill and because such practices would violate doctor-patient trust. Of equal if not greater importance was that Pennypacker opposed the bill on moral grounds; he believed that the proposed law would result in grave injustices and that "to permit such an operation would be to inflict cruelty upon a helpless class of the community which the state has undertaken to protect."[51]

Not all supporters of involuntary sterilization were content to wait for legal approval. One such individual was Harry Sharp, chief surgeon at the Indiana State Reformatory. Sharp, after learning about a new procedure for performing vasectomies, began performing the operation on inmates. Between 1899 and 1907, Sharp—on his own initiative—sterilized nearly five hundred men without their consent. He maintained that the procedure was necessary because it would suppress masturbation (believed to be a leading cause of insanity) and therefore proposed its use to counter the rapid increase in the number of criminals, paupers, and insane and feebleminded persons.[52]

Sharp was cognizant at some level of the procedure's dubious legality and thus lobbied strenuously for the passage of legislation that would permit heads of all state institutions, including almshouses, insane asylums, institutes for the feebleminded, reformatories, and prisons, to "render every male sterile who passes its portals."[53] To this end, Sharp teamed up with John Hurty, Indiana's secretary of the State Board of Health, to enact such legislation. Because of their efforts, in 1907 Indiana became the first state to have an involuntary sterilization law. Of significance, this law—while directed toward inmates and other institutionalized persons—was not imposed as a form of punishment; rather, it was enacted to prevent procreation by confirmed criminals, idiots, imbeciles, and rapists. In short, this law was envisioned as a policy of public health. Indiana's sterilization law was quickly followed by similar laws in twelve other states, and these laws, in turn, were challenged for their constitutionality. The matter was decided in 1927 with the U.S. Supreme Court ruling in *Buck v. Bell*.[54]

In 1924 J. T. and Alice Dobbs committed their adopted daughter, Carrie Buck, to the State Colony for Epileptics and the Feeble-Minded, in Lynchburg, Virginia. Carrie, seventeen years old at the time, had conceived a child (Vivian) out of wedlock, which supposedly demonstrated that she was socially irresponsible and lacking in reproductive "fitness." Such a determination was readily believable by the authorities, given that Carrie was herself the illegitimate daughter of an allegedly feebleminded mother, Emma, who had lived at the colony since 1920. Once Carrie was institutionalized, Dr. Albert S. Priddy petitioned the state to sterilize her on the grounds of sexual immorality; as proof, he offered both her pregnancy and her lineage.

In actuality, Carrie was neither sexually promiscuous nor morally deviant. Carrie had been raped by a relative of her adopted family; one consequence of this violent act was her impregnation. The Dobbses, however, refused to acknowledge or seek punishment for the rapist; instead, they chose to cover up the crime by institutionalizing Carrie and, in turn, supporting her forced sterilization. Carrie's life as an out-of-wedlock child of a supposedly mentally ill mother was considered inconsequential in and of itself. She could be raped with impunity, incarcerated with impunity, and, if the doctors and lawyers had their way, she would be sterilized with impunity.

Proponents of eugenics found in Carrie Buck an ideal test case to determine the constitutionality of sterilization. Harry Laughlin was consulted, and, without ever once personally seeing Carrie, Emma, or

Vivian, he testified to their mental deficiencies. Laughlin argued that Carrie and her mother "belong to the shiftless, ignorant, and worthless class of anti-social whites of the South."[55] Guided by Laughlin's "expertise," combined with testimony from other supposed experts, the circuit court judge of Amherst County upheld the sterilization order, as did the Virginia Supreme Court of Appeals. Ultimately, in 1927 the case was argued before the Supreme Court of the United States. Carrie's defense counsel, I. P. Whitehead, argued against the sterilization statute, warning that under this type of law a "reign of doctors will be inaugurated and in the name of science new classes will be added, even races may be brought within the scope of such a regulation and the worst forms of tyranny practiced."[56] His arguments went for naught, however, as the court declared that sterilization on eugenic grounds was within the police power of the state, that it provided due process of law, and that it did not constitute cruel or unusual punishment.[57] The court's opinion was written by Justice Oliver Wendell Holmes, who (in)famously quipped, "It is better for all the world if, instead of waiting to execute degenerate offspring for crime, or to let them starve for their imbecility, society can prevent those who are manifestly unfit from continuing their kind. . . . Three generations of imbeciles is enough."[58] The argument of Justice Holmes was based on the belief that "future economic necessity could serve as the grounds for a contemporary choice of action or inaction."[59] This decision marked a *legal* confluence of medical ethics and state economics, whereby those rendered by administrative fiat to be "unproductive should willingly sacrifice their care needs for the productive goods of the society whose resources are limited."[60] Thus, when Holmes rendered his opinion in *Buck v. Bell* he articulated a political, social, and economic philosophy, a set of values that could be enacted legally, for, according to Tom Koch, in doing so Holmes promoted an ethic that diminished the rights of the individual in favor of the future economies of the state.[61] This judicial decision, in effect, provided the legal imposition of a distinctive structure of violence, informed by a particular value system, embedded in a specific political economy, that being capitalism.

The decision in *Buck v. Bell* would have far-reaching effects, for the judgment fueled a resurgence of eugenic sterilization lawmaking that led to the enactment of new statutes in sixteen states in the late 1920s and early 1930s; eventually, more than thirty states adopted sterilization laws in an attempt to "protect" American society—and taxpayers' money—from the presumed threat of the feebleminded. The average annual number of operations performed under compulsory sterilization laws increased tenfold, from 230 for the 1907-20 period to 2,273 during the 1930s. It is estimated that in total approximately 60,000 men and women were involuntarily sterilized.[62]

For many writers, the *Buck v. Bell* decision marked the apex of the eugenics movement in American society. To be sure, sterilization and the institutionalization of those deemed unworthy or unfit continued throughout the postwar years. However, it is assumed that eugenics fell into disfavor and, indeed, disrepute when the depravity of the Holocaust became clear. In particular, the passage of the Nuremberg Code in 1964 is believed by some to mark the emergence of an ethically sound medical practice. Despite claims to the contrary, though, eugenic ideas *and practices* did not disappear from contemporary society.[63] What did change was that a veneer of new morality was applied to the practice of medicine.

In 1966 C. Lee Buxton, a physician, published a short commentary in the journal *Northwest Medicine*. Buxton informed readers of the ongoing discussions—and fears—of overpopulation at the global level. But, he warned, the United States was not immune to the threat. He explained that "this population increase affects economics, education, transportation, employment, business, the professions—in fact every walk of life."[64] In the United States, though, Buxton believed that his profession—the medical profession—had not responded accordingly. He lamented that the "medical profession . . . must be aware of this problem but most of us in America have viewed it with the same kind of sympathetic detachment with which we view the existence of localized endemic or epidemic disease in other parts of the world and with an it-can't-happen-here type of thinking."[65]

For Buxton, the biological—and financial—threat of overpopulation not only could happen in the United States, it already was happening.

Poverty, simply put, was a symptom of America's ailment; excessive fertility was the illness. Buxton explained that the "vicious spiral of increasing poverty and increasing fertility is in our midst in this country and is so close to all of us that it is almost incredible that it has carried no greater impact on the general population."[66] It was not a matter of the distribution of resources but rather a problem of personal responsibility: unfit parentage and uncontrolled reproductive behavior. Buxton indicated that "there are 69 million children in the United States under the age of 18" and that of that number, "12 million live in absolute poverty, which means just enough milk, bread, meat, clothing and shelter to keep from starving to death or freezing to death." He continued that "it is safe to say that the majority of these children are unwanted; that they are spawned into a bleak, fatherless and frequently motherless world, and that by the time most of these children reach the age of six they are lost forever."[67]

Foreshadowing the fears that would later be personified as the irresponsible "teenage mom," Buxton decried the "unavailable mother who brings her child home from the hospital and realizes she hates him for being alive."[68] And if the parents—the mothers—were not responsible, it was up to the medical profession, the experts, to do something. Buxton reasoned that "this filthy residue of our culture exists in every city in the United States and the problem is multiplying itself with dreadful predictability, *because the medical profession has controlled the death rate but has done very little about the birth rate*."[69] One should note that the "filthy residue" of which Buxton wrote was in fact, human beings. These were people: fathers, mothers, and children who lived in poverty. But in anticipation of a more conservative—and some would argue, callous—approach to health care, poverty was a mark of personal failure. Increasingly, medicine itself was being subsumed to the market logics of capital, whereby the ethical goal was no longer to do no harm (a position of nonviolence, it should be noted) but to support "the maintenance of economically valuable workers."[70]

Buxton envisioned an apocalyptic world, an Armageddon wrought by uncontrolled fertility. He concluded with a dire question: "are we going to capitulate to an even more incredible pestilence—the destruction of our own civilization by our own progeny?"[71] Despite Buxton's claims to the contrary, the specter of overpopulation—the masses of unwanted children spawned from irresponsible and unfit parents—was pervasive in many policy circles. Indeed, irresponsible parentage was a long-standing fear of many in the medical profession. Consequently, efforts to sterilize the "unfit," of preventing the existence of a generation of morons, imbeciles, and feebleminded persons, did not abate after World War II. Rather, a latent eugenics—including involuntary sterilization—continued throughout the second half of the twentieth century.[72]

As the work of Rebecca Kluchin demonstrates, from the 1950s onward there remained a focus on women's reproductive fitness; a shift, however, was noticeable, in that social anxieties were extended not simply to those deemed mentally defective but also to racialized others. Kluchin affirms that conservative, white, middle-class Americans expressed anger at the "unworthy" poor on the public dole, especially as unwed, nonwhite mothers gained access to public assistance.[73] Consequently, advocates for the regulation of reproduction and the accounting of costs associated with providing for the destitute or disabled converged in maleficent policies that continued to spell the difference between life and death but that are not widely viewed as violent inactions.

CALCULATING THE INEQUALITY OF LIFE

Neoliberalism, as David Harvey explains, "is in the first instance a theory of political economic practices that proposes that human well-being can best be advanced by liberating individual entrepreneurial freedoms and skills within an institutional framework characterized by strong private property rights, free markets, and free trade. The role of the state is to create and preserve an institutional framework appropriate to such practices." However, Harvey notes, in the neoliberal view, if markets do not exist—such as in health care—they must be created, by state action if necessary.[74] Such is the context for the emergence of health-care rationing.

Within the United States the governance of health care and medical procedures exhibits a long and checkered past. Firmly ensconced in the eugenics of industrial capitalism, the "invocation of cost as a rational criterion limiting acceptable levels of care for the chronically and terminally ill is rooted in the late 19th century redefinition of individual worth as a quotient of employability and productivity."[75] Indeed, as Tom Koch explains, the concern with burdensome community costs was the rational motive for Justice Holmes's decision to permit the involuntary sterilization of Carrie Buck.

Throughout the 1970s—as the specter of overpopulation permeated scientific circles and popular culture—state governments began to manage health care. Health care was, and is, promoted as a finite resource— something that is to be rationed.[76] Herein, however, lies a fundamental paradox within the neoliberal state. On the one hand, as Julie Guthman explains, neoliberal governmentality encourages subjects to make few demands on the state and instead to act through the market by exercising consumer choice, being entrepreneurial and self-interested, and striving for self-actualization and fulfillment.[77] On the other hand, the premise of health-care rationing is that patients and physicians, left to their own devices, will make poor health-care decisions.[78] Consequently, to facilitate the calculated management of life and death, some rational, "objective" measure must be employed to balance the scales.

In recent decades questions of cost have generally been assumed to be the appropriate metric of rational treatment in the context of supposedly scarce public resources. Koch elaborates that "even where a failure to care results in a life-threatening or ending decision, the rationalities of cost efficiency are typically assumed to trump the protocols of patient treatment and life prolongation."[79] This is seen clearly in a case involving a five-month-old boy named Maverick. Maverick was born with a severe heart defect and, following two surgeries, was in dire need of a heart transplant. The procedure was denied, however, on the grounds that Maverick had a rare genetic defect that put him at high risk for tumors and infections. Maverick's mother, however, challenged this presumption, claiming instead that Maverick was denied because he had Coffin-Siris syndrome, a rare condition that contributes to delays in cognitive development. It was following this diagnosis that doctors decided that Maverick was not a viable candidate for the life-saving surgery. According to Dr. Linda Addonizio, "It was determined that [Maverick] does not qualify to be a heart transplant candidate at our institution at this time. This decision was based on the medical implications of this Coffin-Siris syndrome, which would limit his survival and *potential benefit* from transplantation."[80] In other words, an infant was denied a potentially life-saving procedure on the presumption of diminished quality of life; a medical procedure that could "make life" was denied, thereby potentially "letting die" a five-month-old boy.

Maverick's case is not the exception but the rule. Upwards of 40 percent of pediatric transplant centers always (or usually) consider a child's neurodevelopmental delays when making transplant decisions according to David Magnus, director of the Center for Biomedical Ethics at Stanford University, even though these children fare just as well medically after a transplant as other children do.[81] This indicates that the supposedly objective and thereby "indifferent" calculations of health-care rationing exhibit a strong preference for the type of (future productive) person to be helped. As Koch concludes, decisions are predominantly made "on the basis of social affordability and utilitarian assumptions about a patient's social value."[82] The withholding of necessary and vital medical procedures, however, is rarely considered a form of violence; indeed, perversely, it is viewed as rational, beneficial, and even compassionate.

Health-care rationing exists as a neoliberal biopolitical practice and exhibits the market logics of letting die. As Manfred Steger and Ravi Roy write, "Rather than operating along more traditional lines of pursuing the public good by enhancing civil society and social justice, neoliberals call for the employment of governmental technologies that are taken from the world of business and commerce: mandatory development of 'strategic plans' and 'risk-management' schemes oriented toward the creation of 'surpluses'; cost-benefit analyses and other efficiency calculations; the shrinking of political governance (so-called 'best-practice governance'); the setting of quantitative targets; the close monitoring of outcomes; the creation of highly individualized, performance-based work plans; and the introduction of 'rational choice' models that internalize and thus normalize market-oriented behavior."[83] These practices have been deeply incorporated throughout the health-care system in the United States—often with tragic and fatal results, for accompanying the neoliberal *practice* of health care has been a transformation in attitudes toward life and death. Indeed, these political economic shifts have witnessed a simultaneous shift in the meaning of life—but not in the meaning of violence. Now, we increasingly hear the medical profession and bioethicists speak of "life-years" as oppose to *life*. We see the application—indeed, substitution—of rating scales and numerical scores to establish a patient's condition. And while harm through inaction (or, more properly, through nonoperations) may result, violence is far removed from the topic of conversation.

At the core of health-care rationing are two concepts predicated on market logics: cost-effectiveness analysis (CEA) and cost-benefit analysis (CBA). Briefly stated, CEA ranks alternative expenditures; it provides a comparison of two or more procedures on the basis of "bang for the buck." CBA, conversely, asks whether the bang is worth the buck. Currently, the medical community has almost universally endorsed both cost-benefit analyses and cost-effectiveness analyses as appropriate guides to medical decision making.[84] To facilitate these analyses, health-care consultants have developed a series of rating scales, such as "Quality-Adjusted Life-Years" (QALYs); "Disability-Adjusted Life-Years" (DALYs), and "Healthy Year Equivalents" (HYEs). In constructing these scales, researchers surveyed thousands of people about their preferences: whether they would "prefer" to be impotent or incontinent, hearing impaired or vision impaired, and so on.[85]

These banal-sounding scales, and their correspondingly trivial acronyms, literally spell the difference between life and death, for underlying these concepts is a calculated management of populations. In short, treatment—whether for prevention or intervention—is predicated on a bio-arithmetic, a calculated trade-off between the cost of a procedure and the anticipated gain. Such decisions, however, are based not at the level of the individual but at the level of the population, for health-care rationing is, at its core, informed by a utilitarian ethics that replaces one abstraction, "sanctity of human life," with a different abstraction, that of "quality of life." As Koch explains, when the ethic of the sanctity of life was dominant, life was to be not merely maintained but also, wherever possible, nurtured.[86] In other words, the attitude to "make life" was preeminent, but such an attitude reflected also a more communitarian approach to life. The transformation toward an attitude of "quality of life," however, reflects a valuation of life that is increasingly subsumed by market logics, for embedded within this transformation is a privileging of abstract normality and competition (in the form of scarce resources).

These bio-logical scales also reflect the subsumption of market logics through the abstract exchangeability of medical conditions. Qualitative differences in the conditions of life, such as vision impairments or kidney failure, are transformed into quantitative indices that permit (in principle) the objective comparison between two or more bodies. In other words, DALYS, QALYS, and HYES assume the role that money plays in capitalist society. Whereas money facilitates the exchange of raincoats for bushels of corn, these medical measures provide a form of equivalency between different ailments and conditions. Presented as such, health-care scales appear as objective, rational, and indifferent to any particular individual, thereby suggesting a seemingly nonpartisan and fair allocation of resources.

Let's look at QALYS—one of the most widely employed rating scales within the medical profession. As explained by Alan Williams, one of the architects of QALYS, the rationale is based on a "quest for efficiency." In presenting his case, Williams maintains that "priority setting is essentially a matter of deciding which are the most valuable things that can be done with the available resources."[87] It bears repeating that in this context, the "things" of which Williams writes are human lives. The purpose, therefore, is to determine which lives are most valuable and hence most deserving of available resources.

Efficiency, for Williams, entails two components: (1) ensuring that no activity costs more than is necessary and (2) ensuring that no activity is pursued beyond the point where the value of the extra benefits it generates outweighs the value of the extra resources it uses.[88] The first component is simple enough and most likely would raise little concern: to not pay too much for a particular service. It is the second component, however, that is decidedly more controversial. Restated, Williams argues that services provided must be cost-effective. He begins by asking various questions: What does it cost to add an extra year to one's life? Is an extra year of life for person x comparable to an extra year of life for person y?

What emerges from these questions is a bio-arithmetic computation known as the quality-adjusted life-year, or QALY. In Williams's own words: "The essence of a QALY is that it takes a year of healthy life expectancy to be worth 1, but regards a year of unhealthy life expectancy as worth less than 1. Its precise value is lower the worse the quality of life of the unhealthy person (which is what the 'quality adjusted' bit is all about). If being dead is worth zero, it is, in principle, possible for a QALY to be negative, i.e., for the quality of someone's life to be judged as worse than being dead."[89]

Williams continues, stating that the "general idea is that a beneficial health care activity is one that generates a positive amount of QALYs, and an efficient health care activity is one where the cost-per-QALY is as low as it can be. A high priority health care activity is one where cost-per-QALY is low, and a low priority activity is one where cost-per-QALY is high."[90] QALYs provide a utilitarian justification for health-care rationing—measured not in human lives but in life-years. Moreover, the rating is determined not by medical science—as problematic as that may be—but through attitudinal and preference surveys. Not surprisingly, as Koch explains, quality-of-life determinations by persons deemed normal and healthy tend to reflect the prejudice, fear, or concerns of the observer, not those of the person whose lived existence is being judged.[91]

QALY scales provide abstract numerical scores for different temporal states or experiences of health; the extremes are straightforward, with a range between "dead" (QALY = 0) and "completely healthy" (QALY = 1.0). However, depending on how individuals respond to survey questions, a year of blindness might score 0.5 QALYs and a year of incontinence might score 0.75 QALYs. Moreover, as Williams acknowledges, it is possible that some health states, such as quadriplegia, might score less than 0 QALYs. In other words, for some respondents—and thus for some health-care decisions—people would rather be dead than be in a wheelchair.[92] Inherent in quality-of-life measures therefore is the view that one cannot be simultaneously disabled and healthy, nor, in theory, can persons with physical conditions deviating negatively from the social norm claim a positive quality of life.[93]

Through the use of market-determined calculations, health-care rationing is predicated not on the value of life per se but instead on economic expediency. Here, good health is, as Koch notes, "defined economically because [capitalist] society is at base an economic system whose accountancies are the single measure of good and worth."[94] Care toward human beings is therefore calculated on a cost-benefit basis, whereby procedures deemed most efficient according to market logics are given priority over less efficient treatments. To this end, Melanie Rock explains that health-care indices invoke "the possibility of exchanging people with disabilities for people without disabilities, and exchanging longer 'normal' lives for 'rehabilitated' bodies."[95] David Dranove provides the following illustrative example. Suppose there exists a medical intervention that offers a blind person a 50 percent chance of fully recovering her eyesight (QALY = 1) and a 50 percent chance of no improvement in vision (QALY = 0.5); bio-calculations quickly reveal that the intervention in question has a QALY score of 0.75.[96] It is readily apparent, moreover, that decisions are made at the level of the population as opposed to that of the individual, despite the neoliberal rhetoric of autonomy and personal choice. Health-care rationing, at its core, is a decidedly utilitarian practice in which the health of one is readily sacrificed for the good of the whole.

One might suspect that comparing different medical interventions is much like comparing apples and oranges. However, as Dranove explains, QALYs (in principle) *justify* such comparisons. For example, consider the cost-effectiveness of two treatments for two different medical conditions: impotence and incontinence. Treatment for the former condition (impotence) costs twenty thousand dollars and is effective for eight years; treatment for the latter costs eighteen thousand dollars but is effective for twelve years. Given a limited budget in an era of health-care rationing, which treatment should be covered? Through the use of QALYs, Dranove demonstrates how such a decision is rendered. Thus, in our example, incontinence carries a QALY score of 0.75 while impotence has a QALY score of 0.9. A patient who is successfully treated for incontinence—elevating his health state from 0.75 to 1.0—gains in effect 0.25 QALYs for each year that the treatment is effective. Multiplied over eight years, the net gain for the treatment is 2 QALYs. With a price tag of twenty thousand dollars, the treatment for incontinence carries a cost-effectiveness ratio of ten thousand dollars per QALY gained. Conversely, a patient who is successfully treated for impotence, again, elevating his health state from 0.9 to 1.0, gains only 0.1 QALYS for each year that the treatment is effective. And multiplied over twelve years, the net gain is just 1.2 QALYs. Therefore, at eighteen thousand dollars per treatment, the cost per QALY gained is fifteen thousand dollars. In this example, the treatment for incontinence has a lower cost per QALY and is therefore more cost-effective than the treatment for impotence.[97]

To facilitate these comparisons, health-care consultants have calculated the cost-effectiveness of thousands of treatments; these are compiled in league tables and are used to determine which procedures are to be promoted. Dranove explains, for example, that hip replacement procedures cost only $2,000 for each QALY gained, while kidney transplants cost $7,500 per QALY gained. Interventions such as erythropoietin treatments for anemia in dialysis patients cost upwards of $86,000 per QALY gained, and neurosurgery for malignant intracranial tumors costs $320,000 for each QALY gained.[98] In short, as Dranove explains, league tables allow policy makers to easily compare many interventions at once and hence allow "disinterested" consultants to determine how best to spend scarce health-care dollars. Underlying this apparently benign and neutral administrative practice, however, is a particular violence that remains unseen, for here is modern neoliberalism in action, whereby "humanity is defined materially" with "the individual and his or her needs disappearing except as a cipher in some impersonal economic analysis."[99]

Consider the statements of Linda Peeno. A physician by training, Peeno worked in the 1980s as a consultant for the health-care giant Humana. She explains that her job was to review hospital requests for admission; more specifically, her job was to keep people *out* of the hospital. In testimony before the U.S. Congress, Peeno detailed how her job performance was itself predicated on a 10 percent denial rate; in other words, bonuses were provided if she (and others) met certain targets. She testified that "in the spring of 1987, as a physician, I denied a man a necessary operation that would have saved his life and thus caused his death. No person and no group has held me accountable for this, because, in fact, what I did was I saved a company a half a million dollars for this."[100] She explained that decisions on coverage and admissions were made in the context of corporate financial gains and losses, that administrators worried incessantly over increases in hospital admissions, the number of outpatient surgeries approved, and the number of emergency-room referrals. It came to a point, according to Peeno, that "sick people were a burden, and we were losing any sense of empathy about the experiences of our fellow human beings." And yet, consultants such as Peeno rarely saw the patients whose lives were in their hands. She explained, "We were removed from the bedside of the patients, distanced from their pain, anxiety, fear, confusion, and other desperate experiences. We no longer looked them in the eye, touched their skin, heard their complaints, examined them for myriad subtleties that told us more than lab values and diagnostic codes could ever do. Our job was to manage care, and simply put, that meant we had to keep the costs of care as low as possible. We reminded ourselves that we could not pay for everything for everybody."[101] Similar procedures—and justifications—were, of course, used by those in the medical profession under the Nazi regime.[102]

The implications of using QALYs to calculate life and death decisions are gravely problematic for the simple reason that these measures are fundamentally both ageist and ableist.[103] John Harris, for example, notes that "maximizing QALYs involves an implicit and comprehensive ageist bias. For saving the life of younger people is, other things being equal, always likely to be productive of more QALYs than saving older people."[104] Even more egregious, however, is the way in which the all-important quality of life is actually measured. Simply put, in constructing these scales, researchers survey thousands of ordinary people about whether they would prefer to be impotent or incontinent, dizzy or nauseated, paraplegic or not.[105] This practice imparts not only a systematic pattern of disadvantage to particular groups of patients, or to people afflicted with particular diseases or conditions, but perhaps also a systematic preference for the survival of some kinds of patients at the expense of others.[106] The idea that each person is as morally important as any other and that the life and interests of each are to be given equal weight plays no part at all in the theory of QALYS. Indeed, an underlying presumption of QALYs and its cousins is that "a person would prefer a shorter, healthier life to a longer period of survival in a state of severe discomfort and disability."[107]

Given that "health states" and "league tables" are, ultimately, derived and ranked by consensus opinion and that health-care dollars are allocated accordingly, it follows that access to treatment for a specific condition depends on what other (usually) nondisabled people think about any particular condition.[108] However, nondisabled persons' attitudes toward the disabled are largely negative; such continued stigmatization of the disabled (and the elderly) has grave implications for access to medical and health care. If consensus opinion in society works against people with disabilities or the elderly, then health-care decisions will correspondingly discriminate against these people. As Jonathan Glover maintains, "It is common to assume that people with disabilities must have a severely reduced quality of life, or even that their lives are likely to be barely worth living."[109] Paul Longmore agrees, noting that "nondisabled physicians, parents, and other nondisabled persons often seem to assume that persons with disabilities see their own lives as inherently diminished due to their disabilities."[110] This, however, is a fallacy, as studies of both disabled and aged respondents reveal. In a study of the will to live among the elderly conducted by Becca Levy and her colleagues, for example, it was found that "those exposed to positive stereotypes tended to choose life, or seek treatment in hypothetical medical situations regardless of the costs. In contrast, those exposed to negative stereotypes tended to refuse these same treatments, even though the scenarios mentioned that without these treatments they would likely die within a month."[111]

These researchers conclude that "the will to live, which is an intensely personal decision, is also a societal decision in old age. Negative stereotypes of aging, which are the prevailing ones, have the capacity to adversely affect not only the quality of life for the aged, but perhaps the duration of it."[112]

Throughout the twentieth century numerous academics have attempted to ascertain, to measure, and to calculate society's acceptance or non-acceptance of the elderly and the "dis-abled."[113] Indeed, researchers have developed innumerable scales that are employed to purportedly measure—and rank—societal levels of acceptance. One of the first was developed in 1925 by the sociologist Emory Bogardus. He forwarded the "social distance scale," in which social distance referred to "the degrees and grades of understanding and feeling that persons experience regarding each other."[114] Bogardus was especially concerned with the acceptance of racial groups, but later his concept of social distance was extended to determine the prejudice exhibited toward disabled groups. John Tringo, for example, developed a "Disability Social Distance Scale" (DSDS), which consisted of a series of nine categories, ranging from "would marry" to "would put to death" to gauge peoples' attitudes toward disabled populations. For Tringo, twenty-one disabilities were selected for study, including arthritis, asthma, blindness, cancer, cerebral palsy, deafness, diabetes, heart disease, spinal curvature, mental illness, and old age. Interestingly, he included ex-convict status and alcoholism as disabilities. Tringo found that common physical ailments, such as ulcers, arthritis, and asthma, were the most "acceptable" forms of disability. Sensory problems (e.g., deafness and blindness) were less acceptable but were perceived as less troubling than brain-related impairments (e.g., mental retardation). The least acceptable disabilities were, according to Tringo, those of "psychogenic" conditions, including mental illness and alcoholism.

In their meta-analysis of these scales, Michael Dear and his colleagues find that "hierarchies have exhibited a fairly high level of stability." Specifically, physical ailments such as asthma, arthritis, and diabetes remain at the top of the acceptance hierarchy; below these are more serious physical conditions—and often those that may have marked aesthetic impacts and sensory limitations (e.g., blindness and deafness). The least acceptable disabilities are those that are brain-related: mental retardation, for example, and cerebral palsy.[115] It is also significant that this latter group includes alcoholics, drug addicts, convicts, and parolees. These are bodies most likely to be portrayed as failures; rendered to a singular, charged attribute, the alcoholic or drug addict is presumed to be solely culpable for his or her condition. A semiotic chain suggests also that these individuals may be dangerous and/or untrusthworthy.[116]

The modern capitalist state reveals a nuanced management of life and death in which decisions to "make live" or to "let die" are made at the level of the population and whereby individuals are reduced to exchangeable units that appear on administrative spreadsheets, only to disappear on hospital bedsheets. This is the realm of thanatopolitics, which, as Nikolas Rose explains, holds that "life itself is subject to a judgment of worth, a judgment that can be made by oneself (suicide) but also by others (doctors, relatives) but is ultimately guaranteed by a sovereign authority (the state)."[117] Indeed, Alan Williams acknowledges as much when he writes, "The issue as to whose values count is not a scientific one but a political one."[118]

PLACING THE DIS-ABLED IN SOCIETY

We are simultaneously many "things": we are gendered, raced, classed, and so forth.[119] We have many tastes, in food, fashion, and so on. And we come in many different sizes: short, tall, wide, thin. On any given day, however, we are asked to suspend these simultaneities, these different facets of our existence. On job applications or loan applications, we exist within the rigid confines of predetermined categories: male or female, married or single. We *become* these categories—at least, from a bureaucratic or administrative standpoint. These supposedly self-determined choices of identity, moreover, render us into manageable and readily exchangeable bodies; we are partitioned into component parts that do not necessarily add up to, well, us. Nevertheless, we routinely participate in a process that Amartya Sen calls "singular affiliation."[120]

Despite our plural affiliations, our involvement in "identities of different kinds in disparate contexts," we are continuously rendered to a singular "affiliation."[121] It is in this context that Sen writes of "the divisive power of classificatory priority" whereby plural identities are submerged by an allegedly primordial way of seeing differences between people.[122] Thus, for example, we may be seen only as "old" or "male" or "disabled." Indeed, as Glover suggests, there is a tendency to think of a disability as a person's main feature.[123] Thus, to ask "What constitutes a disability?" is predicated on one's understanding of how any given body is evaluated within society. Is one who is missing a limb, such as an arm or a leg, to be considered disabled? What of a congenital "dwarf"? Are people who cannot see or hear disabled?

When a person is reduced to a singular attribute, the implications for that person's day-to-day experiences may be profound, for depending on the attribute in question, such myopic perceptions foster prejudice, discrimination, exploitation, and oppression. The "disabled" body for example is not just reduced to a singular attribute or identity: he is deaf, she is blind. Rather, these individuals become infused with what Sen defines as "charged attributions." According to Sen, charged attributions incorporate two distinct but interrelated distortions: first, a "mis-description" of people belonging to a targeted category and, second, the forwarding of this mis-description as the only relevant feature of the targeted person's identity.[124]

"Dis-ability" is a charged attribute.[125] Once a body is medicalized or pathologized into that of a "disabled person" or a "person with disabilities," all other features disappear; plural identities are subsumed by a singular, dominant—and potentially oppressive—descriptor. Our entire lexicon on the ability-disability split is predicated on an individualized, medical abstraction. Consider, for example, both "disabled person" and "person with disability." In each case, it is the body at issue; disability becomes a possession. As Christine Overall explains, "The term 'impairment' itself is given a definition by extension, by picking out certain states of physical features—limbs, organs, and systems—and attributing significance to them as fundamentally defining particular individuals and groups of individuals as abnormal or defective in ways that are believed to be 'biological.'"[126]

As Longmore explains, the "reigning medical model of disability has dominated not only medical treatment decision making regarding persons with disabilities, but also, more broadly, modern cultural definitions of disability, social perceptions of people with disabilities, and the social options and roles permitted to disabled persons."[127] The "disabled" no longer appears as a person; rather, the "disabled" risks becoming an aberration, an outsider, someone who is not *normal*. And, once established, the mis-descriptor serves a semiotic function, whereby the initial label (i.e., "disabled") itself signifies other attributes. The "disabled" is *also and already* nonproductive; the "disabled" is *also and already* dependent; the "disabled" *also and already* poses a risk, a threat, a cost, or a loss to society. Under this medical model, dis-ability appears as human liability.[128] The "dis-abled" becomes "abnormal."

Following the work of Michel Foucault, we recognize that this notion of abnormality has a history and that the appearance of pathological bodies is dependent upon techniques—classifications and calculations—of identification.[129] Hence, "disability categories proliferate as an increasing value is placed upon bodily homogeneity, concepts of quantifiable health measurement, and the workplace standardization of capacities."[130] The establishment, for example, of key disciplines—including, but not limited to demography, anthropology, sociology, and psychology—has contributed to the tendency to pathologize some bodies while privileging others. As Sharon Snyder and David Mitchell explain, "While often parading under the humanist guise of help or sympathy for 'the unfortunate,' they accomplish their debilitating effects through taxonomies of naming, the statistical calculation of average and nonstandard bodies, [and] restrictive public policy implementation."[131]

Throughout the late nineteenth and early twentieth centuries, for example, the nascent disciplines of psychiatry and psychology proposed numerous classification schemes to better manage those deemed abnormal or subnormal. Thus, there emerged particular bodies: the imbeciles, the idiots, and the morons. And yet, these were labels of "discursive production and policy rationale rather than of empirical accuracy."[132] During the apex of the eugenics movement, for example, U.S. statistical researchers calculated that the number of feebleminded bodies increased tenfold between 1850 and 1890; such statistical data provided critical momentum for the movement, because quantitative data, it was presumed, gave the best proof that something, biologically speaking, was going terribly awry with the country's hereditary pool.[133] Indeed, as Snyder and Mitchell remark,

> in the eugenics era, and still today, groups of bodies that house disabilities sport labels that epitomize the idea that disability marks people off as exceptionally, even dramatically, unsuitable in comparison to those occupying the bulky middle of the bell curve—the domain of normalcy constituted by quantitative measures of human appearances and capacities. Terms such as "feebleminded," "subnormal," "non-educable," "crippled," "defective," "monstrous," and "unfit" once infused popular media and served as professional diagnoses.... The updated eugenics of the present day, often called genetics, examines conditions in bodies that are classed as "mutant," "tragic," "coding errors," "suffering," "unhealthy," "deviant," "faulty," and "abnormal."[134]

Which body counts as being dis-abled is far from being a static calculation—although it is always a *statistical* calculation. Well into the twenty-first century, we are witnessing the appearance of another dis-abled figure, this being the "old" person. Indeed, age is a charged attribute, as the biological process of aging has emerged as a medical condition— something to be combated. Death increasingly is becoming portrayed as preferable to growing into old age; aging is the new fate worse than death.[135] Thus, on par with more conventional understandings of disability, age has become a perceived liability, and those who are seen as old are often the recipients of discrimination and prejudice.

Increasingly, the biological process of aging has emerged as a medical condition. And yet, as Overall writes, the biological foundation of old age is itself created conceptually, by selecting particular features and defining these as constituting oldness.[136] For Overall, age is better conceived as relational; what constitutes "old" is both historically and geographically contingent. In the United States, for example, what constitutes old age in the twenty-first century is very different from what constituted old age in the eighteenth century. There is, in other words,

THE VIOLENCE OF REDUNDANCY

considerable cultural flexibility in the designation of the number of years that constitutes old age.[137] However, under a medical model informed by the market logics of capitalism, a "large number of years lived is stigmatized at least partly because people associate it with the supposedly inevitable development of features regarded as impairments."[138] Such prejudices are routinely perpetuated within society. Since the 1990s the use of certain terms—"deadwood" and "burdensome"—has become especially pronounced. Under American capitalism, retirement from paid work shifts the elderly into the ranks of the unproductive; as nonproductive citizens, these bodies are doubly seen as bleeding society of scarce resources.[139]

How society deals with its "dis-abled" population is both historically and geographically contingent. Geographers and other social scientists have written extensively on the place of the disabled within society. Robert Kruse, for example, provides a historical geographical account of dwarfism. He explains that "from mysticism to freak shows, [dwarfism] is an identity of contradictions—an identity that has located adults of extremely short stature in a curious array of places[,] including royal courts, circuses, and institutions."[140] However, he continues, "culturally dominant discourses of dwarfism have resulted from statements made by those individuals and institutions with the power to define dominant notions of *normalcy, deviance, freakishness, comedy,* and *mysticism*" and that such definitions "have material implications in terms of the socio-spatial experiences of little people and their perceived 'place' in society."[141]

Within Western societies throughout the Middle Ages, those people deemed lunatics or disabled often remained either in domestic care— perhaps hidden in a cellar or caged in an animal pen—or were left to wander aimlessly across the land—the "village idiot."[142] Churches, likewise, were utilized to confine the "mad" and other "monsters" of the time. Beginning in the seventeenth century, however, there emerged, according to Foucault, a "great confinement" of the mad and the poor. During this period, enormous houses of confinement—asylums—were built to house those deemed undesirable: paupers, petty criminals, layabouts, streetwalkers, vagabonds, beggars, the insane, and the idiotic.[143]

America too has a long history of defining and confining those deemed abnormal. In the United States, for example, the institutionalization of disabled persons gained popularity in the late eighteenth and early nineteenth centuries. Initially, proponents of institutionalizing the disabled (and also the poor and other social "problems") argued on behalf of "moral treatment" and the curative functions of confinement. It was believed, for example, that healthy environments provided a cure, that immersion in an unspoiled Nature could cure those reeling from the impact of industrialization. Consequently, hundreds of asylums, prisons, almshouses, and poorhouses were erected in rural locations so as to remove the disabled from the degenerating influence of industrializing cities. In time, however, public officials and members of the medical profession recognized that these presumably peaceful settings did not produce the desired results; those deemed insane or abnormal were not miraculously cured because of a change in environment. This realization, in part, contributed to the transformation of these asylums from a rehabilitative, or curative, function to custodial oversight and warehousing.[144] By the middle of the nineteenth century, institutions of almost every type had dropped all pretense of providing therapy or cures; these buildings became nothing more than custodial in function.[145] Regardless of efficacy, however, almost all the helping professions—medical superintendents, jailers, overseers of the poor—continued to favor institutionalization as a form of treatment.[146]

There emerged in the early twentieth century a shift in attitudes toward the dis-abled. In part, this shift is a product of the eugenics movement. David Rothman explains that, while care institutions themselves were "too large, too crowded, too inherently punitive, and too underfinanced to operate in a manner remotely approaching their ideal," the "managers of the institutions, unwilling to accept the responsibility for failure, blamed the victim." Thus, we see that "environmentalism gave way to heredity as the theory of human nature. The problem with the children of the poor, the mentally ill, and the criminals resided in their genes, not in their environment."[147]

The policies and practices of dealing with those perceived as dis-abled varied according to the body in question. In the nineteenth century, for example, there existed numerous categories of dependents. These populations included idiots, lunatics, inebriates, paupers, tramps, vagrants, the aged, the sick, the feebleminded, the disabled, orphans, and criminals. And while on the one hand these classes were conceived of as an undifferentiated whole, there was, on the other hand, a moral division that affected policy responses. Specifically, the "able-bodied were typically castigated as morally corrupt and undeserving of assistance, while lunatics, widows, orphans and the sick were deemed worthy of philanthropic aid."[148] In other words, there was in place an identifiable calculation of a body's worth, a calculus that readily conformed to the nascent industrialization of the United States. Those *able* bodies that *refused* to work—those who shirked their productive responsibilities—were viewed as morally undeserving of assistance; conversely, those who were unable to "normally" participate in society were perceived as more worthy . . . or at least, not as undeserving.

Such supposedly charitable attitudes on the whole, however, faded rapidly with the promotion of eugenics, as the "difference between dependency and deviancy narrowed, with the poor standing as potential criminals."[149] Thus, while so-called unproductive able-bodied men and women attracted considerable scorn from an industrializing society, so too did those men and women classified as feebleminded. The tramp, for example, was seen as a "lazy, shiftless, incorrigible, cowardly, utterly depraved savage."[150] Increasingly, so too were the "mentally defective" cast in amoral terms. As Richard Scheerenberger notes, by the late nineteenth century the "mentally retarded" had become "a great evil of humanity."[151] Indeed, in 1894 Adam Osborne, then-president of the Association of Medical Officers of American Institutions for Idiotic and Feebleminded Persons, explained:

> Is it because there are in the United States an army of perhaps half a million tramps, cranks, and peripatetic beggars crawling like human parasites over our body politic, and feasting upon the rich juices of productive labor? Many of these human parasites have committed no crime and are guilty *per se* of no wrong, unless it is a crime and a wrong

to be brought, without one's volition, into this world, burdened with the accumulated inherent sins of a vitiated and depraved ancestry; to be bred in filth, to be born in squalor and to be raised in an atmosphere tainted of course with crime. Many of these wretches are what they are because they are what they were made, not what they have made themselves. Handicapped by the vices of their inheritance they are simply not strong enough to keep up to the social, civil and moral ethics of the ages, and as an inevitable consequence, just as water seeks its level, they drop back by degrees to become in turn deficient, delinquent, defective and dependent.[152]

This lengthy quote is telling, not so much because of the undisguised loathing and vitriol but rather because of the moral reasoning embedded in its contents. Conforming to the dominant eugenicist beliefs of the time, Osborne conceded that "mental defectives" were not, unlike paupers and tramps, guilty of carelessness or idleness. Instead, these people simply had the misfortune of having been born. Nevertheless, they were still deemed unproductive—burdensome—and thus unable to effectively participate in an urbanizing, industrializing society. Indeed, as Snyder and Mitchell affirm, whereas the country's early agrarian economy had allowed these individuals to perform routine and relatively simple chores on the farm, in a new, manufacturing-based economy those classified as feebleminded were perceived to be incapable of competing with their "normal" peers. And therein lay the economic foundation for society's representation of the "abnormal" and the "unfit": simply put, the "feebleminded became synonymous with incapacity."[153]

Within the United States Longmore maintains that "in everything from freak shows to telethons, movies to medical ethics, people with disabilities have been depicted as the antithesis of what Americans ought to be."[154] Age too has become devalued within society. In an era where youth is privileged, when we are encouraged to wage war against aging, those bodies that evince old age are increasingly perceived as failures. Consequently, as Overall explains, in cases of both ageism and ableism, "social practices and institutions establish and reinforce negative values that make rather ordinary characteristics of some human beings into liabilities and stigmata." She continues that the "systems of ableism and ageism function to make, respectively, certain bodily features (limbs, organs, or systems), and certain numbers of years lived, into social liabilities, rationalizations for subordination, and sources of shame."[155]

Both dis-ability and ability are viewed as two sides of the same economic coin: one is judged dis-abled if one is not abled. However, ability has not been defined, recursively, on not being dis-abled. Ability instead has been measured, calculated, and valued based on a myopic understanding of economic productivity, a market logics if you will. The relationship between dis-ability and ability therefore is not a circular tautology but instead linear: the dis-abled are not abled; they are not able because they (are perceived to) lack certain qualities that are necessary to fully participate in society.

Within capitalism, measurements and calculations of ability and (full) participation are found in the *formal* labor market. Consider, for example, the tripartite division of the feebleminded into idiots, imbeciles, and morons. Whereas we now consider these as nothing more than pejorative—and sometimes interchangeable—labels, for the eugenicists these supposedly empirical classifications carried immense explanatory power and policy prescriptions. To be sure, these groupings (rankings, in fact) were often correlated with educational level, but they were also marked by supposed labor-market capabilities. Morons were perceived as capable of being trained and of working independently; imbeciles, conversely, could perform menial tasks and other productive activities but needed to be kept under constant supervision. At the bottom was the idiot—someone who was "utterly helpless and dependent."[156] In short, what I want to make clear is that *dis-ability* (including, more recently, age) has historically been defined by one's supposed *ability* in the formal, waged labor market and by the appropriate answer to the question, Is the body in question capable of becoming a *productive* member of society?

In turn, both "ableism" (and "ageism") underlie a deeper trend within the American neoliberal state, namely, the flourishing of the idea that certain bodies are literally calculated to be worth less than death, that not only is it acceptable that some bodies will be "let die" but also that some bodies have an *obligation* to die. As Wesley Smith argues, "Our culture is fast devolving into one in which killing is beneficent, suicide is rational, natural death is undignified, and caring properly and compassionately for people who are elderly, prematurely born, disabled, despairing, or dying is a burden that wastes emotional and financial resources."[157] To this end, Longmore explains that the conventional wisdom of the nondisabled seems to be that costly heroic medical interventions frequently keep alive infants and older persons with disabilities who should be allowed or encouraged to die, while the conventional wisdom and common experience in the disability rights community is that adequate and appropriate treatment is frequently denied because of devaluation and discrimination.[158]

PREMATURE DEATH VIA THE DENIAL OF BIRTH

Can violence be directed at someone who is not born? Such a question seems nonsensical, but in fact it is just such a question that confronts today's reproductive politics. Between 1867 and 1920 a series of local ordinances were enacted to rid U.S. streets of beggars, tramps, and other "unsightly" bodies. Known as "ugly laws," many versions of these statutes "made clear in their titles that city leaders aimed the laws at a very particular target, the person who 'exposed' disease, maiming, deformity, or mutilation for the purpose of begging."[159] However, as Susan Schweik details, an engagement with these laws underscores how states intervene in matters of life and death and effectively position "dis-ability" as personal liability. Schweik documents, for example, America's long-standing cultural emphasis on individualism, which enabled the ugly laws' supporters to position disability and begging as individual problems rather than relating them to broader social inequalities.[160] In so doing, Schweik effectively foreshadows the contemporary utilitarian ethos that surrounds the U.S. health-care system and disguises a form of *state* violence that not only remains unseen; it is also legal.

What concerns me most at this point, however, is the central figure of Schweik's study: the "disfigured figure." Schweik begins her book with the tale of a man from Cleveland, Ohio, a man with clubbed hands and feet, a man who was driven off the streets and lost his job selling newspapers because he was considered a "street obstruction." Between the mid-nineteenth century and the early twentieth century, repressive measures were introduced to forcefully remove—and confine—this figure. Now, in the twenty-first century, a more subtle—yet more insidious—form of biopolitical control is being put forward. Now, we must ask *would this man even exist?*

Without doubt, biomedical technologies have altered our understandings, and experiences, of life and death. On the whole, many of us live longer and enjoy healthier lives. These benefits, however, must be tempered with other, more controversial developments that have emerged within the last few decades. Namely, technologies now exist—if one has the financial resources—to not only choose one's baby but to literally design one's baby. As Jonathan Glover writes, "Progress in genetics and in reproductive technologies gives us growing power to reduce the incidence of disabilities and disorders," as well as the potential to give children "a better chance of having abilities—or qualities of temperament and character—that will enrich their lives."[161] There are, accordingly, two issues at hand. On the one hand, we have the ability to prevent certain individuals, for example, those with Down syndrome, spina bifida, cystic fibrosis, or deafness, from ever being born. Hence, many bioethicists are asking not only if parents should deliberately try to *prevent* disabled children from coming into existence but also if parents have an *obligation* to prevent these children from existing. On the other hand, we have also the ability to *create* certain types of children. Likewise, many commentators have considered whether parents have both the right and the responsibility to try to select only the "best" children, that is, those children who are genetically considered to have the most potential for a productive life. Both abilities constitute two sides of the same coin, that of the "designer baby." I consider first the prevention of certain dis-abled bodies followed by the design of "better" babies.

The exclusion of dis-abled children is most simply accomplished through their not being born. This is facilitated through the use of prenatal, or antenatal, testing, which includes such procedures as biochemical screening, genetic screening, and ultrasound screening. All of these practices are widely used in modern obstetrics and gynecology; these services, moreover, are based on population screening to identify people with a genetic risk, or a risk of having a child with a congenital or genetic disorder.[162] Biochemical screening, for example, is used to detect Down syndrome, open neural-tube defects, and anencephaly. In this technique, a single specimen of blood is taken from a pregnant woman at about sixteen to eighteen weeks of pregnancy. Genetic screening is carried out either by amniocentesis or by chorionic villus sampling; these tests are done at fourteen to sixteen weeks and eight to nine weeks, respectively. These procedures screen for possible "abnormalities." Lastly, by defining structural abnormalities, ultrasound screening allows for the identification of fetuses for which treatment in utero may be appropriate.

Antenatal diagnosis has four main purposes: (1) to inform and prepare parents for the birth of an affected infant; (2) to allow in utero treatment or delivery at a special treatment center for immediate postnatal surgery or other care; (3) to allow termination of an "affected" fetus; and (4) to provide information so that parents may choose among the aforementioned choices. Coupled with antenatal diagnosis is the practice of preimplantation diagnosis (PID), a procedure that "aims to avoid the possibility of an affected pregnancy completely. It is based on the simple strategy of sampling genetic material from eggs or embryos within the first week of their development following fertilization."[163]

Both antenatal and preimplantation diagnoses hold the hope or the fear that dis-ability will be eliminated from society by preventing the birth of disabled people. As Julian Savulescu writes, genetic tests are offered to couples to "allow them to select the child—from the best possible children they could have—with the best opportunity of having the best life." And, as such, Savulescu argues that "couples have a moral obligation to select the child with the best prospects."[164] The operative question, of course, is twofold: "How do we determine what is best?" and, related, "Who is to make that determination?"

For philosophers and bioethicists, the answers to these questions are generally found within a balance between parental autonomy and choice, reproductive freedom, obligations to future (and unborn) children, and obligations to society. These discussions, furthermore, are often (though not always) couched within an ideal world of self-determination and free will. Savulescu, for example, maintains that in the case of screening for Down syndrome, each couple should make its own decision about whether or not to have a child with Down syndrome. He believes that his "value judgment should not be imposed on couples who must bear and rear the child. Nor should the value judgment of doctors, politicians, or the state be imposed directly or indirectly (through the denial of services) on them."[165] This sounds good, but it is far from reality.

Aviad Raz explains that such screening "is often neither 'chosen' actively nor 'informed,' but rather stems from compliance to medical authority, particularly for individuals from impoverished or culturally diverse backgrounds." He continues that such screening "that 'naturally' leads to selective abortion in cases of mild or probable embryopathy can be underpinned by normative scripts of 'responsible motherhood' and disguised by the free-market rhetoric of late capitalism."[166] Furthermore, the state does and will continue to intervene. Whether in the form of providing or denying services or supporting the goals of insurance companies, pharmaceutical companies, and so on, the state will serve as final arbiter for reproductive choice. Through the judicial system, it is the state that ultimately determines the legality of any given practice. Far from disappearing—as promoters of a neoliberal doctrine surmise—the government remains ever present. Indeed, its presence is so pervasive, so extensive, that it often remains hidden in plain sight. The state has not relegated its authority to private interests; it has, however, continued to deepen the symbiotic relationship between itself and the corporate world.

State interventions are, more often than not, predicated on a market-based logic and a correlated calculation of a person's worth. And indeed, these calculations are ever present in discussions of designer babies. Bioethicists and health-care consultants, for example, often tout the economic savings associated with antenatal testing and preimplantation diagnosis. Alexandra Murray and Angus Clarke acknowledge that "it has often been argued that it is cheaper to prevent the births of individuals with certain genetic disorders than to care for them, so that screening 'for' these disorders is justified." They note that this "reasoning is particularly applied to the 'prevention' of Down syndrome—on the assumption that terminating a pregnancy in which the fetus has Down syndrome amounts to its 'prevention.'"[167] Sahin Aksoy agrees that the "costs of providing amniocentesis for all expectant mothers over the age of 40 years, and maternal serum AFP screening for all pregnant women, would be more than offset by the economic benefits in terms of savings of expenditure on children and adults with Down's Syndrome and spina bifida." Aksoy does note, however, that "this kind of rational-economic thinking may degrade society's willingness to accept and care for abnormal children, while at the same time enlarging the category of unacceptable abnormality and narrowing the range of acceptable normality."[168] As Glover asks, "What does it do for a disabled person's sense of having equality of respect with other members of society if there are programs designed to prevent the birth of people with his or her disability?" To this end, Glover relates the story of a twelve-year-old girl and sister of a girl (Alice) with Down syndrome. In response to reading an article about guidelines set forth for the prenatal screening for Down syndrome, the girl wrote an editorial that was published in the local newspaper. At the core of her remarks was a single, simple request: " Please tell us what to say to Alice to explain that she is no use to society and that the society she lives in wishes she had been killed.'"[169]

To a large degree, these practices have called into question not only our understanding of (and prejudices regarding) "dis-abilities" but also our valuation of persons with disabilities and with it, the place of violence in society. As indicated earlier, until very recently the conception of disability most people had was a purely medical one: some physiological or chemical system might be missing or atrophied or might have been damaged through illness, accident, or some other trauma.[170] And yet, current biopolitical thinking continues to expand the range of what is considered to be dis-abled. Accordingly, ever-shifting definitions of normality or abnormality, disability or difference, will greatly inform what is considered cost effective. As Aksoy questions, "If Down's syndrome and spina bifida are 'too' expensive today, what will become 'too' expensive if the economic climate becomes gloomy?"[171] What other designated defects or disabilities will be targeted for prevention?

And is there actually choice, or autonomy, with prenatal genetic screening? What of parents who choose to bring into this world a child with a particular disability? Are they (the parents) to be considered irresponsible and hence not deserving of assistance? Should society pay for the possibly extensive medical care required for these babies? For many bioethicists, the answer is a resounding "no." Indeed, as Savulescu concedes, "requests to deliberately select a disabled child push respect for autonomy to its limits."[172] The decision not to have a child with a disability therefore may be an expression of ugly attitudes toward people with disabilities.[173] Likewise, criticism of those parents who consciously choose to have a child with a disability may also be an expression of ugly attitudes. This is made clear in the vociferous debates surrounding deafness as either a disability or a difference. In 2002, for example, Sharon Duchesneau and Candy McCullough, who are both deaf, used sperm donated by a friend with hereditary deafness to have a deaf baby.[174] Duchesneau said during her pregnancy that having a "hearing baby" would be a blessing but that having a "deaf baby" would be a special blessing. For this couple, deafness was not a disability but instead a difference.[175] Indeed, the couple viewed "deafness as a cultural identity"; their preferential decision, as such, was thus no different from other parents trying to have a girl.[176]

The choice made by Duchesneau and McCullough was, to many commentators, a significant injustice; the couple, it was argued, acted irresponsibly in their deliberate attempt to bring into the world a child with a supposedly severe physical impairment. As Alta Charo, professor of law and bioethics at the University of Wisconsin, responded, "I'm loath to say it, but I think it's a shame to set limits on a child's potential."[177] Likewise, Ken Connor, president of the Family Research Council, criticized their actions, explaining that "to intentionally give a child a disability, in addition to all the disadvantages that come as a result of being raised in a homosexual household, is incredibly selfish."[178] The statements of Connor are informative on at least two issues. The first centers on the presumption that deafness is a disadvantage and, hence, must be corrected if present or prevented through genetic screening. The second ties into a deeper question of responsibility and stems from the fact that the couple in question was lesbian. Here, it is not possible to adequately consider the many facets of parental choice and homosexuality. Suffice it to say that for many commentators, the fact that these parents may potentially raise their children outside of the traditional nuclear family will undoubtedly influence their position.

There is, finally, another, equally troubling procedure currently in use that prevents the dis-abled from living: the promotion of active infanticide. In part, this is another practice associated with recent advances in biomedical technologies. It is routine, for example, that newborn babies undergo a series of diagnostics to identify key disorders and abnormalities. On the positive side, the "most important and widely accepted goal of newborn screening is to improve health outcomes in the screened population of newborns."[179] On the negative side, critics point out, such screening procedures facilitate the killing of dis-abled babies. Consider, for example, the statements of Joseph Fletcher, a bioethicist who, as early as the 1970s, advocated the killing of disabled children. For Fletcher, the justification for killing disabled babies was determined on utilitarian grounds: "this view assigns value to human *life* rather than merely being *alive* and holds that it is better to be dead than to suffer too much or to endure too many deficits of human function."[180] Contemporary bioethicists, such as Peter Singer, likewise argue that dis-abled infants have no moral right to live. In his widely adopted text on practical ethics, for example, Singer explains why he supports the deliberate killing of a newborn with hemophilia: "When the death of a disabled infant will lead to the birth of another infant with better prospects of a happy life, the total amount of happiness will be greater if the disabled infant is killed. The loss of the happy life for the first infant is outweighed by the gain of a happier life for the second. Therefore, if the killing of the hemophiliac infant has no adverse effect on others it would . . . be right to kill him."[181]

A neoliberal underpinning is readily apparent in the attitudes of Singer and other bioethicists, namely, that (1) infants are replaceable and

(2) that individuals should strive for the promotion of a good with the most potential, as measured by productivity. In forwarding a "replacement view" of reproduction, Jonathan Glover explains that "if a mother is resolved to have exactly one child and no more, the death of her first baby may cause her to have another. If the second baby has just as good a life as the first one would have done, then, in terms of the worthwhile life objection, the death of the first baby has not mattered at all. And, if the first baby would have had a less good life, its death was in this respect a good thing."[182] Glover continues that "perhaps there are people who . . . would think that for them any kind of life would be preferable to death," but "those of us who think that we would opt for death rather than some kinds of lives have a good reason for holding that some lives are not worth living. In these cases, depending on the degree of impairment, the quality of the life either simply ceases to be an objection to killing or else becomes a positive argument in favor of it."[183] Accordingly, Glover concludes that selective infanticide should be permissible—if the calculations warrant such actions. Stated differently, Glover is advocating that the criminal offense of infanticide be waived in the case of "defective" babies.

In current practice, both the taking of life and the letting die of dis-abled infants occur regularly in the United States, England, the Netherlands, and elsewhere. Children with Down syndrome and spina bifida in particular have been "allowed" to die through a lack of medical care; other infants have been actively killed through lethal injections. These practices often arise in the midst of deeply traumatic cases in which parents, doctors, and, ultimately, legal professionals determine the "best" course of action. What warrants discussion is how biotechnologies are used in the calculation of life and death in the neoliberal state. In the Netherlands, for example, the "livableness" of an infant's life depends on a combination of factors, including the expected measure of suffering, the expected potential for communication and human relations, the potential for independent living, and overall life expectancy. According to guidelines, if the infant's prospects don't measure up to what the doctor and parents believe is a life worth living, then the child can be medically neglected to death or killed by the doctor via lethal injection.[184] Guidelines such as these highlight the salience of how we—as a society—calculate the worth of some lives over others, as well as what these calculations suggest about our values and attitudes toward those classified as dis-abled.

As indicated earlier, there are two correlated issues involved in the controversy over prenatal testing: the prevention of supposedly unworthy or unfit babies and the design of babies that are better because they have been screened for flaws. To what extent have advances in biotechnologies altered this side of the equation and what are the implications for contemporary reproductive rights? Julian Savulescu identifies a fundamental paradox of reproductive choice, resources, and governmental intervention. While, on the one hand, he argues that "reproduction should be about having children who have the best prospects" and that "we must give individual couples the freedom to act on their own value judgment of what constitutes a life of prospect," he notes on the other hand the limitations of such freedoms.[185] He writes, "Either such freedom is important, in which case it should be supported with taxpayers' money. Or it is not important, and there is no problem with allowing only people with the personal resources to buy it. The only legitimate ground for interference in reproductive decisions would be an important detrimental social impact of such choices."[186] A similar position is held by Thomas Lemke, who suggests that "we might witness a process in which it will be more and more problematic to opt out of the personal usage of genetic information, since this might be seen as an objective sign of lacking subjective competence or as an indisputable fact of irrational behavior."[187] My assessment is that, rhetorically, while reproductive rights are promoted as important, ultimately such freedom will be granted only to those individuals deemed responsible and productive.

EXCEPTIONAL VIOLENCE AND THE DUTY TO DIE

"We all accept that killing is in general wrong," Jeff McMahan writes, "but virtually all of us also recognize certain exceptions—that is, we conceded that there can be instances in which killing is permissible."[188] Killing in self-defense, for example, is often ruled as an acceptable, defensible, and hence legal reason—justification—for taking another's life. Likewise, killing in defense of one's country—such as in war—is also considered to be just. Other forms of killing may be justified—such as physician-assisted suicide—but these cases are often subject to intense debate.

Euthanasia figures prominently in current debates surrounding the moral distinction between "killing" and "letting die." Derived from two Greek words, *eu*, meaning "good," and *thanatos*, meaning "death," euthanasia is thus simply defined as "good death." Conceptually, the practice of ending one's life—properly—has occupied the attention of Western philosophers since at least the time of ancient Greece. Both Socrates and Plato, for example, regarded suffering as the result of a painful disease to be a sufficient reason for ending one's life. Likewise, and following the example set forth by Socrates, who himself committed suicide, there emerged a long-standing tradition that the taking of one's life may, under the proper conditions, be considered both moral and justifiable. That said, other Greek philosophers, notably Aristotle, Pythagoras, and Epicurus, condemned the practice.[189]

Christian theology prohibited euthanasia. Saint Augustine, for example, argued that suicide was in contradiction to the commandment against murder and that life and suffering were divinely ordained by God; to take one's life was to go against God, for only God had the right to decide when a person would die. However, associated with the Protestant Reformation and the subsequent separation of church and state, other philosophers and political theorists began to reconsider the morality of the practice. Increasingly, the right of life or death became associated with the sovereign and, as such, the management and cultivation of a healthy population might identify situations where euthanasia was acceptable. Indeed, both Thomas More and David Hume argued that euthanasia was acceptable for terminally ill patients.[190] Within Western society, the debate over euthanasia has continued into the twentieth and twenty-first centuries. In 1935 the British Voluntary Euthanasia Society was founded, followed three years later by the establishment of the Euthanasia Society of America.[191] Today, there are numerous organizations devoted to the legalization of euthanasia.

Euthanasia, as a practice, entails a variety of different forms. First, it is possible to distinguish euthanasia based on the actions involved. Killing an individual, ostensibly for his or her own good, is referred to as *active* euthanasia; "letting die," conversely, is considered a form of *passive* euthanasia. An example of active euthanasia would be the administration of a lethal injection by a physician, while examples of passive euthanasia include removing life-support systems (e.g., respirators) or not providing hydration. Euthanasia may also be classified by various relations of consent. For example, *voluntary* euthanasia refers to a situation in which a person freely and autonomously requests or consents to being killed or allowed to die. However, the notion of free choice is highly contentious and itself becomes a legal decision. Infants, for example, are often considered by bioethicists to lack autonomy and thus are unable to make their own decisions; the elderly, likewise, are in a process of losing this condition. *Nonvoluntary* euthanasia exists when it is not possible for an individual who is killed or allowed to die either to give or to withhold consent. In this situation, which would include infants and "congenitally severely impaired" persons, some other legally responsible individual makes the final decision. Lastly, euthanasia is said to be *involuntary* when an individual who is competent to give or to withhold consent is killed or allowed to die either contrary to his or her expressed will or when his or her consent has not been sought.[192] In anticipation of later arguments, we might also consider the denial of treatment to requesting patients by the medical community—or insurance companies—to be a form of involuntary euthanasia. However, unless negligence is legally established, the fact of letting die is increasingly viewed as a noncriminal act.

Opponents of euthanasia fear that a pervasive culture of death is spreading throughout American society, a cultural trend that promotes some lives at the expense of others. Indeed, owing to both ableism and ageism, it is already taken to be self-evident that people with so-called impairments and people that are elderly are of lesser value than lives without so-called impairments or lives that are youthful. These lives are even considered, in some cases, not worth living.[193] Christine Overall explains that because both disability and aging are often represented as shameful, weak, and low in value, people "of all ages internalize the negative valuations of impairment and old age and, as a result, almost everyone participates in the social conspiracy to pretend that there are no impaired or aged people."[194] One way that this is accomplished is through the near ubiquitous discourse of burdensomeness, a highly negative value that is incorporated in both ageism and ableism. People who have lived many years, along with people with features deemed to be impairments, are regarded as being nonfunctional and nonproductive—hence, they become burdens.[195] As Marilyn Golden and Tyler Zoanni caustically write, "Have we gotten to the point that we will abet suicides because people need help using the toilet?"[196] From such a conservative, bioethical standpoint, prolonging human life, whether individually or collectively, and supporting individual people with features deemed to be impairments becomes problematic and even morally unjustified.[197]

The coordinates of "burdensomeness" are determined by the parameters of the capitalist labor market. Those who do not conform to the demands of the market are marginalized—relegated to the periphery of society. Both the aged and the disabled have little place in contemporary society. They are simultaneously conceived as not being productive enough and also as being too expensive. Likewise, aging itself has emerged as a matter of personal responsibility: it is within one's power to stave off chronic illnesses associated with getting older. As Rose Galvin explains, "It is the transformation of the notion of behavioral culpability into our current obsession with health and fitness, and the accompanying belief that both are a matter of individual choice, which now predominates and results in a new culture of victim blaming."[198]

In this penultimate section I consider in depth the "duty-to-die" movement.[199] Coupled with the aforementioned practices of preventing the dis-abled from coming into existence, I maintain that the duty-to-die movement underscores a deeper animus, and violence, toward the dis-abled and the elderly—two figures that are progressively understood as market failures within the neoliberal state. Indeed, for both dis-abled and elderly bodies, the "injunction to 'die sooner' is becoming hauntingly clear."[200]

As of 2015, only two states in the United States permit physician-assisted suicide: Oregon and Washington. This is not for lack of attempts, however, to make the practice more widely available. Indeed, health-care consultants, bioethicists, and a surprisingly large number of medical professionals have gone on record in their support of physician-assisted suicide. As Margaret Morganroth Gullette explains, the rhetoric of the duty-to-die proponents already influences many medical systems. In the United States, despite systemic incentives to overtreat, some doctors already treat some older patients differently than younger ones, by withholding information, diagnostic services, or treatment, with sometimes negative or even lethal consequences.[201] Similar observations may be made regarding the treatment of disabled infants and adults.

Modern assisted suicide advocacy arose out of the struggle to permit people to refuse unwanted life-extending medical treatment.[202] It is legal, for example, in every U.S. state for an individual to create an advance directive that requires the withdrawal of treatment under any conditions the person wishes and for a patient to refuse any treatment or to require any treatment to be withdrawn. Likewise, it is legal in the United States for anyone who is dying in discomfort to receive palliative sedation, whereby the dying person is sedated so discomfort is relieved.[203] What differs with the current duty-to-die movement is the contention that some people have an obligation to die. This obligation, I will argue, arises from either an inability to contribute as a productive member of society or the overconsumption of scarce resources. Debates surrounding physician-assisted suicide, however, have more often than not redirected attention, away from market considerations to that of autonomy, self-determination, and personal choice. In so doing, these debates reflect the overriding neoliberal rationale of the duty-to-die movement.

Consider those who are eligible for physician-assisted suicide. Supporters of the practice emphasize that safeguards are in place, that only certain people will be eligible. However, as opponents are quick to point out, the definition of eligibility has been expanding continuously. The Oregon Death with Dignity Act (1994), for example, allows terminally ill adult patients to make a written request for a prescription for medication to end their life. According to the act, patients must be adults who are capable of medical decision making; patients, also, must be considered terminally ill. In Oregon, a terminal disease was defined as one leading to death within six months.[204] However, more recent efforts to legalize physician-assisted suicide have proposed definitions with considerably more flexibility. In a bill introduced in New Hampshire in 2009, for example, a terminal condition was defined as "an incurable and irreversible condition, for the end stage of which there is no known treatment which will alter its course to death, and which, in the opinion of the attending physician and consulting physician competent in that disease category, will result in premature death." Likewise, in Montana, the suicide advocacy group Compassion & Choices proposed its own definition of a terminally ill adult patient: "[An adult] who has an incurable or irreversible condition that, without the administration of life-sustaining treatment, will, in the opinion of his or her attending physician, result in death within a relatively short time."[205] In both instances, people who *are not dying*, including those who are paraplegic or diabetic, fall under the proposed definition.

Within an environment of health-care rationing, "once a person is labeled 'terminal' the argument can be made that his or her treatment should be denied in favor of someone more deserving."[206] Indeed, the neoliberal foundation of health-care rationing should not be discounted. On this point, Oregon's act is especially instructive. In 1994 Oregon voters approved Ballot Measure 16, which legalized physician-assisted suicide—to be effective in 1997. Not coincidentally, in 1994 Oregon also instituted health-care rationing for the poor. That year, the Oregon Medical Assistance Program (OMAP) ranked more than 700 health services and terminated funding for 167 of them. This action itself marked the culmination of years of political struggles to ration health care in the state. Beginning in the early 1980s, reeling from a deep recession and rising costs within its health-care system, the state began looking for ways to reduce costs; Oregon's Medicaid program was a particular target.

Various cost analyses and cost-benefit procedures were used, including the shift of enrollees into managed-care programs, an overall reduction in enrollments, and the elimination of services. Likewise, coverage of certain costly medical services and procedures was limited. Then, in 1987, Oregon began to limit access to organ transplants—an exceptionally costly procedure. This decision, however, backfired when a seven-year-old boy, Coby Howard, required a bone marrow transplant for his leukemia—a procedure that promised a 20 percent chance of survival. Howard's mother, though, was unemployed and on welfare. Medicaid elected not to pay for the $100,000 surgery. When it became publicly known that a young boy was being disallowed life, public outcry sparked a massive effort to raise the necessary funds. By the time sufficient funds were raised, however, it was too late, and Coby Howard died.[207]

Given the firestorm that was ignited by the life and death of Coby Howard, supporters of health-care rationing in Oregon needed to revise their strategies. Policy makers went on the offensive in promoting a utilitarian rationale for budget cuts to health care. They argued, in part, that Oregon was already rationing care by limiting enrollments and payments to providers. But policy makers also argued on the basis of whether certain procedures *in general* were cost-effective or not. And the costs were tied directly to taxpayers' wallets. Citizens were questioned whether state lawmakers should spend $100,000 on a bone marrow transplant for an elderly man, for example, as opposed to spending the same amount of money to immunize ten thousand children against the measles.[208] In short, advocates for health-care rationing primed the citizens of Oregon to think of the economic bottom line and to rationalize whose lives were worth saving and whose lives should be sacrificed.

Between the late 1980s and early 1990s the state's Health Services Commission developed league tables to facilitate the rationing of medical services. Initially, the committee identified more than 1,600 condition-treatment pairs; this figure was finally rendered to a list of 709. At the top of the list were medical treatments for bacterial pneumonia and tuberculosis. Appendectomies, the repair of ruptured intestines, and surgery for ectopic pregnancies also made the top 10. In the middle of the list were other routine and well-accepted treatments, such as medical therapy for sinusitis and repair of open wounds. Toward the bottom of the list were procedures directed toward support for extremely low birth-weight babies and medical therapy for patients with end-stage AIDS. Life support for anencephaly ranked last.[209] But where, on this list, was coverage to end? In the end, the state of Oregon drew the line by setting a budget and seeing how much health care it could afford to buy; those patients whose procedures were among the ones the state deemed affordable received treatment, while those who needed care the state deemed unaffordable did not receive it.[210]

Oregon's move to legalize physician-assisted suicide must be understood within this history of health-care rationing. In 1997, for example, when the Death with Dignity Act went into effect, OMAP directors placed lethal prescriptions on the list of treatments categorized as "comfort care"; at the same time, OMAP slashed Medicaid funding for more than 150 services crucial for people with disabilities, people with terminal illnesses, and older adults.[211] At this point, the battle lines were drawn: whose lives were worth saving, and which lives had an obligation to die? Into this maelstrom entered Barbara Wagner.[212]

Barbara Wagner, sixty-four years old and divorced, worked as a home health-care worker, waitress, and school bus driver. In 2005 she was diagnosed with lung cancer. Unable to pay for her medicines out of pocket, she received chemotherapy, radiation, and a special bed and wheelchair from the Oregon Health Plan (OHP, the state's Medicaid program). Her cancer went into remission and she continued on with her life until May 2008, when a CT scan revealed that her cancer had returned. Her physician prescribed Tarceva, a medicine that slows cancer growth and extends life. Previous studies had indicated that Tarceva provided a 30 percent increase in median survival rate for patients like Wagner who had advanced lung cancer. However, Wagner soon received a letter from OHP informing her that her plan would not cover Tarceva but would "cover palliative, or comfort care, including if she chose, doctor-assisted suicide."[213] In other words, her plan would not provide the means to extend her life but would pay for "letting die," that is, it would pay for her to actively kill herself. In turn, Wagner's oncologist appealed to Genentech, the company that marketed Tarceva. In June, Wagner received notification from the company that they would cover her medicine for one year; afterwards, she could reapply. Wagner, how-ever, passed away in October of that year.

As detailed earlier, in 1994 Oregon's health-care system began establish-ing league tables that determined when, and if, any particular treatment would be covered. One of the established guidelines was that treatments (including radiotherapy and chemotherapy) for patients with less than a 5 percent expected five-year survival were not covered. In other words, if the cost-benefit calculations indicated that a patient had less than a 5 percent chance to live another five years, the treatment would not be cov-ered. Patients could pay for the medicine out of pocket, which, of course, constitutes a built-in class dimension to health-care rationing, a feature that is too often masked by rhetoric of self-determination, autonomy, and choice.

Both supporters and detractors of physician-assisted suicide agree on the specifics of the Wagner case. The difference lies in the interpretation and is reflected in countervailing points of view with respect to life and death. For example, Barbara Coombs Lee, president of Compassion & Choices, has described the entire situation as "an easy media 'gotcha'" story.[214] While conceding that "it was insensitive for the Oregon Health Plan to include Aid in Dying in its lists of available care for Ms. Wagner," Lee maintains that "it was one option in a long list." More to the point, Lee finds fault *with the physician* for attempting to extend Wagner's life. Lee explains that "Wagner's doctor did her no favors by recommending she take a highly toxic, futile drug treatment that had minuscule chance of extending her life."[215] To clarify, the toxic effects include diarrhea and rash. And as for the bio-arithmetic, 8 percent of advanced lung cancer patients respond to the drug, with life extended on average four to six months. Thus, according to the 5 percent/five-year guideline, the pre-scribed treatment was not cost-effective.

Supporters of the duty-to-die movement, such as John Hardwig, argue that recent advances in biomedical technology have contributed to the "obligation" for the elderly and the disabled to die. Hardwig explains that our current medical practices enable many people "to survive longer than we can take care of ourselves, longer than we know what to do with ourselves, longer than we even are ourselves."[216] In other words, the elderly are simply sitting around, waiting to die, all the while consuming precious resources that could be used for more productive—and hence, more deserving—able-bodied people. Within a society rife with ableism and ageism, dignity is extended to the disabled or elderly only when it comes to ending one's life. There is, in other words, dignity in death but not in life. The presumed shame of being cared for is recast as becoming a burden, something to be avoided—even if this avoidance occurs through dying.

Retrospective studies of patients who to all appearances chose assisted suicide are especially noteworthy.[217] Silvia Canetto and Janet Hollenshead, for example, in a study of 75 suicides that were "assisted" by Jack Kevorkian, found that 54 were women and that the majority of them were suffering from a chronic, disabling but nonterminal-stage condition. These authors also reviewed the cases of 112 persons who were the target of "mercy killings" between 1960 and 1993. In this study, Canetto and Hollenshead found that of the 73 cases in which the age and sex of the person mercy killed was known, 63 percent were older adult women. Furthermore, they determined that of all individuals (men and women) who had a physical illness, only 35 percent were classified as having a terminal illness. For Canetto and Hollenshead, these findings are particularly troubling in that they highlight the gendered context of assisted suicide. In the study of assisted suicide deaths between 1960 and 1993, for example, they conclude that "the mercy killed typically were physically-ill older women, while the mercy killers were usually male family members, often the husbands of the mercy killed."[218] Similar patterns have been found elsewhere.[219]

Despite these findings, supporters of euthanasia and the duty to die continue to focus on superficial issues of choice and self-determination, thereby masking the possibility of direct violence.[220] Hardwig, for example, believes that "many of us now worry that death will come too late—long after life has lost its usefulness and its savor, long after we have ceased to have a 'life.'" Consequently, following this argument, we must be rational in our calculations of personal life and death, with Hardwig explaining that today, dying well requires wisdom, skill, and prudential virtues.[221] And thus, while one may no longer be a productive member of society, one can still do the rational thing and die. Of course, as of this writing, Hardwig himself has not taken his own life, despite his own claims. He writes, "At my age I should be ready to die" and "I have already had a full life. . . . If I am not yet ready to die, something is deeply amiss in my outlook on life."[222] So Hardwig is presumably ready to die—but has *not* yet chosen to end his life. One wonders about his own presumed obligation to live.

Regardless of the all too apparent hypocrisy of Hardwig's promotion of a duty to die as choice, other commentators have disputed the supposed logic of autonomy. R. J. D. George and coauthors, for example, counter that the "autonomy argument is thin"; they explain that in actuality "the final decision for physician assisted suicide or therapeutic killing rests with the doctor." Consequently, in their opinion, "patients' perception of total control over this type of death is illusory."[223] The illusion of choice is also tempered by health-care insurers. Recall the case of Barbara Wagner. With Oregon's Medicaid rule, which denies medical treatment coverage for patients with less than a 5 percent expectation of a five-year survival, where is the choice? It certainly does not exist for those patients who, like Wagner, are unable to pay for medical care. Indeed, the tendency under current policy arrangements for aging to become more of an individual "risk" and less of a collective responsibility means that increasing numbers of people are compelled to care for themselves, whether economically or physically, as they age.[224] And when persons are no longer capable of either preventing aging or living on their own, it becomes their responsibility to die. It is therefore hypocritical when supporters of physician-assisted suicide promote autonomy when it comes to dying but not to living. In practice, legalized physician-assisted suicide would create a two-tiered system: nondisabled or non-elderly individuals who express suicidal wishes would receive suicide prevention services or palliative care, while individuals with disabilities—or those who are perceived to be too old— would receive lethal prescriptions.[225]

Proponents of the duty-to-die movement attempt to downplay accusations of ageism and ableism. Supporters, consequently, promote the idea of responsible management of one's life. For Hardwig, "there is no disrespect or devaluing of the elderly in this." He explains that "it is simple acknowledgment of the implications of being alive, and aware that we are alive."[226] The aforementioned Barbara Coombs Lee agrees. She maintains that "in order for society to overcome its collective denial of mortality, we desperately need a public dialogue that shuns superficial sensationalism and leads us to, and through, the hard questions." Ultimately, she suggests, "the burning health policy question is whether we inadvertently encourage patients to act against their own self-interest, chase an unattainable dream of cure, and foreclose the path of acceptance that curative care has been exhausted and the time for comfort care is at hand."[227] It would seem that one must not follow the advice of Dylan Thomas to "not go gentle into that good night" nor to "rage, rage against the dying of the light." Rather, much like the citizens of the world of *Logan's Run*, we must meekly submit to the metaphoric hourglasses embedded in our palms.

Ironically, supporters of physician-assisted suicide at times counter their own argument of autonomy. Lee, for example, queries, "What do patients like Wagner really understand about the 'last hope' treatments their doctors offer?"[228] In other words, Lee implies that patients *should not* have a choice, for the reason that they are not qualified to make informed, reasonable decisions. It would seem as if the "irrational" desire to live—even for a few extra months—clouds one's mind about making the responsible choice to die. Other bioethicists likewise argue that despite the advance of medical technologies that may lengthen one's life, these advanced treatments should not be pursued.[229] Hardwig, for example, laments that biotechnologies have simply "given us more debility, dementia, and protracted chronic and terminal illnesses."[230] He worries that "advances in medicine have given us tremendous new powers, but we do not yet know how to use our new capabilities wisely."[231] Rather, we should, following Hardwig, recognize that "suicide is sometimes perfectly fitting and morally acceptable—sometimes even morally praiseworthy."[232]

Both ableism and ageism, despite claims to the contrary, are intertwined in malignantly effective ways that result in disrespect, reduction of autonomy, and the disregard of the rights of those targeted.[233] For example, the overwhelming majority of the people in Oregon who have reportedly used that state's assisted suicide law wanted to die not because of pain but for reasons associated with disability, including the loss of dignity and the loss of control of bodily functions.[234] It is worth recalling, therefore, that "if the elderly are influenced by negative stereotypes in considering death, they may make decisions to forgo medical interventions that could prolong their lives."[235] Likewise, subjected to constant negative valuations of their worth, the elderly (and disabled) may "choose" to submit to physician-assisted suicide.[236] Therein lies the "choice" behind physician-assisted suicide and health-care rationing. As George and coauthors warn, "Once promoted to a medical good, therapeutic killing becomes a legitimate consideration in resource management."[237]

It is noteworthy that Hardwig, among others, uses the terms "duty," "obligation," and "responsibility" interchangeably.[238] Hardwig, for example, proposes an ever-expansive rubric under which people are obligated to die. His recommendation extends well beyond the (legal) refusal of life-prolonging medical treatment and the completion of advance directives refusing life-prolonging treatment. Indeed, Hardwig suggests that "a duty to die can go well beyond that. There can be a duty to die before one's illnesses would cause death, even if treated only with palliative measures." He concludes that "*there may be a fairly common responsibility to end one's life in the absence of any terminal illness at all*" and that "*there can be a duty to die when one would prefer to live.*"[239] Let us be perfectly clear as to the implications of Hardwig's position. People *not* suffering from a terminal illness, who want to live, have an obligation—a responsibility—to die. Here, simply deciding to live is refashioned as being "irresponsible": one's mere existence becomes a burden to others. I quote Hardwig at length:

> The lives of our loved ones can be seriously compromised by caring for us. The burdens of providing care or even just supervision twenty-four hours a day, seven days a week are often overwhelming. When this kind of caregiving goes on for years, it leaves the caregiver exhausted, with no time for herself or life of her own. Ultimately, even her health

is often destroyed. But it can also be emotionally devastating simply to live with a spouse who is increasingly distant, uncommunicative, unresponsive, foreign, and unreachable. Other family members' needs often go unmet as the caring capacity is exceeded. Social life and friendships evaporate, as there is no opportunity to go out to see friends and the home is no longer a place suitable for having friends in.[240]

Let us take this statement slowly. First, the gender bias is palpable, with the presumption that the caregiver is a female—presumably a daughter or wife or niece. Second, there is the conception of "caring capacity," suggesting that one's ability to care for another is a finite resource; having expended so much energy in caring, the caregiver (e.g., family member or friend) is simply too spent to care anymore. Third, there is the notion that having a person in palliative need somehow diminishes the livability of a household, to such an extent that even friends no longer visit. Fourth, while Hardwig is clearly speaking of the elderly, one should note that it is possible to make the same arguments for infants and the disabled: they require continuous care and supervision. This is especially salient when one recalls Hardwig's earlier statement that a duty-to-die ethos *should* be extended to include those *without* terminal illness and wanting to live.

At what point is this decision made? And who makes that determination if the "life" in question is neither consulted nor considered? As George et al. caution, "Coercion is a real, immeasurable risk."[241] For example, in both Oregon and Washington, despite assurances to the contrary, "neither act requires witnesses at the death. Without disinterested witnesses, the opportunity is created for someone else to administer the lethal dose to the person without his consent. Even if he struggled, who would know?"[242] Consequently, legalization of assisted suicide, broadly promoted, is a recipe for both elder abuse and the abuse of dis-abled people, especially women. Moreover, it opens the door for murder. As Margaret Dore relates, "Nationwide, elder financial abuse is a crime growing in intensity, with perpetrators often family members, but also strangers and new 'best friends.' Victims are even murdered for their funds."[243] Canetto and Hollenshead likewise argue that elderly and dis-abled women are most at risk of "choosing" to die. This risk, moreover, is intimately related to the aforementioned sexism inherent in Hardwig's argument. Canetto and Hollenshead, to this point, argue that the female preponderance among the mercy killed may result, on the one hand, from the "pervasive cultural devaluing of women, particularly older women" and, on the other hand, from the husband's unwillingness or inability to accept an almost complete role reversal in the household—namely, that he should take care of her.[244]

Neoliberal and neoconservative ideologies, however, obfuscate the potential ageist, ableist, *and* sexist attitudes that surround mercy killing and the legalization of physician-assisted suicide. Martin Gunderson, for example, supports both physician-assisted suicide and the "responsibility" to refuse life-prolonging treatments lest one become a burden on others. He notes that numerous studies have shown how caring for family members with such conditions as severe depression, Alzheimer's disease, traumatic brain injury, and vascular dementia can lead to anxiety, depression, social isolation, and physical illness, as well as financial problems.[245] Consequently, Gunderson concludes that these afflicted bodies should refuse to become a burden and thus refuse to live. Note, however, that such a proposition conforms readily to the medical model of disability (and age). Rather than emphasizing the structural limitations of society that preclude palliative care, and rather than focusing on the budgetary limitations that restrict options for care, class-determined and market solutions are embodied in the "dis-abled" bodies. Following Gunderson's logic, it should be perfectly legal—and morally justified—to take the life of those with severe depression, dementia, or traumatic brain injuries. And, as studies of assisted suicides and homicides indicate, if the burdensome body does not "choose" to die, there is always the option of hastening death through "mercy" killing.

Such reasoning elides easily with the cost-benefit analyses promoted by bioethicists and other health-care consultants. Hardwig, again, is informative. He explains that "if talking about money sounds venal or trivial, remember that much more than money is normally at stake here. When someone has to quit work, she may well lose her career. Savings decimated late in life cannot be recouped in the few remaining years of employability, so the loss compromises the quality of the rest of the caregiver's life. For a young person, the chance to go to college may be lost to the attempts to pay debts due to an illness in the family, and this decisively shapes an entire life."[246] Sidestepping the (again) gendered component of Hardwig's statement, one is struck by the apparent refusal to engage in the deeper, systemic problems of American society. In parallel with long-standing debates over child care, why aren't additional provisions made available for caregiving? This fundamental question hinges, of course, on the presumption that health care *must* be rationed. Under such a scenario, it makes perfect sense (for Hardwig and his supporters) to conclude that dying is the most economically sensible practice. If fact, for Hardwig, the *poor* have an even greater obligation to cease to exist, as when he writes, "There is greater duty to die if your loved ones' lives have already been difficult or impoverished, if they have had only a small share of the good things that life has to offer."[247] Hence, rather than address the structural inequalities and societal injustices that exist, it is better (and cheaper) for the impoverished to die.

And therein lies the gist of the issue. One's obligation to die is, in the (literally) final analysis, predicated upon an ageist and ableist market logic—a point that Hardwig himself acknowledges yet seemingly refuses to entertain. Hardwig agrees that the "claim that there is a duty to die will seem to some a misplaced response to social negligence." He concedes that, "if our society were providing for the debilitated, the chronically ill, and the elderly as it should be, there would be only very rare cases of a duty to die." But, Hardwig concludes, this is not the case, and, accordingly, he is "asking the sick and debilitated to step in and accept responsibility because society is derelict in its responsibility to provide for the incapacitated."[248] One is hard-pressed to fathom the logic of Hardwig's argument; because society has failed to address social injustices, he reasons, those who are exploited and oppressed should commit suicide. Is Hardwig's logic so completely illogical? Or does it instead reflect a market-based rationale deeper than any heretofore addressed?

Within the neoliberal state, the elderly and the disabled are no longer perceived to embody any worth—as defined by the market. They are presumably beyond any productive function for our modern, postindustrial economy. Hardwig, for example, supposes that a duty to die "becomes greater as you grow older" because "as we age, we will be giving up less by giving up our lives, if only because we will sacrifice fewer remaining years of life and a smaller portion of our life plans."[249] The ageism implicit in this sentiment is all the more palpable when juxtaposed with the aforementioned discussion of life-extending biotechnologies. As Walter Glannon explains, "A world in which everyone's life span was extended beyond 85 years might increase competition for scarce resources and lower the quality of life for all. The moral and prudential argument against this would be that a longer life for all would mean the defeat of people's interest in having good lives. In this regard, living longer might be not just undesirable but bad."[250]

Able-bodied infants, conversely, while likewise requiring constant care and supervision, hold the promise—the potential—to become productive members of society. It is this ageist balance that informs the support (by the likes of Peter Singer) for the euthanasia of disabled infants and the elderly. Here, I believe that Hardwig's own statement regarding the death of his mother is telling. Hardwig writes, "Throughout most of her miserable stay in a very nice nursing home, she had little physical pain and no terminal illness. She felt stuck—there was nothing for her do to but wait for death to show up."[251] Why was there nothing for her to do? More broadly, why does society, as a whole, consider the elderly, as well as the disabled, as having little value? Could not policies be pursued that could tap into the accumulated wisdom and experiences of those deemed elderly? Might not we think beyond the labor market to consider other ways to integrate *all* members of society?

The message is clear: those who are considered to be economically nonproductive, and thus presumably with nothing left to contribute to society, should willingly embrace death. However, one must not forget that within the neoliberal market it is not simply productivity that is vital but also responsibility. Earlier, I indicated that responsibility is couched in one's obligation to not unduly consume precious resources or to become a financial burden on others. The classist dimensions are self-evident—but incomplete, for Hardwig, among others, does note that the wealthy may also be irresponsible and thus have an obligation to die. Hardwig explains that "there is a greater duty to die to the extent that you have lived a relatively lavish lifestyle instead of saving for illness or old age. . . . It is a greater wrong to come to your family for assistance if your need is the result of having chosen leisure or a spendthrift lifestyle."[252] Consequently, those who act irresponsibly within the capitalist market, those who did not adequately prepare for their postretirement years, are undeserving of assistance—even from family members. And having made one's choice to consume and not to save, one should become (belatedly) responsible and choose to die.

The duty-to-die movement, in sum, brings to light a series of highly contested issues that revolve around societal perceptions and attitudes toward the disabled and the elderly, but the movement also directs attention toward our valuation of some bodies over others. The legality, and acceptance, of these practices—prenatal screening, selective abortion, and physician-assisted suicide—will literally mean the difference between life and death. Therein lies the slippery-slope argument. If it becomes morally accepted and expected that *some* bodies—the disabled, the aged—have an obligation, a responsibility, to die, what is to prevent *other* bodies from likewise becoming targets? Moreover, as Diane Coleman explains, "assisted suicide laws ensure legal immunity for [some] physicians who already devalue the lives of older and disabled people and have significant economic incentives to at least agree with their suicides, if not encourage them, or worse." Consequently, "since these same physicians are already empowered by 'futility' laws and policies to overrule patient decisions to receive life-sustaining treatment and thus impose involuntary passive euthanasia, there is no basis to assume that they will uniformly prevent involuntary active euthanasia, even if they could."[253] And this is why the role of the state should remain salient— but tempered. As John Harris correctly observes, "One of the prime functions of the State is to protect the lives and fundamental interests of its citizens and to treat each citizen as the equal of any other. This is why the State has a basic obligation, *inter alia*, to treat all citizens as equals in the distribution of benefits and opportunities which affect their civil rights."[254]

CONCLUSIONS

No doubt the ethical issues raised in this chapter are difficult, but they have profound implications for our understanding—and abstraction—of violence. We are confronted with a dizzying array of medical and technological advances that intersect within contemporary society in complex ways: politically, economically, and socially. As Tom Koch writes, "We live not alone but in society and the issues of ethics are as much about communal activities and impediments as they are about personal preferences and reasons."[255] Our values are shaped by the historical and geographical moment in which we live. This is what Karl Marx means when he states that "we make our own history" but that it is not entirely of our own choosing.

The steady commodification of society, the interpenetration of the market logics of capitalism into our daily lives, imparts a particular valuation of life itself. This greatly informs our abstractions of violence and definition of crime, for it is not so much *when* we see violence as it is *what* we see as violence. There exist many actions and inactions that impinge upon one's ability to survive—practices that harm, injure, and result in premature death. Koch ponders "the means by which care of the fragile and sick is advanced or withheld." He concludes that "the real question is the degree and nature of our communal responsibility for the care of this or that individual."[256] It is within this question that our understanding of violence should be situated. For when we fail to take responsibility for the plight of the less fortunate—for those who have heretofore been declared redundant—we ourselves are engaging in, and abetting, violence.

5

The Reality of Violence

The first clue, lesson number one from human history on the subject of nonviolence, is that there is no word for it. The concept has been praised by every major religion. Throughout history there have been practitioners of nonviolence. Yet, while every major language has a word for violence, there is no word to express the idea of nonviolence except that it is not another idea, it is not violence.

—MARK KURLANSKY, *Nonviolence: Twenty-Five Lessons from the History of a Dangerous Idea*

Mark Kurlansky effectively highlights the difficulties with articulating the concept of nonviolence. As an idea, a practice, or condition, nonviolence is understood by what it is not. Nonviolence is the absence, or lack, or even opposite of violence. A similar conundrum exists for the concept of peace. Peace is widely (and erroneously) understood as the absence of war. And yet, as many commentators have noted, a society not at war is not necessarily peaceful.

The problem when we begin with a negative—nonviolence—is that we presume to know its counterpart: violence. Despite claims to the contrary, violence is not self-evident, as indicated by the voluminous writings on violence. In a seminal essay from 1921 the theorist Walter Benjamin distinguished between "law-making" and "law-preserving" violence. The former, also understood as foundational violence—is associated with the moments of the investiture of law; the latter, conversely, constitutes an administratively enforced violence, as exemplified by the establishment of judicial and police apparatuses. This raises a fundamental tension in that violence appears not only as a method of enforcement—manifest, for example, in armed conflict and the use of police repression—but also as a means of enforcing political legitimacy, as exhibited in the establishment of torture and execution. Later in his essay Benjamin introduces the concept of mythic violence, which includes both law-making and law-preserving violence. His ideas are complex, but in essence Benjamin calls attention to the mythical aspects of law and violence whereby mythic violence is "the creator and the protector of the prevailing political and legal order."[1] Divine violence, conversely, is pure violence in that it challenges and destroys mythic violence. How divine violence *appears* has generated considerable controversy. For Judith Butler, divine violence is equated with noncoercive and nonviolent action; for Slavoj Žižek, it is the opposite.[2]

Hannah Arendt similarly works through the idea of violence.[3] She begins with a critique of Mao Zedong's aphorism that power comes out of the barrel of a gun. Arendt's conceptualization of violence is considerably more nuanced in that she distinguishes power from violence. For Arendt, power is not something that is possessed but rather is an expression of a collective will. This view counters more conventional approaches—including that of Max Weber—that conceive of power as having power over someone. Violence, on the other hand, is instrumental. Thus defined, for Arendt, power and violence are antithetical concepts; violence may lead to change, but it can never lead to power.

The forwarding of power as opposed to violence by Arendt complements the approach taken by Michel Foucault. For Foucault, power is not some*thing* that is held by any one person, group, or state; rather, power circulates; power is relational. Discipline is a type of power, and, while it is not simply a matter of consent, it is also not a renunciation of freedom or a transfer of rights from the powerless to the powerful. Violence, conversely, is, according to Foucault, totalizing. When violence is engaged, it removes the possibilities for active subjects (agents) to act autonomously.

Benjamin, Arendt, and Foucault provide three theoretical approaches to violence; there are literally dozens of others, for almost every political philosopher has had something to say at some point about violence. There has been no consensus on the definition of violence, however, because *violence does not exist independently in material form*. Violence is an abstraction—akin to the concept "fruit"—and by extension "nonviolence" is also an abstraction. This has profound implications, for scholars routinely study the aftermath of violence, the legal response to violence, crime and the criminalization of violence, the fear of violence, the representation of violence, and the memorialization of violence. However, the act of violence—for it is invariably understood as an action, not an inaction—and the social conditions that produce and are produced by violence become a black box, assumed, acknowledged, but rarely theorized in such a way as to afford a critical evaluation of its constitution.[4]

This is a serious lacuna because it makes violence appear to be natural, enduring, and aspatial to the human condition, thus hiding many other actions (and inactions) that harm, injure, kill, or let die. In the United States of America, for example, the Patient Protection and Affordable Care Act (PPACA) was signed into law by Pres. Barack Obama on March 23, 2010.[5] Highly controversial and mired in partisan politics, the PPACA was intended to make health insurance more accessible to approximately 47 million uninsured Americans. This was to be accomplished, in part, by requiring states to expand Medicaid eligibility to people with income less than 138 percent of the federal poverty level. In June 2012, however, the Supreme Court of the United States ruled that states could opt out of Medicaid expansion. As of November 2013, twenty-five states had in fact opted out, leaving millions of Americans uninsured who otherwise would have been covered by Medicaid. Sam Dickman and coauthors estimate that approximately 8 million men, women, and children would be uninsured because of the court's opt-out decision. As a result, they calculate that Medicaid expansion in those states that opted out "would have resulted in 422,553 more diabetics receiving medication for their illness, 195,492 more mammograms among women aged 50–64 years and 443,677 more pap smears among women age 21–64. Expansion would have resulted in an additional 658,888 women in need of mammograms gaining insurance, as well as 3.1 million women who should receive regular pap smears." They put the number of potential deaths attributable to the lack of Medicaid expansion in opt-out states at between 7,115 and 17,104. In other words, upwards of 17,000 people in the United States may die as a result of governmental decision making.

My point in raising the PPACA is not to engage in partisan politics or to argue either for or against the notion that the Affordable Care Act is the best way of addressing Americans' health-care needs. Rather, my point is simply this: if the projections of Dickman et al. are accurate, people who might otherwise live will die. They will die as a result of an omission—an inaction on the part of a handful of politicians who for various reasons do not support the PPACA but also do not provide any alternative. Phrased differently, the state will let die a not insignificant number of men, women, and children who might otherwise have lived.

The potential deaths of seventeen thousand people because a few politicians elect to have their state opt out of Medicaid expansion generally is *not* considered violent. Moreover, in an ironic, perverted twist, the decisions that will lead to these deaths are not only not considered criminal but they epitomize legality in that they are upheld by the highest court of law in the United States. And because those decisions are viewed as neither violent nor criminal, one suspects that the issue of health-care reform does not occupy the attention of many well-meaning individuals who promote nonviolence.

The inability to see violence in the face of potential or actual harm goes to the heart of my argument that violence is a fetish, that violence—understood as something natural and obvious—appears as something that is already knowable. We know violence when we see it; violence appears as the husband beating his wife, the gang member shooting a stranger, the serial killer stalking another victim. With violence conceived as such, we do not always see it, even when it is most apparent. We do not necessarily see the violence of war, because wars are supposedly just; we do not see the violence of capital punishment, because the execution of criminals has been upheld by law. More problematic still is that we do not see the violence of a lack of health care or welfare because, seemingly, there is no intentionality to the premature deaths that might result.

Before we study the aftermath or the response to violence, or the criminalization, fear, representation, or memorialization of violence, we need to better understand that "violence" is an abstraction. Rather than beginning with an essentialist working of violence, we must critique the ontology of violence itself. Here, ontology has two distinct meanings.[6] On the one hand, it refers to the fundamental nature of reality—of what exists, and, on the other hand, it refers to the systematic study of this nature.[7] With regard to the first usage, ontology is understood as the sedimented and normally taken-for-granted background of everyday life. It is, in other words, the common world in which we live. From this vantage point, violence is a fact of life; it simply exists. This is the violence of empiricism, in which we focus on measurable, mappable acts that are labeled "violent" or "criminal."

Conversely, it is possible to critique the ontology that violence exists. What we take as the everyday—including our understanding of the reality of violence—is itself the outcome of the political. As Johanna Oksala writes, the political "is not a distinct realm of social reality, but its precondition."[8] She elaborates that "to be able to argue that entities such as homosexual, delinquent, and pervert are not natural phenomena which human sciences could simply discover, describe, and refer to objectively, but effects of power relations and political struggles, requires a profound denaturalization of ontology: we have to sever any direct, natural, or necessary link between scientific concepts and their referents."[9]

Reality—or, rather, what we take as reality—is an assemblage of political, economic, and social practices; it is always and already the effect of power relations. As Foucault asserts, "Power produces; it produces reality; it produces domains of objects and rituals and truth."[10] Thus, when we consider the reality of violence, of what is counted (homicide and rape) and discounted (health-care and welfare reform), of what is criminalized (gang activity) and not criminalized (again, health-care and welfare reform), we do so through an understanding of how power and difference are constituted by and of society. Violence assumes real, concrete form through political, economic, and social practice.

That the reality of violence is structured by political, economic, and social practice directs attention to the proposition that the abstraction of violence must be situated within particular historical and geographical contexts. As John Rees explains, "Theoretical concepts arise from and relate to the real world, but not in a direct and simplistic way."[11] Thus, eschewing an idealist, Hegelian understanding, I have argued that violence must be understood dialectically and as being a determinant of dominant modes of production. Capitalism, for example, is a specific historical form of social relations; it is founded on the separation of direct producers from the means of production. This is why workers—although formally free— are (with very few exceptions) compelled by material circumstances to sell their labor power to the capitalist. Capitalism, in this sense, appears as an economic system whereby a person's capacity to work becomes a commodity that can be bought and sold on the market. The fetishism of capitalism, however, disguises the fact that capitalism—or any other mode of production—is not *just* an economic system, for *any mode of production*, and not just capitalism, is first and foremost a constellation of myriad social relations.

This last statement cannot be overemphasized: all modes of production are characterized by particular social relations. This is vitally important because violence—as abstraction—is likewise relational. The relation between perpetrator and victim is most obvious, but we can readily observe other abstractions of violence as relational. Those men, women, and children who are lacking in food, for example, *are related to other members of society that are not lacking*. To what extent do these other members have an obligation, legal or otherwise, to provide assistance? Or, conversely, to what extent are these other members responsible for the unequal and unjust distribution of food? The answers to all of these questions are conditioned by the society at hand, and just as social relations under feudalism differ from those of capitalism (both of which

THE REALITY OF VIOLENCE

are broadly conceived here), so too are obligations and responsibilities conditioned by these relations.

Under capitalism—and specifically its neoliberal and neoconservative variant, as seen in the United States—violence is abstracted according to the market logics of letting die. Within a commodified society, the waged labor market becomes the model on which social relations are structured. A competitive, atomistic worldview is promoted, and it is a worldview predicated on assumptions of scarce and finite resources to be fought over in an unending struggle for personal survival. Individuals are posited as rational decision makers, and decisions are rendered based on profit maximization and the valorization of surplus value.

Capitalism is indifferent to use value, and this may result in an indifference to life itself. On September 21, 2013, a fifty-seven-year-old woman, Lynne Spalding Ford, was reported missing.[12] She had been admitted to San Francisco General Hospital two days earlier for a bladder infection. Upon notification of her disappearance, authorities made a perimeter check but, apparently, did not conduct a full search; she was not classified as a missing person. Days later, on October 1, a hospital orderly informed a nurse that he had seen an unconscious woman on a locked exterior stairwell. He reportedly stepped over her body twice while going up and down the stairs. The nurse subsequently contacted the sheriff's department. "We'll take care of it," was the response. That same day another employee reported hearing banging coming from the same stairwell. On October 8, more than two weeks after Ford went missing, her body was found on an exterior stairwell of the hospital—the very same stairwell where the orderly had reported stepping over an unconscious woman, the same stairwell where another employee had reported hearing knocking sounds.

I relate the tragic and needless death of Ford because it encapsulates the indifference to use value that I suggest permeates contemporary society. The actions and inactions, whether ultimately determined to be criminal or not, speak to the callousness with which some bodies are valued and other bodies are discarded. Why was there not an immediate response to the orderly's report of discovering an unconscious person on a hospital stairwell? Why did the orderly himself not do more? Is it because the person or body, located on an exterior stairwell, was presumed to be that of just another homeless person? Ford was not directly killed, but her unconscious body was intentionally neglected, left, in this case, to die. It is for this specific reason that I abstract violence under capitalism according to the market logics of letting die.

The moral difference between killing and letting die is found most often in debates surrounding euthanasia, itself a long-standing practice that is currently viewed from the standpoint of scarce resources and freedom of choice. Both philosophers and bioethicists have offered many points of argument on the issue; in general, the arguments are framed around the *intent* to kill or to let die as a means of relieving suffering. In contradistinction, my suggestion is that the morality distinguishing the act of killing from the non-act of letting die actually constitutes two sides of the same coin, that, following Marx, we may look to the *unity of these two opposites*, and that the presumption of the wrongness to kill hinges on a conservative understanding of agency.

According to Will Cartwright, a plausible account of the difference between killing and letting die may be that one kills someone if one initiates a causal sequence that ends in one's death, whereas one lets another die if one allows an already existing causal sequence to culminate in that person's death.[13] In effect, Cartwright is addressing the broader context, or conditions, that may result in death. These conditions in fact underlie Johan Galtung's well-known distinction between direct/personal violence and structural violence and greatly inform our moral—and legal—distinction between acts of commission and acts of omission.

Intentionality is the fetishized pivot upon which direct violence diverges from structural violence, with the former referring to concrete acts committed by and on particular people and the latter occurring when apparently *unintentional* inequalities are structured into society. Examples of the latter include differences in access to gainful employment or adequate medical care. The act of letting die is not always reducible to not doing something to prevent death.[14] Rather, to let die may be understood as a failure to act—it is intentional; it is to refrain from acting otherwise. To let die is an active inaction.

This argument rests on three conditions readily apparent in Engels's critique of society: ability, opportunity, and awareness. First, to refrain from performing an action is predicated on the presumed ability of one to perform an action but, for whatever reason, choosing not to perform that action. Stated in the form of a question, Is an individual in a position to prevent harm but (through inaction) does not do so? Second, does a person have the opportunity to prevent harm? To take an obvious geographic example, suppose a doctor living in New York has the ability—the skills—to save a person suffering from an illness in Los Angeles but has not the opportunity to do so. Lastly, is an individual *aware* of the conditions that contribute to harm befalling another person? I maintain that if an individual (or, for that matter, an institution or government) has the ability, the opportunity, and awareness of conditions that will let die and one still chooses to refrain from taking actions to prevent that consequence, then that person has reduced the other to a status of bare life.

At a societal level we are aware of the gross inequalities that lead to stark differences in life expectancies. Corporations and the government are aware of the deplorable conditions confronting those who die prematurely; they also have the ability and opportunity to positively intervene. Such intervention, however, is precluded within a political-economic system that tolerates but does not promote positive duties and maintains that there is no moral difference between taking life and letting die. We promote negative rights to the exclusion of positive rights. We are thus under no obligation to help those less fortunate, and we increasingly fail to consider that the plight of the downtrodden might stem from systemic failings of our contemporary political-economic system. When it is presumed that workers willingly and fairly enter the waged labor market, that they get paid a fair wage for a fair day's work, and that as long as they (the poor, the destitute, the downtrodden) are not directly killed by corporations (e.g., negligence), they will remain as homo sacer: their deaths in the labor market will have little to no meaning beyond the necessity of finding a suitable (laboring) replacement.

Given this pervasive attitude, embedded within both law and the economy, the premature deaths of the abandoned are considered neither morally nor legally wrong, nor are these deaths readily viewed as violent. If, as Marx suggests, society creates the conditions under which wealth is created, so too does society create the conditions under which some may live and others must die. And it is not solely the material deprivation of those who are marginalized that is at issue. As Robert Young explains, because those who have been economically marginalized—the old, the poor, the mentally or physically disabled—depend on bureaucratic institutions for support or services, they are subject also to patronizing, punitive, demanding, and arbitrary treatment; being dependent in our society implies being legitimately subject to often arbitrary and invasive authority of social service providers—the state.[15] The marginalized are, in fact, outside political life.

Under neoliberalism, neither corporations nor the state take responsibility for the plight of any particular individuals, who, as totally free agents, are assumed to be fully responsible for their condition.[16] Indeed, as Katharyne Mitchell, Sallie Marston, and Cindi Katz argue, the "devolution of more and more 'choice' to a seemingly ever more autonomous individual who must rationally calculate the benefits and costs of all aspects of life . . . is part of a much broader set of practices that tend to increase productivity and profits for the employer while reducing the responsibility of both the employer and the state in managing and sustaining the reproduction of labor-power."[17] In other words, within neoliberal capitalism, as long as capitalists and the state are presumed to refrain from direct harm, they are under no obligation to promote (costly) positive duties. Marx is clear on this point: "Capital . . . takes no account of the health and the length of life of the worker, unless society forces it to do so. Its answer to the outcry about the physical and mental degradation, the premature death, the torture of over-work, is this: Should that pain trouble us, since it increases our pleasure (profit)?"[18] As such, those individuals deemed redundant—the unemployed, the homeless, the welfare recipient—are abandoned by a pervasive indifference that is systemic to capitalism itself.

Untold numbers of people are being consigned to the margins of society; they are increasingly blamed for their own premature deaths. As Rose Galvin explains,

With the collapse or, at the very least, shrinking of the welfare state and the emergence of neoliberalism and economic rationalism as guiding principles of government in contemporary western culture, the concepts of social engineering and tutelage have been swept aside by the belief that individuals should be empowered to take control of their lives outside of the patronage of a large, complex and benevolent state apparatus. At the heart of this shift in political posture is the neoliberal resurrection of the classical liberal concept of "negative liberty" which seeks to minimize the intervention of political administration in the lives of citizens and, in the current context, casts them as "consumers" and "enterprising individuals" who make choices and who, consequently, are responsible for the outcomes of these choices.[19]

Within such a political-economic climate, those who become ill, or old, or give birth to disabled children are increasingly deemed irresponsible and thus excluded from consideration. This is because, under our current political and economic system, it is *believed* that people can choose to avoid getting too sick, or too old, or too poor. And couched within this pervasive victim blaming is a fear that society must secure itself against those deemed irresponsible, that those unproductive, burdensome populations must be eliminated.

PATHS FORWARD

Where do we go from here? A first step is to recast the theorization of violence within an explicit framework of social injustice. Theories of (in)justice generally begin with the assumption that the most fundamental problem is how to distribute fairly the burdens and benefits of society.[20] An engagement with social justice, however, entails more than a simple recognition that some people are better off than others; it calls for a conscious effort to promote change. A promotion of social justice requires both change and transformation: to change those conditions—both structural and institutional—that produce inequalities and injustices and to transform society—both individually and collectively—to not accept the

existence of inequalities and injustices. In short, social justice is normative, concerned with what should be as opposed to what actually exists.[21]

That said, there is no widespread agreement as to what constitutes
either violence or an injustice. In the United States, as indicated earlier,
the top 1 percent of the population accounts for approximately 40 percent
of the country's wealth. In addition, one in one hundred Americans is
currently incarcerated, paroled, or on probation—with African Americans
disproportionately represented in these numbers. Do these numbers, at
face value, indicate an injustice? For some commentators, as we have seen,
the discrepancies in health and wealth, imprisonment and homelessness,
lie solely with the decisions made by individuals. Inequalities in society are
presumed to be the explicit result of avoiding personal responsibilities—
men and women *choosing* to not work or *choosing* to commit crimes. Much
like Horatio Alger, the top 1 percent of Americans thus believe they are
just harder working, more frugal with their resources, and making better
choices as to education and occupation. Indeed, in the United States,
there is a long-standing discourse that poverty, crime, and even sickness
and death occur because of the moral degeneracy and personal failings
of *individuals* as opposed to the existence of structural and institutional
conditions that might generate such results.[22]

The presumption of personal responsibility and moral failings is seen
clearly in the ongoing debates surrounding health care. We know, for
example, that not all people in the United States have equal access to
health care and that this results in stark differences in life expectancy.
How these inequalities are framed, however, is not agreed upon. As Daniel
Wikler explains, "If social and economic inequalities are as powerful in
determining health expectancies as current research indicates they are,
then [governments] would seem obligated to narrow these inequalities,
or to find ways to reduce their effect on health and longevity." However,
he notes that, "if we assign responsibility for the excess mortality and
morbidity associated with socioeconomic inequality to individuals (on
the premise that these misfortunes stem from differences in lifestyle that
reflect different personal priorities, tastes, and character traits), then we
cannot demand remedial action by [government]."[23]

The discourse of personal responsibility is not only misplaced; it is deliberately invoked to maintain and exacerbate structural inequalities in society. To forward the claim that poverty, for example, stems from individual failings is to obfuscate the deeply entrenched practices that constrain one's ability to obtain a decent education, job, or even a healthy life. Ascriptions of responsibility, as Wikler writes, presuppose freedom of action. However, "actions only rarely have all the attributes—informed, voluntary, uncoerced, spontaneous, deliberated, and so on—that, in the ideal case, are preconditions for full personal responsibility."[24]

Needed therefore is a continued critique of the *processes* that create unequal conditions and distributions *within the space of the exception*. Such a critique is necessary to further disentangle those "structures of violence" that limit the opportunity to fully participate in society and to redress the practices of oppression that permeate contemporary society. Consider one such practice, that of exploitation. As an oppressive condition, exploitation is endemic to capitalism; indeed, exploitation is the catalyst for the accumulation of surplus value, and it is for this reason I maintain that calculations of life and death must always and already be situated within the capitalist labor market. As educators, we can begin by bringing to light how poverty, for example, is *not* always and already the result of personal failings but rather a necessary component of our current economic system.[25] We can direct attention to ongoing efforts that *humanize* rather than *dehumanize*, to understand, for example, the "humanity and agency of poor people in a manner that [works toward] actual and potential emancipatory politics."[26] As Don Mitchell and Nik Heynen write, the saga of survival in the United States "is not a one-way story of oppression, restriction, and decline. . . . It is also a story of both coping in the shadowed interstices . . . and of fighting back."[27]

We must continue also to deconstruct the abstract categories that work to marginalize. As Evelyn Ruppert explains, "People are not governed in relation to their individuality but as members of populations. The embodied individual is of interest to governments insofar as the individual can be identified, categorized and recognized as a member of a population."[28] Accordingly, we must critically interrogate those calculated bodies that become the object—the target—of governmental interference: those identified as the teenage mom, the pre-pregnant woman, and the overweight. We must challenge those impersonal statistical machinations that purport to ascribe failings onto the personal. It becomes necessary, also, to identify those practices—buttressed by the construction of marginal categories—that render some people powerless, to the benefit of others. We must deconstruct efforts, for example, that disenfranchise voters or rescind welfare on account of racist, classist, and sexist ideology. We must challenge those state interventions that render invisible the lives and contributions of racial minorities, the disabled, and the elderly. We must promote a culture of acceptance and empathy. No person should be considered a burden, and no person should be obligated to die. And lastly, we must challenge the widespread promotion and acceptance of violence within society. We must teach differently; we must teach peace rather than promote fear. Above all, we must take seriously the calculations of life and death within our contemporary society.

"We have learned from historical experience," Howard Zinn writes, "that people can change their opinions dramatically if they get new information."[29] We can provide that information, to demonstrate that people are not "market failures" and hence undeserving of our care and our compassion. In order to redress the varied structures of oppression, we must, as Zinn concludes, "expose the motives of our political leaders, point out their connections to corporate power, show how huge profits are being made out of death and suffering."[30] Patricia Calderwood echoes these sentiments when she writes, "When change does finally come about, it is often because public sentiment has moved, so that formerly radical ideas seem reasonable and just and former norms seem unjust and in need of revision."[31] The gross inequalities of American society, as expressed most gravely in the differences of life expectancy, are not natural, normal, or just, but they are violent. The stark discrepancies between the wealthy and the poor do not reflect personal failings but rather systemic oppressive structures embedded within our current political-economic system. To advocate for change is not radical; it is just.

NOTES

1. THE ABSTRACTION OF VIOLENCE

1. This account is drawn from Chuck Currie, "Jessica Williams Did Not Have to Die: A Faith Perspective on Violence and Homelessness in America," 1–17, *Rev. Chuck Currie*, accessed November 3, 2011, www.chuckcurrie.blogs.com; Chuck Currie, "All God's Children: How Rene Denfeld Distorts the Truth About Homeless Youth," *Rev. Chuck Currie*, accessed November 4, 2011, www.chuck currie.blogs.com/chuck_currie/2007/01/all_gods_childr.html; Nick Budnick, "Street Life—and Death," *Portland Tribune*, January 26, 2007, http://www .portlandtribune.com/news/print_story.php?story_id=116977293184887200; and Tracy Jan, "Homicide Victim Was Childlike," accessed November 3, 2011, http://come-over.to/fas/HomicideVictimChildlike.htm.
2. Mark Price's story is drawn from Mary K. Reinhart, "2nd Person Denied Arizona Transplant Coverage Dies," *Arizona Republic*, January 5, 2011, www .azcentral.com/news/articles/2011/01/05/20110105arizona-second-patient -denied-coverage-dies.htm.
3. Reinhart, "2nd Person Denied Arizona Transplant Coverage Dies."
4. See, for example, Tyner and Inwood, "Violence as Fetish."
5. "Independent Spending in Arizona, 2006–2010," National Institute on Money in State Politics, accessed November 3, 2011, http://www.followthemoney .org/press/ReportView.phtml?r=456.
6. Krug et al., "World Report on Violence and Health," 1084.
7. Krug et al., "World Report on Violence and Health," 1083, 1085.
8. World Health Organization, *Global Burden of Disease*; United Nations Children's Fund/World Health Organization, *Diarrhoea*.

9. Families USA, *Dying for Coverage*. See also Dorn, *Uninsured and Dying Because of It*.

10. Rita Webb, "Reproductive Health Disparities for Women of Color," National Association of Social Workers, December 2004, http://www.naswdc.org /diversity/Equity1204.pdf.

11. Galtung, "Violence, Peace, and Peace Research." See also Galtung and Höivik, "Structural and Direct Violence."

12. Galtung, "Violence, Peace, and Peace Research," 168.

13. Galtung, "Violence, Peace, and Peace Research," 170.

14. Galtung, "Violence, Peace, and Peace Research," 170–71.

15. Opotow, "Reconciliation in a Time of Impunity," 151.

16. Loyd, "'Microscopic Insurgent,'" 865–66. See also Loyd, "Geographies of Peace and Antiviolence."

17. Sutherland, "White-Collar Criminality."

18. Garver, "What Violence Is," 817.

19. See Audi, "On the Meaning and Justification of Violence"; Betz, "Violence"; Coady, "Idea of Violence"; Bäck, "Thinking Clearly about Violence"; Bufacchi, "Two Concepts of Violence"; De Haan, "Violence as an Essentially Contested Concept"; and Krause, "Beyond Definition."

20. Betz, "Violence," 341.

21. Coady, "Idea of Violence," 4.

22. Coady, "Idea of Violence," 12.

23. Albritton, *Economics Transformed*, 168.

24. Ollman, *Alienation*, 62.

25. Foucault, *Birth of Biopolitics*, 3.

26. Rees, *Algebra of Revolution*, 23.

27. Rees, *Algebra of Revolution*, 23.

28. Strawson, *Bounds of Sense*, 35.

29. Rees, *Algebra of Revolution*, 25.

30. Althusser and Balibar, *Reading "Capital"*; Hartsock and Smith, "On Althusser's Misreading of Marx's 1857 'Introduction'"; Hall, "Marx's Notes on Method"; Ollman, "Marx's Dialectical Method."

31. Ollman, *Dance of the Dialectic*, 12.

32. Ollman, *Dance of the Dialectic*, 15.

33. Ingersoll, Matthews, and Davison, *Philosophic Roots of Modern Ideology*, 118.

34. Kirk, "Natural Change in Heraclitus," 38.

35. Ingersoll, Matthews, and Davison, *Philosophic Roots of Modern Ideology*, 119.

36. Sortal concepts are classificatory concepts. McMahan, *Ethics of Killing*, 6.

37. McMahan, *Ethics of Killing*, 6.

38. Rees, *Algebra of Revolution*, 43.
39. Rees, *Algebra of Revolution*, 43–44.
40. Marx and Engels, *German Ideology*, 42 (emphasis added).
41. Marx, *Capital*, 1:103.
42. Marx and Engels, *German Ideology*, 42.
43. Marx and Engels, "Holy Family," 150.
44. Marx and Engels, "Holy Family," 150.
45. Rees, *Algebra of Revolution*, 63.
46. Alvarez and Bachman, *Violence*, 7.
47. Hall, "Marx's Notes on Method," 117.
48. U.S. Census Bureau, "How the Census Bureau Measures Poverty," accessed January 21, 2014, http://www.census.gov/hhes/www/poverty/about/overview /measure.html.
49. McCormack, "Geography and Abstraction," 715.
50. Marx, *Contribution to the Critique of Political Economy*, 210.
51. Ollman, *Dance of the Dialectic*, 60.
52. Ollman, *Dance of the Dialectic*, 12.
53. Harvey, *Justice, Nature and the Geography of Difference*, 51.
54. Paolucci, *Marx's Scientific Dialectics*, 159–88.
55. Paolucci, *Marx's Scientific Dialectics*, 159.
56. Paolucci, *Marx's Scientific Dialectics*, 160.
57. Paolucci, *Marx's Scientific Dialectics*, 165.
58. Paolucci, *Marx's Scientific Dialectics*, 165.
59. Paolucci, *Marx's Scientific Dialectics*, 167.
60. Ollman, *Dance of the Dialectic*, 100.
61. Muchembled, *History of Violence*, 1.
62. Muchembled, *History of Violence*, 5.
63. Mitchell, "Political Violence, Order, and the Legal Construction of Public Space," 156.
64. Harvey, *Social Justice and the City*, 298.
65. Marx, *Grundrisse*, 105.

2. MATERIALISM AND MODE OF PRODUCTION

1. Rees, *Algebra of Revolution*, 64.
2. Marx was heavily influenced by the writings of Charles Darwin, and, in turn, Marx applied various evolutionary concepts in his writings. Marx's appropriation of evolutionary principles is not to be equated, however, with the vulgarities apparent in the social Darwinism that characterized much eugenic and neo-eugenic thought. Marx likewise did not forward a teleological,

determinist account of history—despite what many critics (continue to) say. Rather, Marx postulated that societies evolve—and here, note that the words *evolve* and *evolution* do not suggest "progress" or a fixed, linear path but instead mean "adaptation." In other words, individuals (and, by extension, societies) respond and adapt to changing material realities, which, in dialectic fashion, are subsequently transformed through human action.

3. Marx and Engels, *German Ideology*, 36–37.
4. Marx and Engels, *German Ideology*, 37.
5. Peet, *Global Capitalism*, 59.
6. Garland, *Culture of Control*, 90.
7. Harcourt, *Illusion of Free Markets*, 48.
8. Lea, *Crime and Modernity*.
9. It is worth noting that both Adam Smith and David Ricardo used similar analogies, including the Robinson Crusoe story, and, interestingly, Marx was critical (or at least suspicious) of such approaches. Furthermore, I am aware that in my example I have imagined individuals who "descend" to the island fully formed and with previous experiences in alternative modes of production from which to draw upon.
10. Marx and Engels, *German Ideology*, 37.
11. Marx, *Contribution to the Critique*, 20.
12. Paolucci, *Marx's Scientific Dialectics*, 194. See also Somerville, "Marxist Ethics, Determinism, and Freedom."
13. Marx and Engels, *German Ideology*, 38.
14. See, for example Banaji, *Theory as History*.
15. It is just such an erroneous and simplistic reading that has caused much confusion over the years.
16. Marx and Engels, *German Ideology*, 38.
17. Marx, *Contribution to the Critique*, 20–21 (emphasis added).
18. Peet, "Materialism, Social Formation, and Socio-Spatial Relations," 149. See also Paolucci, *Marx's Scientific Dialectics*, 76–77.
19. Horvath and Gibson, "Abstraction in Marx's Method," 15.
20. Peet, *Global Capitalism*, 58.
21. Marx, *Capital*, 1:286.
22. Peet, *Global Capitalism*, 59.
23. Marx, *Capital*, 1:290 (emphasis added).
24. Marx, *Capital*, 1:284.
25. Peet, *Global Capitalism*, 59.
26. Marx, *Capital*, 3:927–28.
27. Peet, "Materialism, Social Formation, and Socio-Spatial Relations," 150.

28. Marx, "Poverty of Philosophy," 219-20.
29. Marx, "Poverty of Philosophy," 220.
30. Paolucci, *Marx's Scientific Dialectics*, 90.
31. Peet, "Materialism, Social Formation, and Socio-Spatial Relations," 150.
32. Wood, *Empire of Capital*, 9.
33. Heinrich, *Introduction to the Three Volumes of Karl Marx's "Capital,"* 181.
34. Marx, *Capital*, 1:873.
35. Marx, *Capital*, 1:874.
36. Marx, *Capital*, 1:271.
37. Marx, *Capital*, 1:272.
38. Reiman, "Marxian Critique of Criminal Justice," 37.
39. Reiman, "Marxian Critique of Criminal Justice," 37.
40. Marx, *Capital*, 1:874.
41. Marx, *Capital*, 1:875.
42. Marx, *Capital*, 1:875.
43. Knox and Agnew, *Geography of the World Economy*, 149.
44. Jackson, *Sovereignty*, 30.
45. Knox and Agnew, *Geography of the World Economy*, 149-50.
46. Federici, *Caliban and the Witch*, 23.
47. Federici, *Caliban and the Witch*, 24.
48. Knox and Agnew, *Geography of the World Economy*, 154.
49. Knox and Agnew, *Geography of the World Economy*, 157.
50. Marx, *Capital*, 1:915-16.
51. Federici, *Caliban and the Witch*, 68.
52. Federici, *Caliban and the Witch*, 72.
53. Aitken, *Family Fantasies and Community Space*, 39.
54. Eviota, *Political Economy of Gender*, 12.
55. Eviota, *Political Economy of Gender*, 13.
56. Lea, *Crime and Modernity*, 59.
57. Saunders and Williams, "Constitution of the Home," 85.
58. Domosh and Seager, *Putting Women in Place*, 3-4.
59. Aitken, *Family Fantasies and Community Space*, 27.
60. Federici, *Caliban and the Witch*, 75.
61. Aitken, *Family Fantasies and Community Space*, 46.
62. See Glassman, "Primitive Accumulation, Accumulation by Dispossession"; and Neocleous, "War on Waste."
63. Federici, *Caliban and the Witch*, 12.
64. Fortunati, *Arcane of Reproduction*, 30.
65. Fortunati, *Arcane of Reproduction*, 30-31.

66. Domosh and Seager, *Putting Women in Place*, 5.
67. Aitken, *Family Fantasies and Community Space*, 46.
68. Federici, *Caliban and the Witch*, 75.
69. Federici, *Caliban and the Witch*, 72.
70. Marx, *Capital*, 1:896.
71. Marx, *Capital*, 1:897-98.
72. Foucault, *Discipline and Punish*, 82.
73. Wrightson, *English Society, 1580-1680*, 166.
74. Foucault, *Discipline and Punish*, 85.
75. Blomley, "Law, Property, and the Geography of Violence," 122.
76. Foucault, *Discipline and Punish*, 86.
77. Lea, *Crime and Modernity*, 37.
78. Lea, *Crime and Modernity*, 3.
79. Garland, *Culture of Control*, 118.
80. May, *Philosophy of Foucault*, 70.
81. Foucault, *Discipline and Punish*, 80.
82. Lea, *Crime and Modernity*, 29.
83. Foucault, *Discipline and Punish*, 80-81.
84. Foucault, *Discipline and Punish*, 82.
85. Lea, *Crime and Modernity*, 30-31.
86. Foucault, *Discipline and Punish*, 220-21.
87. Marx, *Capital*, 1:899.
88. Foucault, *Discipline and Punish*, 138.
89. Foucault, *Discipline and Punish*, 138.
90. Foucault, *Discipline and Punish*, 10.
91. Lea, *Crime and Modernity*, 30.
92. Dean, *Governmentality*, 128.
93. Lemke, *Biopolitics*, 37. See also Legg, "Foucault's Population Geographies"; and Philo, "Sex, Life, Death, Geography."
94. Foucault, *Security, Territory, Population*, 70-71.
95. Foucault, "Governmentality," 216-17.
96. Curtis, "Foucault on Governmentality and Population," 508.
97. Bailey, *Making Population Geography*, 118.
98. Curtis, "Foucault on Governmentality and Population," 508-9.
99. Curtis, "Foucault on Governmentality and Population," 529.
100. Dean, *Governmentality*, 43.
101. Dean, *Governmentality*, 120.
102. Marx, *Capital*, 1:273.
103. Baradat, *Political Ideologies*, 87.

104. A. Smith, *Wealth of Nations*, 278.
105. A. Smith, *Wealth of Nations*, xv.
106. Peet, *Theories of Development*, 25.
107. A. Smith, *Wealth of Nations*, 3, 4.
108. Peet, *Theories of Development*, 25.
109. A. Smith, *Wealth of Nations*, 45, 46.
110. Baradat, *Political Ideologies*, 87.
111. Baradat, *Political Ideologies*, 87.
112. N. Smith, *Endgame of Globalization*, 31.
113. Steger, *Globalism*, 9.
114. N. Smith, *Endgame of Globalization*, 32.
115. A. Smith, *Wealth of Nations*, 300.
116. David Ricardo (1772-1823), following both Adam Smith and Robert Torrens (1780-1864), further developed the concept of comparative advantage. The law of comparative advantage holds that a state will benefit by exporting a good that it produces at a lower relative cost than other states; conversely, a state will benefit by importing a good that it could produce at a higher relative cost. Consequently, all states within the international economy would—in principle—specialize only in the production of those commodities for which they held a comparative advantage.
117. Baradat, *Political Ideologies*, 87.
118. Baradat, *Political Ideologies*, 87.
119. A. Smith, *Wealth of Nations*, 399 (emphasis added to first quote).
120. A. Smith, *Wealth of Nations*, 399.
121. A. Smith, *Wealth of Nations*, 406.
122. A. Smith, *Wealth of Nations*, 408.
123. A. Smith, *Wealth of Nations*, 409.
124. A. Smith, *Wealth of Nations*, 410.
125. A. Smith, *Wealth of Nations*, 419, 430 (emphasis added).
126. Of course, depending on the historical period under question, women, children, and persons of color were not considered full participants in society and were thus excluded from these protections.
127. Harcourt, *Illusion of Free Markets*, 37.
128. Baradat, *Political Ideologies*, 87.
129. Steger, *Globalism*, 10.
130. Steger, *Globalism*, 8-9.
131. Harvey, *Brief History of Neoliberalism*, 2.
132. Peters, *Poststructuralism, Marxism, and Neoliberalism*, 19.
133. Harcourt, *Illusion of Free Markets*, 27.

134. Peters, *Poststructuralism, Marxism, and Neoliberalism*, 19.

135. Harcourt, *Illusion of Free Markets*, 34.

136. Steger, *Globalism*, 16.

137. Bacevich, *New American Militarism*, 70.

138. Bacevich, *New American Militarism*, 73-74.

139. Beckett and Sasson, *Politics of Injustice*, 45.

140. Jenkins, *Decade of Nightmares*, 134.

141. Bacevich, *New American Militarism*, 75.

142. Marx, *Capital*, 1:926.

143. Albritton, *Economics Transformed*.

144. Marx, *Capital*, 1:344.

145. D'Amato, *Meaning of Marxism*, 43.

146. Marx, *Capital*, 1:280.

3. THE MARKET LOGICS OF LETTING DIE

1. Albritton, *Economics Transformed*, 9.

2. Foucault, *Discipline and Punish*, 25.

3. Foucault, *Discipline and Punish*, 25-26.

4. Dean, *Governmentality*, 29. See also Barker, *Michel Foucault*, 58.

5. Foucault, *History of Sexuality*, 140-41.

6. Foucault, *Society Must Be Defended*, 249.

7. Foucault, *Society Must Be Defended*, 240.

8. Foucault, *History of Sexuality*, 138.

9. Nally, "Biopolitics of Food Provisioning," 38 (emphasis added).

10. Thurschwell, "Ethical Exception," 572.

11. Blencowe, "Foucault's and Arendt's 'Insider View' of Biopolitics," 122.

12. Sarat and Culbert, "Introduction," 6.

13. Agamben, *Homo Sacer*, 16.

14. Agamben, *Homo Sacer*, 1.

15. Agamben, *Homo Sacer*, 11.

16. Agamben, *Homo Sacer*, 83.

17. Rose, *Politics of Life Itself*, 57.

18. Agamben, *Homo Sacer*, 142.

19. S. Murray, "Thanatopolitics," 198.

20. Agamben, *Homo Sacer*, 115.

21. Beckett and Sasson, *Politics of Injustice*, 58-59.

22. Beckett and Sasson, *Politics of Injustice*, 45.

23. Jenkins, *Decade of Nightmares*, 134.

24. Reiman and Leighton, *Rich Get Richer and the Poor Get Prison*, 65.

25. Reiman and Leighton, *Rich Get Richer and the Poor Get Prison*, 86–92.
26. Li, "To Make Live or Let Die?," 66.
27. Davis, "Priority of Avoiding Harm," 301.
28. Steinbock, "Introduction."
29. Pollock, *Criminal Law*, 7.
30. Pollock, *Criminal Law*, 37.
31. Hale quoted in Pollock, *Criminal Law*, 214.
32. Pollock, *Criminal Law*, 219. According to Pollock, no state in the United States currently recognizes a marital exemption; however, some states have retained the concept for "lesser" sexual assault crimes (220).
33. See, e.g., Pollock, *Criminal Law*, 49.
34. There are "Good Samaritan" laws in the United States, but they are designed to protect citizens from civil liability if they stop and render assistance and are sued as a result of their actions. Pollock, *Criminal Law*, 51. This is very different from the legal obligation to render assistance. In other words, for the most part, it is not legally wrong to stand by idly while someone bleeds to death.
35. See, for example, Rachels, "Killing and Starving to Death"; Young, "What Is So Wrong with Killing People?"; Green, "Killing and Letting Die"; McMahan, "Killing, Letting Die, and Withdrawing Aid"; Davis, "Priority of Avoiding Harm"; Lichtenberg, "Moral Equivalence of Action and Omission"; Steinbock, "Introduction"; Cartwright, "Killing and Letting Die"; and Asscher, "Moral Distinction between Killing and Letting Die in Medical Cases."
36. Foot, "Killing and Letting Die."
37. Foot, "Killing and Letting Die," 283.
38. Foot, "Killing and Letting Die," 288.
39. Foot, "Killing and Letting Die," 286.
40. Quinn, "Actions, Intentions, and Consequences," 358.
41. Galvin, "Disturbing Notions of Chronic Illness and Individual Responsibility," 109.
42. Trammell, "Saving Life and Taking Life," 290.
43. Trammell, "Saving Life and Taking Life," 292.
44. Trammell, "Saving Life and Taking Life," 293.
45. Trammell, "Saving Life and Taking Life," 294.
46. Trammell, "Saving Life and Taking Life," 296.
47. Agamben, *Homo Sacer*, 107.
48. Matthaei, "Why Feminist, Marxist, and Anti-Racist Economists Should be Feminist-Marxist-Anti-Racist Economists," 36.
49. Peck, *Work-Place*.

50. Postone, *Time, Labor, and Social Domination*, 44.
51. Wright, "Dialectics of Still Life," 461.
52. Albritton, *Economics Transformed*, 26.
53. Marx, *Capital*, 1:138.
54. Marx, *Capital*, 2:156.
55. Albritton, *Economics Transformed*, 22.
56. Marx, *Capital*, 3:297.
57. Albritton, *Economics Transformed*, 26.
58. Clearly, many firms will diversify their market base and produce multiple products; that said, no corporation can always produce everything. Choices still have to be made.
59. Albritton, *Economics Transformed*, 24.
60. Marx, *Capital*, 1:274.
61. Marx, *Capital*, 1:188.
62. Marx, *Capital*, 1:200.
63. Marx, *Capital*, 1:203.
64. Marx, *Capital*, 1:248.
65. Marx, *Capital*, 1:250.
66. Marx, *Capital*, 1:251.
67. Harvey, *Companion to Marx's "Capital,"* 85.
68. Weeks, *Problem with Work*, 53 (emphasis added).
69. Weeks, *Problem with Work*, 6.
70. Weeks, *Problem with Work*, 8.
71. Weeks, *Problem with Work*, 10.
72. McDowell, *Gender, Identity & Place*, 75.
73. Piore, "Notes for a Theory of Labor Market Stratification," 2.
74. See, for example, Hartmann, "Unhappy Marriage of Marxism and Feminism"; Glenn, "Racial Ethnic Women's Labor"; and Matthaei, "Why Feminist, Marxist, and Anti-Racist Economists Should Be Feminist-Marxist-Anti-Racist Economists."
75. Marx, *Capital*, 1:1038 (emphasis added).
76. Marx, *Capital*, 1:1039 (emphasis added).
77. Marx, *Capital*, 1:1039.
78. Marx, *Capital*, 1:1039.
79. Marx, *Capital*, 1:1040.
80. Marx, *Capital*, 1:1041.
81. Marx, *Capital*, 1:1044.
82. Marx, *Capital*, 1:1044.
83. Marx, *Capital*, 1:1044.

84. Marx, *Capital*, 1:1046.
85. Marx, *Capital*, 1:270.
86. Marx, *Capital*, 1:271.
87. Marx, *Capital*, 1:293.
88. Marx, *Capital*, 1:302.
89. Marx, *Capital*, 1:279.
90. Harvey, *Companion to Marx's "Capital,"* 128.
91. Harvey, *Companion to Marx's "Capital,"* 129.
92. Marx, *Capital*, 1:274.
93. D'Amato, *Meaning of Marxism*, 56.
94. Marx, *Capital*, 1:711.
95. Marx, *Capital*, 1:375.
96. Marx, *Grundrisse*, 90.
97. Marx, *Capital*, 1:376.
98. Mies, *Patriarchy and Capital Accumulation*, 31.
99. Myslik, "Renegotiating the Social/Sexual Identities of Places," 159.
100. Domosh and Seager, *Putting Women in Place*, 4.
101. Mies, *Patriarchy and Capital Accumulation*, 31.
102. Marx, *Capital*, 1:376.
103. See, for example, Harris, "Marxist Conception of Violence," 197.
104. Matthaei, "Why Feminist, Marxist, and Anti-Racist Economists Should Be Feminist-Marxist-Anti-Racist Economists," 32.
105. Marx, *Capital*, 1:449.
106. Marx, *Capital*, 1:353.
107. Marx, *Capital*, 1:717.
108. Marx, *Capital*, 1:1067.
109. Marx, *Capital*, 1:342.
110. Marx, *Capital*, 1:717.
111. Marx, *Capital*, 1:718.
112. Marx, *Capital*, 1:719.
113. Marx, *Capital*, 1:718.
114. D'Amato, *Meaning of Marxism*, 55.
115. Marx, *Economic and Philosophic Manuscripts of 1844*, 20.
116. Marx, *Capital*, 1:348.
117. Li, "To Make Live or Let Die?," 67.
118. Marx, *Capital*, 1:275.
119. Albritton, *Let Them Eat Junk*, 37.
120. Harvey, *Companion to Marx's "Capital,"* 145–46.
121. Nadesan, *Governmentality, Biopower, and Everyday Life*, 41.

122. The event was sponsored by a variety of conservative groups, including the Family Research Council and the Heritage Foundation. See William Rivers Pitt, "Sick Bastards," *Truthout*, September 22, 2010, http://archive.truthout .org/sick-bastards63456.
123. Huckabee quoted in Pitt, "Sick Bastards."
124. Pitt, "Sick Bastards." Huckabee did suggest, later in his speech, that people are of equal worth. However, it is difficult to consider how this notion of worth will materialize when health care is to be rationed and only those who can afford health care will obtain coverage. It would appear that Huckabee's attitude is that people of the same income group are of equal worth and that there is not to be equality in care or compassion across class divisions.
125. Giroux, *Terror of Neoliberalism*, xv–xvi.
126. Giroux, *Terror of Neoliberalism*, xvii.
127. A. Smith, *Wealth of Nations*, 300.
128. Jared Bernstein, "The Tyranny of Zombie Economics in America," *The Atlantic*, September 6, 2011, http://www.theatlantic.com/business/archive/2011/09 /the-tyranny-of-zombie-economics-in-america/244588/.
129. Dieter Plehwe, interview by Tom Mills, in "Defending Capitalism: The Rise of Neoliberal Thought Collective (Part 2)," *New Left Project*, March 14, 2012, http://www.newleftproject.org.
130. Malloy, "Mortgage Market Reform," 79, 82.
131. Malloy, "Mortgage Market Reform," 83.
132. Joseph Stiglitz, "Of the 1%, by the 1%, for the 1%," *Vanity Fair*, May 2011, http:// www.vanityfair.com/society/features/2011/05/top-one-percent-201105.
133. See, for example, Blau, "Theories of the Welfare State"; O'Campo and Rojas-Smith, "Welfare Reform and Women's Health"; A. M. Smith, "Politicization of Marriage"; Hays, *Flat Broke with Children*; Reese, *Backlash against Welfare Mothers*; and Wacquant, *Punishing the Poor*.
134. Wacquant, *Punishing the Poor*, 85.
135. O'Campo and Rojas-Smith, "Welfare Reform and Women's Health," 422.
136. Wacquant, *Punishing the Poor*, 89.
137. A. M. Smith, "Politicization of Marriage," 312.
138. Reese, *Backlash against Welfare Mothers*, 4.
139. Wacquant, *Punishing the Poor*, 89.
140. Wacquant, *Punishing the Poor*, 91.
141. A. M. Smith, "Politicization of Marriage," 306.
142. Hays, *Flat Broke with Children*, 66.
143. Reese, *Backlash against Welfare Mothers*, 4.

144. Gilbert, "Identity, Space, and Politics." See also Roberts, *Killing the Black Body*, 219.

145. Reese, *Backlash against Welfare Mothers*, 18.

146. Reese, *Backlash against Welfare Mothers*, 22.

147. Reese, *Backlash against Welfare Mothers*, 26.

148. Wacquant, *Punishing the Poor*, 85.

149. Roberts, *Killing the Black Body*, 222.

150. O'Campo and Rojas-Smith, "Welfare Reform and Women's Health," 428.

151. Roberts, *Killing the Black Body*, 223.

152. Wacquant, *Punishing the Poor*, 85.

153. O'Campo and Rojas-Smith, "Welfare Reform and Women's Health," 428-29.

154. Wacquant, *Punishing the Poor*, 79.

155. Hays, *Flat Broke with Children*, 12-13.

156. Wacquant, *Punishing the Poor*, 80.

157. Wacquant, *Punishing the Poor*, 80.

158. Wacquant, *Punishing the Poor*, 85.

159. Reese, *Backlash against Welfare Mothers*, 18.

160. A. M. Smith, "Politicization of Marriage," 315.

161. Wacquant, *Punishing the Poor*, 88.

162. A. M. Smith, "Politicization of Marriage," 315.

163. Reese, *Backlash against Welfare Mothers*, 12.

164. Roberts, *Killing the Black Body*, 203.

165. O'Campo and Rojas-Smith, "Welfare Reform and Women's Health," 423.

166. Harvey, *Spaces of Hope*, 106.

167. Peck, *Work-Place*, 3.

168. Nadesan, *Governmentality*, 32.

4. THE VIOLENCE OF REDUNDANCY

1. Bauman, *Wasted Lives*, 11, 12.

2. Bauman, *Wasted Lives*, 12.

3. Cacho, *Social Death*, 19, 33 (emphasis added).

4. See Tyner, "Population Geography I."

5. Haller, *Outcasts from Evolution*; Livingston, *Geographical Tradition*.

6. Schiebinger, *Nature's Body*, 117.

7. Edelman, *Political Language*, 123.

8. Tucker, *Science and Politics of Racial Research*, 22. See also Miles, *Racism*.

9. Crookshank, *Mongol in Our Midst*.

10. Schiebinger, *Nature's Body*, 147.

11. Schiebinger, *Nature's Body*, 156.

12. Schiebinger, *Nature's Body*, 134–36.
13. Paul, *Controlling Human Heredity*, 40.
14. Castree, *Nature*, 53.
15. Paul, *Controlling Human Heredity*, 41.
16. Paul, *Controlling Human Heredity*, 31.
17. Paul, *Controlling Human Heredity*, 41. See also Stepan, *"Hour of Eugenics,"* 24.
18. Stepan, *"Hour of Eugenics,"* 26. See also Kevles, *In the Name of Eugenics*; Trent, *Inventing the Feeble Mind*; and Kluchin, *Fit to Be Tied*.
19. T. Koch, "Eugenics and the Genetic Challenge, Again," 197.
20. Kevles, *In the Name of Eugenics*, 78. Lewis Terman, a professor at Stanford University, would later modify the test, which became known as the Stanford-Binet test.
21. Goddard took the term "moron" from the Greek word meaning "dull" or "stupid." See Kevles, *In the Name of Eugenics*, 78.
22. Paul, *Controlling Human Heredity*, 59; Trent, *Inventing the Feeble Mind*, 157–60.
23. Paul, *Controlling Human Heredity*, 42–43.
24. Ekland-Olson, *Who Lives, Who Dies, Who Decides*, 30.
25. Davenport quoted in Paul, *Controlling Human Heredity*, 44.
26. Kevles, *In the Name of Eugenics*, 78.
27. Paul, *Controlling Human Heredity*, 49.
28. Ekland-Olson, *Who Lives, Who Dies, Who Decides*, 21.
29. Ekland-Olson, *Who Lives, Who Dies, Who Decides*, 18.
30. Commons, *Races and Immigrants in America*, 70.
31. Hummel, *Emancipating Slaves, Enslaving Free Men*, 298.
32. Winston, "Relation of the Whites to the Negroes," 108.
33. Belin, "Southern View of Slavery," 517.
34. Belin, "Southern View of Slavery," 519.
35. See, for example, Mencke, *Mulattoes and Race Mixture*; Hodes, *White Women, Black Men*; and Tyner and Houston, "Controlling Bodies."
36. Ekland-Olson, *Who Lives, Who Dies, Who Decides*, 21.
37. Dubow, *Scientific Racism in Modern South Africa*, 101.
38. Baker, *Race Improvement or Eugenics*.
39. Burleigh, *Death and Deliverance*; Kühl, *Nazi Connection*.
40. Paul, *Controlling Human Heredity*, 10–11.
41. Popenoe and Johnson, *Applied Eugenics*, 241, 260.
42. Ross quoted in Tucker, *Science and Politics of Racial Research*, 60.
43. Grant, *Passing of the Great Race*, 60.
44. Popenoe and Johnson, *Applied Eugenics*, 147.
45. Popenoe and Johnson, *Applied Eugenics*, 218.

46. Popenoe and Johnson, *Applied Eugenics*, 294–96.

47. Grant, *Passing of the Great Race*, 60.

48. Grant, *Passing of the Great Race*, 53.

49. Davenport quoted in Paul, *Controlling Human Heredity*, 78.

50. Ekland-Olson, *Who Lives, Who Dies, Who Decides*, 42.

51. Ekland-Olson, *Who Lives, Who Dies, Who Decides*, 36–37 (Pennypacker quote, 37).

52. Paul, *Controlling Human Heredity*, 81.

53. Paul, *Controlling Human Heredity*, 82.

54. See, for example, Kevles, *In the Name of Eugenics*, 110–12; and Kluchin, *Fit to Be Tied*, 15–16.

55. Laughlin quoted in Kevles, *In the Name of Eugenics*, 110.

56. Whitehead quoted in Kevles, *In the Name of Eugenics*, 111.

57. Kevles, *In the Name of Eugenics*, 111.

58. Holmes quoted in Paul, *Controlling Human Heredity*, 83.

59. T. Koch, *Thieves of Virtue*, 42.

60. T. Koch, "Care, Compassion, or Cost," 132.

61. T. Koch, *Thieves of Virtue*, 111.

62. Larson, *Sex, Race, and Science*, 28.

63. Lemke, "Genetic Testing, Eugenics and Risk"; L. Koch, "Meaning of Eugenics"; Ekberg, "Old Eugenics and the New Genetics Compared"; Raz, "Eugenic Utopias/Dystopias, Reprogenetics, and Community Genetics."

64. Buxton, "Doctor's Responsibility in Population Control," 112.

65. Buxton, "Doctor's Responsibility in Population Control," 113.

66. Buxton, "Doctor's Responsibility in Population Control," 114.

67. Buxton, "Doctor's Responsibility in Population Control," 115.

68. Buxton, "Doctor's Responsibility in Population Control," 115.

69. Buxton, "Doctor's Responsibility in Population Control," 116 (emphasis in original).

70. T. Koch, *Thieves of Virtue*, 67.

71. Buxton, "Doctor's Responsibility in Population Control," 116.

72. Kluchin, *Fit to Be Tied*.

73. Kluchin, *Fit to Be Tied*, 3.

74. Harvey, *Brief History of Neoliberalism*, 2.

75. T. Koch, "Care, Compassion, or Cost," 131.

76. Dranove, *What's Your Life Worth?*

77. Guthman, *Weighing In*, 18.

78. Dranove, *What's Your Life Worth?*, 81.

79. T. Koch, "Care, Compassion, or Cost," 130.

80. Addonizio quoted in Elizabeth Cohen, "Disabled Baby Denied Heart Transplant," *CNN News*, November 30, 2013, http://www.cnn.com/2013/11/30/health/disabled-transplants/index.html.
81. Magnus cited in Cohen, "Disabled Baby Denied Heart Transplant."
82. T. Koch, "Care, Compassion, or Cost," 130.
83. Steger and Roy, *Neoliberalism*, 12.
84. Dranove, *What's Your Life Worth?*, 85.
85. Dranove, *What's Your Life Worth?*, 98.
86. T. Koch, "Life Quality vs the 'Quality of Life,'" 419.
87. Williams, "Value of QALYs," 3.
88. Williams, "Value of QALYs," 3.
89. Williams, "Value of QALYs," 3.
90. Williams, "Value of QALYs," 3.
91. T. Koch, "Life Quality vs the 'Quality of Life,'" 422.
92. Dranove, *What's Your Life Worth?*, 99.
93. T. Koch, "Life Quality vs the 'Quality of Life,'" 422.
94. T. Koch, *Thieves of Virtue*, 65.
95. Rock, "Discounted Lives?," 414.
96. Dranove, *What's Your Life Worth?*, 100.
97. Dranove, *What's Your Life Worth?*, 100–101.
98. Dranove, *What's Your Life Worth?*, 101. Prices listed are in 1998 dollars and are used for illustrative purposes only.
99. T. Koch, *Thieves of Virtue*, 66.
100. "HMO Whistleblower Dr. Linda Peeno on the Subordination of Healthcare to a For-Profit System," Democracy Now!, June 21, 2007, http://www.democracynow.org/2007/6/21/hmo_whistleblower_dr_linda_peeno_on.
101. Peeno quoted in "What Is the Value of a Voice?" *U.S. News and World Report*, March 9, 1998, http://www.lexisnexis.com/hottopics/Inacademic/?csi+8065&sr=headline(What%20is%20the%20value%20of%20a%20voice%3f)+and+date=+1998.
102. See, for example, Tyner, *Genocide and the Geographical Imagination*.
103. Harris, "QALYfying the Value of Life"; Cubbon, "Principle of QALY Maximisation"; Harris, "Unprincipled QALYs"; Anand and Hanson, "DALYs"; Gold, Stevenson, and Fryback, "HALYs and QALYs and DALYs, Oh My"; Brock, "Cost-Effectiveness and Disability Discrimination."
104. Harris, "QALYfying the Value," 119.
105. Dranove, *What's Your Life Worth?*, 98.
106. Harris, "QALYfying the Value," 119.
107. Harris, "QALYfying the Value," 118.

108. Dranove, *What's Your Life Worth?*, 103.
109. Glover, *Choosing Children*, 30.
110. Longmore, "Medical Decision Making and People with Disabilities," 84.
111. Levy, Ashman, and Dror, "To Be or Not to Be," 416.
112. Levy, Ashman, and Dror, "To Be or Not to Be," 417.
113. Bogardus, "Measuring Social Distances"; Tringo, "Hierarchy of Preference toward Disability Groups"; Grand, Bernier, and Strohmer, "Attitudes toward Disabled Persons as a Function of Social Context."
114. Bogardus, "Measuring Social Distances," 299.
115. Dear et al., "Seeing People Differently," 465–66.
116. Dear et al., "Seeing People Differently," 466.
117. Rose, *Politics of Life Itself*, 57.
118. Williams, "Value of QALYs," 5.
119. The following is based on Tyner, *Space, Place, and Violence*, 155–56.
120. Sen, *Identity and Violence*.
121. Sen, *Identity and Violence*, 23–24.
122. Sen, *Identity and Violence*, 11.
123. Glover, *Choosing Children*, 30.
124. Sen, *Identity and Violence*, 7.
125. Longmore, "Medical Decision Making and People with Disabilities"; Dear et al., "Seeing People Differently"; Pain et al., *Introducing Social Geographies*; Hansen and Philo, "Normality of Doing Things Differently."
126. Overall, "Old Age and Ageism, Impairment and Ableism," 127.
127. Longmore, "Medical Decision Making and People with Disabilities," 82.
128. Snyder and Mitchell, *Cultural Locations of Disability*, 18.
129. Snyder and Mitchell, *Cultural Locations of Disability*, 12.
130. Snyder and Mitchell, *Cultural Locations of Disability*, 23.
131. Snyder and Mitchell, *Cultural Locations of Disability*, 5.
132. Snyder and Mitchell, *Cultural Locations of Disability*, 18.
133. Snyder and Mitchell, *Cultural Locations of Disability*, 76.
134. Snyder and Mitchell, *Cultural Locations of Disability*, 19.
135. Gullette, *Agewise*, 24.
136. Overall, "Old Age and Ageism," 131.
137. Overall, "Old Age and Ageism," 129.
138. Overall, "Old Age and Ageism," 132.
139. Gullette, *Agewise*, 49.
140. Kruse, *How Dwarfs Experience the World*, 1.
141. Kruse, *How Dwarfs Experience the World*, 5–6 (emphasis added).
142. Porter, *Madness*, 90.

143. Porter, *Madness*, 92.
144. Snyder and Mitchell, *Cultural Locations of Disability*, 71.
145. Dear and Wolch, *Landscapes of Despair*, 34.
146. Dear and Wolch, *Landscapes of Despair*, 33.
147. Rothman, *Discovery of the Asylum*, 164.
148. Dear and Wolch, *Landscapes of Despair*, 30.
149. Rothman, *Discovery of the Asylum*, 164.
150. As quoted in Katz, *Poverty and Policy in American History*, 160.
151. Scheerenberger, *History of Mental Retardation*, 116.
152. Osborne quoted in Scheerenberger, *History of Mental Retardation*, 116.
153. Snyder and Mitchell, *Cultural Locations of Disability*, 84.
154. Longmore, "Medical Decision Making and People with Disabilities," 84.
155. Overall, "Old Age and Ageism," 131.
156. Snyder and Mitchell, *Cultural Locations of Disability*, 81.
157. W. Smith, *Culture of Death*, xiii.
158. Longmore, "Medical Decision Making and People with Disabilities," 84.
159. Schweik, *Ugly Laws*, 2.
160. Schweik, *Ugly Laws*, 5.
161. Glover, *Choosing Children*, 1.
162. Aksoy, "Antenatal Screening." The following discussion of antenatal techniques is derived from this source.
163. Aksoy, "Antenatal Screening."
164. Savulescu, "Deaf Lesbians," 772.
165. Savulescu, "Deaf Lesbians," 772.
166. Raz, "Eugenic Utopias/Dystopias, Reprogenetics, and Community Genetics," 605.
167. A. Murray and Clarke, "Ethics of Population Screening," 449.
168. Aksoy, "Antenatal Screening."
169. Glover, *Choosing Children*, 33.
170. Glover, *Choosing Children*, 6.
171. Aksoy, "Antenatal Screening."
172. Savulescu, "Deaf Lesbians," 773.
173. Glover, *Choosing Children*, 33.
174. Glover, *Choosing Children*, 5. See also Spriggs, "Lesbian Couple Create a Child Who Is Deaf"; and Stainton, "Identity, Difference and the Ethical Politics of Prenatal Testing."
175. Glover, *Choosing Children*, 5.
176. Spriggs, "Lesbian Couple Create a Child Who Is Deaf," 283.
177. Charo quoted in Glover, *Choosing Children*, 5.

178. Connor quoted in Spriggs, "Lesbian Couple Create a Child Who Is Deaf," 283.

179. Moyer et al., "Expanding Newborn Screening," 34.

180. Fletcher, *Humanhood*, 144.

181. Singer, *Practical Ethics*, 186.

182. Glover, *Causing Death*, 159.

183. Glover, *Causing Death*, 162.

184. W. Smith, *Culture of Death*, 63.

185. Savulescu, "Deaf Lesbians," 772.

186. Savulescu, "Deaf Lesbians," 773.

187. Lemke, "Genetic Testing, Eugenics and Risk," 287.

188. McMahan, *Ethics of Killing*, vii.

189. Admiraal, "Euthanasia and Assisted Suicide," 207.

190. Admiraal, "Euthanasia and Assisted Suicide," 208–9.

191. Admiraal, "Euthanasia and Assisted Suicide," 210.

192. McMahan, *Ethics of Killing*, 457.

193. Overall, "Old Age and Ageism," 131.

194. Overall, "Old Age and Ageism," 132.

195. Overall, "Old Age and Ageism," 133.

196. Golden and Zoanni, "Killing Us Softly," 18.

197. Overall, "Old Age and Ageism," 133.

198. Galvin, "Disturbing Notions of Chronic Illness and Individual Responsibility," 109.

199. There is an extensive literature on this topic. See, for example, Hardwig, "Is There a Duty to Die?"; Corlett, "Is There a Moral Duty to Die?"; Gunderson, "Being a Burden"; George, Finlay, and Jeffrey, "Legalised Euthanasia Will Violate the Rights of Vulnerable Patients"; Hardwig, "Going to Meet Death"; Cholbi, "Duty to Die and the Burdensomeness of Living"; Enck, "Physician-Assisted Dying"; Golden and Zoanni, "Killing Us Softly"; and Dore, "Physician-Assisted Suicide."

200. Gullette, *Agewise*, 50.

201. Gullette, *Agewise*, 51.

202. W. Smith, *Culture of Death*, 98.

203. Golden and Zoanni, "Killing Us Softly," 17.

204. Alpers and Lo, "Physician-Assisted Suicide in Oregon."

205. Dore, "Physician-Assisted Suicide," 2.

206. Dore, "Physician-Assisted Suicide," 2.

207. Dranove, *What's Your Life Worth?*, 120–21.

208. Dranove, *What's Your Life Worth?*, 121–22.

209. Dranove, *What's Your Life Worth?*, 128.
210. Dranove, *What's Your Life Worth?*, 135.
211. Golden and Zoanni, "Killing Us Softly," 18.
212. The vignette that follows is derived from multiple sources, including Physicians for Compassionate Care Education Foundation (PCCEF), "Oregon Rationing Cancer Treatment but Offering Assisted Suicide to Cancer Patients Paying to Die But Not to Live," Physicians for Compassionate Care Education Foundation (PCCEF), accessed April 17, 2012, http://www.pccef.org/articles/art67htm; and Compassion & Choices, "Myth vs. Fact: Barbara Wagner Was Not Harmed by Oregon's Death with Dignity Act," accessed April 17, 2012, http://www.compassionandchoices.org.
213. PCCEF, "Oregon Rationing Cancer Treatment."
214. Barbara Coombs Lee, "Sensationalizing a Sad Case Cheats the Public of Sound Debate," *Oregon Live* (blog), accessed April 17, 2012, http://www.blog.oregonlive.com/opinion_impact.
215. Compassion & Choices, "Myth vs. Fact."
216. Hardwig, "Is There a Duty to Die?," 35.
217. Canetto and Hollenshead, "Older Women and Mercy Killing"; Canetto and Hollenshead, "Men's Mercy Killing of Women"; and Canetto and Hollenshead, "Gender and Physician-Assisted Suicide."
218. Canetto and Hollenshead, "Older Women and Mercy Killing," 91.
219. Otlowski, "Mercy Killing Cases in the Australian Criminal Justice System"; Humphrey and Wickett, *Right to Die.*
220. Golden and Zoanni, "Killing Us Softly," 16.
221. Hardwig, "Going to Meet Death," 38.
222. Hardwig, "Going to Meet Death," 38–39.
223. George, Finlay, and Jeffrey, "Legalised Euthanasia," 684.
224. Neilson, "Ageing, Experience, Biopolitics," 45.
225. Golden and Zoanni, "Killing Us Softly," 18. See also Coleman, "Assisted Suicide Laws Create Discriminatory Double Standard."
226. Hardwig, "Going to Meet Death," 39.
227. Lee, "Sensationalizing a Sad Case." Note that in Lee's statement about patients acting "against their own self-interest," not choosing suicide—in other words, living—becomes a selfish act.
228. Coombs Lee, "Sensationalizing a Sad Case."
229. See, for example, Glannon, "Identity, Prudential Concern, and Extended Lives"; and Horrobin, "Value of Life and the Value of Life Extension."
230. Hardwig, "Going to Meet Death," 38.
231. Hardwig, "Going to Meet Death," 44.

232. Hardwig, "Going to Meet Death," 42.
233. Overall, "Old Age and Ageism," 131.
234. Golden and Zoanni, "Killing Us Softly," 17.
235. Levy, Ashman, and Dror, "To Be or Not to Be," 417.
236. Numerous studies have documented the prevalence of negative stereotypes of the elderly within a variety of settings. See, for example, Miller et al., "Stereotypes of the Elderly in Magazine Advertisements"; Robinson et al., "Portrayal of Older Characters in Disney Animated Films"; and Fealy et al., "Constructing Ageing and Age Identities."
237. George et al., "Legalised Euthanasia," 685.
238. Hardwig, "Is There a Duty to Die?," 34.
239. Hardwig, "Is There a Duty to Die?," 35 (emphasis added).
240. Hardwig, "Is There a Duty to Die?," 36.
241. George, Finlay, and Jeffrey, "Legalised Euthanasia," 684.
242. Dore, "Physician-Assisted Suicide," 1.
243. Dore, "Physician-Assisted Suicide," 2.
244. Canetto and Hollenshead, "Older Women," 93. See also Easteal, "Homicide-Suicides between Adult Sexual Intimates."
245. Gunderson, "Being a Burden," 37.
246. Hardwig, "Is There a Duty to Die?," 36.
247. Hardwig, "Is There a Duty to Die?," 39.
248. Hardwig, "Is There a Duty to Die?," 40.
249. Hardwig, "Is There a Duty to Die?," 39.
250. Glannon, "Identity, Prudential Concern, and Extended Lives," 282.
251. Hardwig, "Going to Meet Death," 38.
252. Hardwig, "Is There a Duty to Die?," 39.
253. Coleman, "Assisted Suicide Laws Create Discriminatory Double Standard," 48.
254. Harris, "QALYfying the Value," 121.
255. Koch, Thieves of Virtue, 13.
256. Koch, Thieves of Virtue, 19.

5. THE REALITY OF VIOLENCE

1. Springer, "Violence Sits in Places?," 95.
2. Butler, Precarious Life; Žižek, Violence.
3. Arendt, On Violence.
4. Tyner and Inwood, "Violence as Fetish."
5. This account is based on Sam Dickman, David Himmelstein, Danny McCormick, and Steffie Woolhandler, "Opting Out of Medicaid Expansion: The

Health and Financial Impacts," *Health Affairs* (blog), January 30, 2014, http://healthaffairs.org/blog.

6. This section is based on Tyner and Inwood, "Violence as Fetish."

7. Oksala, *Foucault, Politics, and Violence*, 34.

8. Oksala, *Foucault, Politics, and Violence*, 16.

9. Oksala, *Foucault, Politics, and Violence*, 19.

10. Foucault, *Discipline and Punish*, 194.

11. Rees, *Algebra of Revolution*, 99.

12. The following is based on Holly Yan, "Body Found in Hospital Stairwell: San Francisco Sheriff Details What Went Wrong," *CNN.com*, November 7, 2013, http://www.cnn.com/2013/11/07/us/California-body-in-stairwell; and "Orderly Reported a Woman in Hospital Stairwell Week before Body Found," *ABCNews.com*, accessed December 11, 2013, http://abcnews.go.com/US/orderly-reported-woman-hospital-stairwell-week-body-found.

13. Cartwright, "Killing and Letting Die."

14. Green, "Killing and Letting Die," 196.

15. Young, *Justice*, 54.

16. Albritton, *Let Them Eat Junk*, 147.

17. Mitchell, Marston, and Katz, "Life's Work," 418.

18. Marx, *Capital*, 1:381.

19. Galvin, "Disturbing Notions of Chronic Illness and Individual Responsibility," 117.

20. Buchanan et al., *From Chance to Choice*, 20. See also D. Smith, *Geography and Social Justice*; and Barry, *Why Social Justice Matters*.

21. D. Smith, *Geography and Social Justice*, 2.

22. See, for example, Gilbert, "Identity, Space, and Politics."

23. Wikler, "Personal and Social Responsibility for Health," 49.

24. Wikler, "Personal and Social Responsibility for Health," 50.

25. See, for example, Leitner, Peck, and Sheppard, *Contesting Neoliberalism*.

26. Gilbert, "Place, Space, and Agency," 152.

27. Mitchell and Heynen, "Geography of Survival and the Right to the City," 613.

28. Ruppert, "Population Objects," 218.

29. Zinn, *Just War*, 54.

30. Zinn, *Just War*, 55.

31. Calderwood, "Toward a Professional Community for Social Justice," 305.

BIBLIOGRAPHY

Admiraal, Pieter. "Euthanasia and Assisted Suicide." In *Birth to Death: Science and Bioethics*, edited by David C. Thomasma and Thomasine Kushner, 207-17. Cambridge: Cambridge University Press, 1996.

Agamben, Giorgio. *Homo Sacer: Sovereign Power and Bare Life*. Translated by Daniel Heller-Roazen. Stanford CA: Stanford University Press, 1998.

Aitken, Stuart C. *Family Fantasies and Community Space*. New Brunswick NJ: Rutgers University Press, 1998.

Aksoy, Sahin. "Antenatal Screening and Its Possible Meaning from Unborn Baby's Perspective." *BMC Medical Ethics* 2, no. 3 (2001). http://www.biomedcentral.com/1472-6939/2/3.

Albritton, Robert. *Economics Transformed: Discovering the Brilliance of Marx*. Ann Arbor MI: Pluto, 2007.

———. *Let Them Eat Junk: How Capitalism Creates Hunger and Obesity*. New York: Pluto, 2009.

Alpers, Ann, and Bernard Lo. "Physician-Assisted Suicide in Oregon: A Bold Experiment." *Journal of the American Medical Association* 274, no. 6 (1995): 483-87.

Althusser, Louis, and Étienne Balibar. *Reading "Capital."* New ed. London: Verso, 1997.

Alvarez, Alex, and Ronet Bachman. *Violence: The Enduring Problem*. Los Angeles: SAGE, 2008.

Anand, Sudhir, and Kara Hanson. "DALYs: Efficiency versus Equity." *World Development* 26, no. 2 (1998): 307-10.

Arendt, Hannah. *On Violence*. New York: Harvest Books, 1970.

Asscher, Joachim. "The Moral Distinction between Killing and Letting Die in Medical Cases." *Bioethics* 22, no. 5 (2008): 278–85.

Audi, Robert. "On the Meaning and Justification of Violence." In *Violence*, edited by Jerome Shaffer, 45–99. New York: David McKay, 1971.

Bacevich, Andrew J. *The New American Militarism: How Americans Are Seduced by War.* Oxford: Oxford University Press, 2005.

Bäck, Allan. "Thinking Clearly about Violence." *Philosophical Studies* 117, no. 1–2 (2004): 219–30.

Bailey, Adrian. *Making Population Geography.* London: Hodder Arnold, 2005.

Baker, L. H. M. *Race Improvement or Eugenics.* New York: n.p., 1912.

Banaji, Jairus. *Theory as History: Essays on Modes of Production and Exploitation.* Chicago: Haymarket Books, 2011.

Baradat, Leon P. *Political Ideologies: Their Origins and Impact.* 7th ed. Upper Saddle River NJ: Prentice Hall, 2000.

Barker, Philip. *Michel Foucault: An Introduction.* Edinburgh: Edinburgh University Press, 1998.

Barry, Brian. *Why Social Justice Matters.* Malden MA: Polity, 2005.

Bauman, Zygmunt. *Wasted Lives: Modernity and Its Outcasts.* Malden MA: Polity, 2004.

Beckett, Katherine, and Theodore Sasson. *The Politics of Injustice: Crime and Punishment in America.* 2nd ed. Thousand Oaks CA: SAGE, 2004.

Belin, H. E. "A Southern View of Slavery." *American Journal of Sociology* 13, no. 4 (1908): 513–522.

Betz, Joseph. "Violence: Garver's Definition and a Deweyan Correction." *Ethics* 87, no. 4 (1977): 339–51.

Blau, Joel. "Theories of the Welfare State." *Social Service Review* 63, no. 1 (1989): 26–38.

Blencowe, Claire. "Foucault's and Arendt's 'Insider View' of Biopolitics: A Critique of Agamben." *History of the Human Sciences* 23, no. 5 (2010): 113–30.

Blomley, Nicholas. "Law, Property, and the Geography of Violence: The Frontier, the Survey, and the Grid." *Annals of the Association of American Geographers* 93, no. 1 (2003): 121–41.

Bogardus, Emory S. "Measuring Social Distances." *Journal of Applied Sociology* 9 (1925): 299–308.

Brock, Dan W. "Cost-Effectiveness and Disability Discrimination." *Economics and Philosophy* 25, no. 1 (2009): 27–47.

Buchanan, Allen, Dan W. Brock, Norman Daniels, and Daniel Wikler. *From Chance to Choice: Genetics & Justice.* Cambridge: Cambridge University Press, 2000.

Bufacchi, Vittorio. "Two Concepts of Violence." *Political Studies Review* 3, no. 2 (2005): 193–204.

Burleigh, Michael. *Death and Deliverance: "Euthanasia" in Germany 1900–1995.* Cambridge: Cambridge University Press, 1994.

Butler, Judith. *Precarious Life: The Powers of Mourning and Violence.* New York: Verso, 2006.

Buxton, C. Lee. "The Doctor's Responsibility in Population Control." *Northwest Medicine* 65, no. 2 (1966): 112–16.

Cacho, Lisa Marie. *Social Death: Racialized Rightlessness and the Criminalization of the Unprotected.* New York: New York University Press, 2012.

Calderwood, Patricia E. "Toward a Professional Community for Social Justice." *Journal of Transformative Education* 1, no. 4 (2003): 301–20.

Canetto, Silvia Sara, and Janet D. Hollenshead. "Gender and Physician-Assisted Suicide: An Analysis of the Kevorkian Cases, 1990–1997." *Omega* 40, no. 1 (2000): 165–208.

———. "Men's Mercy Killing of Women: Mercy for Whom? Choice for Whom?" *Omega* 45, no. 3 (2002): 291–96.

———. "Older Women and Mercy Killing." *Omega* 42, no. 1 (2001): 83–99.

Cartwright, Will. "Killing and Letting Die: A Defensible Distinction." *British Medical Bulletin* 52, no. 2 (1996): 354–61.

Castree, Noel. *Nature.* New York: Routledge, 2005.

Cholbi, Michael. "The Duty to Die and the Burdensomeness of Living." *Bioethics* 24, no. 8 (2010): 412–20.

Coady, C. A. J. "The Idea of Violence." *Journal of Applied Philosophy* 3, no. 1 (1986): 3–19.

Coleman, Diane. "Assisted Suicide Laws Create Discriminatory Double Standard for Who Gets Suicide Prevention and Who Gets Suicide Assistance: Not Dead Yet Responds to Autonomy, Inc." *Disability and Health Journal* 3, no. 1 (2010): 39–50.

Commons, John R. *Races and Immigrants in America.* New York: Macmillan, 1907.

Corlett, J. Angelo. "Is There a Moral Duty to Die?" *Health Care Analysis* 9, no. 1 (2001): 41–63.

Crookshank, F. G. *The Mongol in Our Midst: A Study of Man and His Three Faces.* New York: E. P. Dutton, 1924.

Cubbon, John. "The Principle of QALY Maximisation as the Basis for Allocating Health Care Resources." *Journal of Medical Ethics* 17, no. 4 (1991): 181–84.

Curle, James H. *Our Testing Time: Will the White Race Win Through?* New York: George H. Doran, 1926.

Curtis, Bruce. "Foucault on Governmentality and Population: The Impossible Discovery." *Canadian Journal of Sociology* 27, no. 4 (2002): 505–33.

D'Amato, Paul. *The Meaning of Marxism*. Chicago: Haymarket Books, 2006.

Davis, N. Ann. "The Priority of Avoiding Harm." In *Killing and Letting Die*, edited by Bonnie Steinbock and Alastair Norcross, 298–354. 2nd ed. New York: Fordham University Press, 1994.

Dean, Mitchell. *Governmentality: Power and Rule in Modern Society*. 2nd ed. Thousand Oaks CA: SAGE, 2010.

Dear, Michael, Robert Wilton, Sharon L. Gaber, and Lois Takahashi. "Seeing People Differently: The Sociospatial Construction of Disability." *Environment and Planning D: Society and Space* 15, no. 4 (1997): 455–80.

Dear, Michael, and Jennifer Wolch. *Landscapes of Despair: From Deinstitutionalization to Homelessness*. Princeton NJ: Princeton University Press, 1987.

De Haan, Willem. "Violence as an Essentially Contested Concept." In *Violence in Europe*, edited by S. Body-Gendrot and P. Spierenburg, 27–40. New York: Springer, 2008.

Domosh, Mona, and Joni Seager. *Putting Women in Place: Feminist Geographers Make Sense of the World*. New York: Guilford, 2001.

Dore, Margaret K. "Physician-Assisted Suicide: A Recipe for Elder Abuse and the Illusion of Personal Choice." *Vermont Bar Journal* 27, no. 1 (2011): 1–4.

Dorn, Stan. *Uninsured and Dying Because of It: Updating the Institute of Medicine Analysis on the Impact of Uninsurance on Mortality*. Washington DC: Urban Institute, 2008.

Dranove, David. *What's Your Life Worth? Health Care Rationing . . . Who Lives? Who Dies? And Who Decides?* Upper Saddle River NJ: Prentice Hall, 2003.

Dubow, Saul. *Scientific Racism in Modern South Africa*. Cambridge: Cambridge University Press, 1995.

Easteal, P. "Homicide-Suicides between Adult Sexual Intimates: An Australian Study." *Suicide and Life-Threatening Behavior* 24, no. 2 (1994): 140–51.

Edelman, Murray. *Political Language: Words That Succeed and Policies That Fail*. New York: Academic Press, 1977.

Ekberg, Merryn. "The Old Eugenics and the New Genetics Compared." *Social History of Medicine* 20, no. 3 (2007): 581–93.

Ekland-Olson, Sheldon. *Who Lives, Who Dies, Who Decides: Abortion, Neonatal Care, Assisted Dying, and Capital Punishment*. New York: Routledge, 2012.

Enck, Robert E. "Physician-Assisted Dying." *American Journal of Hospice & Palliative Medicine* 27, no. 7 (2010): 441–43.

Eviota, Elizabeth U. *The Political Economy of Gender: Women and the Sexual Division of Labor in the Philippines*. London: Zed Books, 1992.

Families USA. *Dying for Coverage: The Deadly Consequences of Being Uninsured*. Washington DC: Families USA, 2012.

Fealy, Gerard, Martin McNamara, Margaret P. Treacy, and Imogen Lyons. "Constructing Ageing and Age Identities: A Case Study of Newspaper Discourses." *Ageing & Society* 32, no. 1 (2012): 85–102.

Federici, Silvia. *Caliban and the Witch: Women, the Body and Primitive Accumulation.* Brooklyn NY: Autonomedia, 2004.

Fletcher, Joseph. *Humanhood: Essays in Medical Ethics.* Buffalo NY: Prometheus Books, 1979.

Foot, Philippa. "Killing and Letting Die." In *Killing and Letting Die,* edited by Bonnie Steinbock and Alastair Norcross, 280–89. 2nd ed. New York: Fordham University Press, 1994.

Fortunati, Leopoldina. *The Arcane of Reproduction: Housework, Prostitution, Labor and Capital.* Brooklyn NY: Autonomedia, 1995.

Foucault, Michel. *The Birth of Biopolitics: Lectures at the Collège de France, 1978–1979.* New York: Picador, 2008.

——. *Discipline and Punish: The Birth of the Prison.* New York: Vintage, 1977.

——. "Governmentality." In *Power,* volume 3 of *The Essential Works of Foucault, 1954-1984,* edited by James D. Faubion, 201–22. New York: New Press, 2001.

——. *The History of Sexuality: An Introduction.* New York: Vintage, 1990.

——. *Security, Territory, Population: Lectures at the Collège de France, 1977-1978.* New York: Picador, 2007.

——. *Society Must Be Defended: Lectures at the Collège de France, 1975-1976.* Edited by Mauro Bertani and Alessandro Fontana. Translated by David Macey. New York: Picador, 2003.

Galtung, Johan. "Violence, Peace, and Peace Research." *Journal of Peace Research* 6, no. 3 (1969): 167–91.

Galtung, Johan, and T. Höivik. "Structural and Direct Violence: A Note on Operationalization." *Journal of Peace Research* 8, no. 1 (1971): 73–76.

Galvin, Rose. "Disturbing Notions of Chronic Illness and Individual Responsibility: Towards a Genealogy of Morals." *Health: An Interdisciplinary Journal for the Social Study of Health, Illness and Medicine* 6, no. 2 (2002): 107–37.

Garland, David. *The Culture of Control: Crime and Social Order in Contemporary Society.* Chicago: University of Chicago Press, 2012.

Garver, Newton. "What Violence Is." *The Nation,* June 24, 1968, 817–22.

George, R. J. D., I. G. Finlay, and David Jeffrey. "Legalised Euthanasia Will Violate the Rights of Vulnerable Patients." *British Medical Journal* 331, no. 7518 (2005): 684–85.

Gilbert, Melissa R. "Identity, Space, and Politics: A Critique of the Poverty Debates." In *Thresholds in Feminist Geography: Difference, Methodology, Representation,* edited by John Paul Jones III, Heidi J. Nast, and Susan M. Roberts, 29–45. Lanham MD: Rowman & Littlefield, 1997.

———. "Place, Space, and Agency: Moving Beyond the Homogenous 'Ghetto.'" *Urban Geography* 31, no. 2 (2010): 148–52.

Giroux, Henry A. *The Terror of Neoliberalism*. Boulder CO: Paradigm, 2004.

Glannon, Walter. "Identity, Prudential Concern, and Extended Lives." *Bioethics* 16, no. 3 (2002): 266–83.

Glassman, Jim. "Primitive Accumulation, Accumulation by Dispossession, Accumulation by 'Extra-Economic' Means." *Progress in Human Geography* 30, no. 5 (2006): 608–25.

Glenn, Evelyn N. "Racial Ethnic Women's Labor: The Intersection of Race, Gender and Class Oppression." *Review of Radical Political Economics* 17, no. 3 (1985): 86–108.

Glover, Jonathan. *Choosing Children: Genes, Disability, and Design*. Oxford: Oxford University Press, 2006.

Gold, Marthe R., David Stevenson, and Dennis G. Fryback. "HALYs and QALYs and DALYs, Oh My: Similarities and Differences in Summary Measures of Population Health." *Annual Review of Public Health* 23 (2002): 115–34.

Golden, Marilyn, and Tyler Zoanni. "Killing Us Softly: The Dangers of Legalizing Assisted Suicide." *Disability and Health Journal* 3, no. 1 (2010): 16–30.

Grand, Sheldon A., Joseph E. Bernier, and Douglas C. Strohmer. "Attitudes toward Disabled Persons as a Function of Social Context and Specific Disability." *Rehabilitation Psychology* 27, no. 3 (1982): 165–74.

Grant, Madison. *The Conquest of a Continent, or the Expansion of Races in America*. New York: Charles Scribner's Sons, 1933.

———. *The Passing of the Great Race, or the Racial Basis of European History*. New York: Charles Scribner's Sons, 1920.

Green, O. H. "Killing and Letting Die." *American Philosophical Quarterly* 17, no. 3 (1980): 195–204.

Gullette, Margaret Morganroth. *Agewise: Fighting the New Ageism in America*. Chicago: University of Chicago Press, 2011.

Gunderson, Martin "Being a Burden: Reflections on Refusing Medical Care." *Hastings Center Report* 34, no. 5 (2004): 37–43.

Guthman, Julie. *Weighing In: Obesity, Food Justice, and the Limits of Capitalism*. Berkeley: University of California Press, 2011.

Hall, Stuart. "Marx's Notes on Method: A 'Reading' of the '1857 Introduction.'" *Cultural Studies* 17, no. 2 (2003): 113–49.

Haller, John S., Jr. *Outcasts from Evolution: Scientific Attitudes of Racial Inferiority, 1859–1900*. Carbondale: Southern Illinois University Press, 1971.

Hansen, Nancy, and Chris Philo. "The Normality of Doing Things Differently: Bodies, Spaces and Disability Geography." *Tijdschrift voor Economische en Sociale Geografie* 98, no. 4 (2007): 493–506.

Harcourt, Bernard E. *The Illusion of Free Markets: Punishment and the Myth of the Natural Order*. Cambridge MA: Harvard University Press, 2011.

Hardwig, John. "Going to Meet Death: The Art of Dying in the Early Part of the Twenty-First Century." *Hastings Center Report* 39, no. 4 (2009): 37–45.

———. "Is There a Duty to Die?" *Hastings Center Report* 27, no. 2 (1997): 34–42.

Harris, John. "The Marxist Conception of Violence." *Philosophy & Public Affairs* 3, no. 2 (1974): 192–220.

———. "QALYfying the Value of Life." *Journal of Medical Ethics* 13, no. 3 (1987): 117–23.

———. "Unprincipled QALYs: A Response to Cubbon." *Journal of Medical Ethics* 17, no. 4 (1991): 185–88.

Hartmann, Heidi. "The Unhappy Marriage of Marxism and Feminism: Towards a More Progressive Union." *Capital & Class* 3, no. 2 (1979): 1–33.

Hartsock, Nancy, and Neil Smith. "On Althusser's Misreading of Marx's 1857 'Introduction.'" *Science & Society* 43, no. 4 (1979): 486–89.

Harvey, David. *A Brief History of Neoliberalism*. Oxford: Oxford University Press, 2005.

———. *A Companion to Marx's "Capital."* New York: Verso, 2010.

———. *Justice, Nature and the Geography of Difference*. Oxford: Blackwell, 1996.

———. *Social Justice and the City*. Rev. ed. Athens: University of Georgia Press, 2009.

———. *Spaces of Hope*. Berkeley: University of California Press, 2000.

Hays, Sharon. *Flat Broke with Children: Women in the Age of Welfare Reform*. New York: Oxford University Press, 2003.

Heinrich, Michael. *An Introduction to the Three Volumes of Karl Marx's "Capital."* New York: Monthly Review Press, 2012.

Hodes, Martha. *White Women, Black Men: Illicit Sex in the Nineteenth-Century South*. New Haven CT: Yale University Press, 1997.

Horrobin, Steven. "The Value of Life and the Value of Life Extension." *Annals of the New York Academy of Science* 1067, no. 1 (2006): 94–105.

Horvath, Ron J., and Katherine D. Gibson. "Abstraction in Marx's Method." *Antipode* 16, no. 1 (1984): 12–25.

Hummel, Jeffrey R. *Emancipating Slaves, Enslaving Free Men: A History of the American Civil War*. Chicago: Open Court, 1996.

Humphrey, Derek, and Ann Wickett. *The Right to Die: Understanding Euthanasia*. New York: Harper & Row, 1986.

Ingersoll, David E., Richard K. Matthews, and Andrew Davison. *The Philosophic Roots of Modern Ideology: Liberalism, Communism, Fascism, Islamism*. 3rd ed. Upper Saddle River NJ: Prentice Hall, 2001.

Jackson, Robert. *Sovereignty*. Malden MA: Polity, 2007.

Jenkins, Philip. *Decade of Nightmares: The End of the Sixties and the Making of Eighties America*. Oxford: Oxford University Press, 2006.

Katz, Michael B. *Poverty and Policy in American History*. New York: Academic Press, 1983.

Kevles, Daniel J. *In the Name of Eugenics: Genetics and the Uses of Human Heredity*. Cambridge MA: Harvard University Press, 1995.

Kirk, G. S. "Natural Change in Heraclitus." *Mind* 60, no. 237 (1951): 35–42.

Kluchin, Rebecca M. *Fit to Be Tied: Sterilization and Reproductive Rights in America, 1950–1980*. New Brunswick NJ: Rutgers University Press, 2011.

Knox, Paul, and John Agnew. *Geography of the World Economy*. 2nd ed. New York: Edward Arnold, 1994.

Koch, Lene. "The Meaning of Eugenics: Reflections on the Government of Genetic Knowledge in the Past and the Present." *Science in Context* 17, no. 3 (2004): 315–31.

Koch, Tom. "Care, Compassion, or Cost: Redefining the Basis of Treatment in Ethics and Law." *Journal of Law, Medicine & Ethics* 39, no. 2 (2011): 130–39.

———. "Eugenics and the Genetic Challenge, Again: All Dressed Up and Just Everywhere to Go." *Cambridge Quarterly of Healthcare Ethics* 20, no. 2 (2011): 191–203.

———. "Life Quality vs the 'Quality of Life': Assumptions Underlying Prospective Quality of Life Instruments in Health Care Planning." *Social Science & Medicine* 51, no. 3 (2000): 419–27.

———. *Thieves of Virtue: When Bioethics Stole Medicine*. Cambridge MA: MIT Press, 2012.

Krause, Keith. "Beyond Definition: Violence in a Global Perspective." *Global Crime* 10, no. 4 (2009): 337–55.

Krug, Etienne G., James A. Mercy, Linda L. Dahlberg, and Anthony B. Zwi. "The World Report on Violence and Health." *The Lancet* 360, no. 9339 (2002): 1083–88.

Kruse, Robert J. *How Dwarfs Experience the World Around Them: The Personal Geographies of "Disabled" People*. Lewiston NY: Edwin Mellen Press, 2007.

Kühl, Stefan. *The Nazi Connection: Eugenics, American Racism, and German National Socialism*. Oxford: Oxford University Press, 1994.

Kurlansky, Mark. *Nonviolence: Twenty-Five Lessons from the History of a Dangerous Idea*. New York: Modern Library, 2006.

Larson, Edward J. *Sex, Race, and Science: Eugenics in the Deep South*. Baltimore: Johns Hopkins University Press, 1995.

Lea, John. *Crime and Modernity: Continuities in Left Realist Criminology*. Thousand Oaks CA: SAGE, 2002.

Legg, Stephen. "Foucault's Population Geographies: Classifications, Biopolitics and Governmental Spaces." *Population, Space and Place* 11, no. 3 (2005): 137-56.

Leitner, Helga, Jamie Peck, and Eric Sheppard, eds. *Contesting Neoliberalism: Urban Frontiers*. New York: Guilford, 2007.

Lemke, Thomas. *Biopolitics: An Advanced Introduction*. New York: New York University Press, 2011.

———. "Genetic Testing, Eugenics and Risk." *Critical Public Health* 12, no. 3 (2002): 283-90.

Levy, Becca, Ori Ashman, and Itiel Dror. "To Be or Not to Be: The Effects of Aging Stereotypes on the Will to Live." *Omega* 40, no. 3 (2000): 409-420.

Li, Tania Murray. "To Make Live or Let Die? Rural Dispossession and the Protection of Surplus Populations." *Antipode* 41, no. 1 (2009): 66-93.

Lichtenberg, Judith. "The Moral Equivalence of Action and Omission." In *Killing and Letting Die*, edited by Bonnie Steinbock and Alastair Norcross, 210-29. 2nd ed. New York: Fordham University Press, 1994.

Livingston, David. *The Geographical Tradition: Episodes in the History of a Contested Enterprise*. Cambridge MA: Blackwell, 1993.

Longmore, Paul K. "Medical Decision Making and People with Disabilities: A Clash of Cultures." *Journal of Law, Medicine & Ethics* 23, no. 1 (1995): 82-87.

Loyd, Jenna. "Geographies of Peace and Antiviolence." *Geography Compass* 6, no. 8 (2012): 477-89.

———. "'A Microscopic Insurgent': Militarization, Health, and Critical Geographies of Violence." *Annals of the Association of American Geographers* 99, no. 5 (2009): 863-73.

Malloy, Robin Paul. "Mortgage Market Reform and the Fallacy of Self-Correcting Markets." *Pace Law Review* 30, no. 1 (2009): 79-123.

Marx, Karl. *Capital: A Critique of Political Economy, Volume 1*. Translated by Ben Fowkes. 1867. New York: Penguin Books, 1990.

———. *Capital: A Critique of Political Economy, Volume 2*. Translated by David Fernbach. New York: Penguin Books, 1992.

———. *Capital: A Critique of Political Economy, Volume 3*. Translated by David Fernbach. New York: Penguin Books, 1991.

———. *A Contribution to the Critique of Political Economy*. New York: International Publishers, 1970.

———. *Economic and Philosophic Manuscripts of 1844*. Amherst NY: Prometheus Books, 1988.

———. *Grundrisse: Foundations of the Critique of Political Economy*. New York: Penguin, 1973.

———. "The Poverty of Philosophy." In *Karl Marx: Selected Writings*, edited by David McLellan, 219–20. 2nd ed. Oxford: Oxford University Press, 2000.

Marx, Karl, and Friedrich Engels. *The German Ideology*. Amherst NY: Prometheus Books, 1998.

———. "The Holy Family." In *Karl Marx: Selected Writings*, edited by David McLellan, 146–70. 2nd ed. Oxford: Oxford University Press, 2000.

Matthaei, Julie. "Why Feminist, Marxist, and Anti-Racist Economists Should Be Feminist-Marxist-Anti-Racist Economists." *Feminist Economics* 2, no. 1 (1996): 22–42.

May, Todd. *The Philosophy of Foucault*. Montreal and Kingston: McGill-Queen's University Press, 2006.

McCormack, Derek. "Geography and Abstraction: Towards an Affirmative Critique." *Progress in Human Geography* 36, no. 6 (2012): 715–34.

McDowell, Linda. *Gender, Identity & Place: Understanding Feminist Geographies*. Minneapolis: University of Minnesota Press, 1999.

McMahan, Jeff. *The Ethics of Killing: Problems at the Margins of Life*. Oxford: Oxford University Press, 2002.

———. "Killing, Letting Die, and Withdrawing Aid." *Ethics* 103, no. 2 (1993): 250–79.

Mencke, J. G. *Mulattoes and Race Mixture: American Attitudes and Images, 1865–1918*. Ann Arbor MI: UMI Research Press, 1976.

Mies, Maria. *Patriarchy and Capital Accumulation on a World Scale: Women in the International Division of Labor*. New York: Palgrave Macmillan, 1998.

Miles, Robert. *Racism*. London: Routledge, 1989.

Miller, Patricia N., Darryl W. Miller, Eithne M. McKibbin, and Gregory L. Pettys. "Stereotypes of the Elderly in Magazine Advertisements 1956-1996." *International Journal of Aging and Human Development* 49, no. 4 (1999): 319–37.

Mitchell, Don. "Political Violence, Order, and the Legal Construction of Public Space: Power and the Public Forum Doctrine." *Urban Geography* 17, no. 2 (1996): 152–78.

Mitchell, Don, and Nik Heynen. "The Geography of Survival and the Right to the City: Speculations on Surveillance, Legal Innovation, and the Criminalization of Intervention." *Urban Geography* 30, no. 6 (2009): 611–32.

Moyer, Virginia A., Ned Calonge, Steven M. Teutsch, and Jeffrey R. Botkin. "Expanding Newborn Screening: Process, Policy, and Priorities." *Hastings Center Report* 38, no. 3 (2008): 32–39.

Muchembled, Robert. *A History of Violence: From the End of the Middle Ages to the Present*. Malden MA: Polity Press, 2012.

Murray, Alexandra, and Angus Clarke. "The Ethics of Population Screening." *Current Paediatrics* 12, no. 6 (2002): 447–52.

Murray, Stuart J. "Thanatopolitics: On the Use of Death for Mobilizing Political Life." *Polygraph* 18 (2006): 191–215.

Myslik, Wayne D. "Renegotiating the Social/Sexual Identities of Place: Gay Communities as Safe Havens or Sites of Resistance? In *BodySpace: Destabilizing Geographies of Gender and Sexuality*, edited by Nancy Duncan, 156–69. London: Routledge, 1996.

Nadesan, Majia H. *Governmentality, Biopower, and Everyday Life*. New York: Routledge, 2010.

Nally, David. "The Biopolitics of Food Provisioning." *Transactions of the Institute of British Geographers* 36, no. 1 (2011): 37–53.

Neilson, Brett. "Ageing, Experience, Biopolitics: Life's Unfolding." *Body & Society* 18, no. 3–4 (2012): 44–71.

Neocleous, M. "War on Waste: Law, Original Accumulation and the Violence of Capital." *Science & Society* 75, no. 4 (2011): 506–28.

O'Campo, Patricia, and Lucia Rojas-Smith. "Welfare Reform and Women's Health: Review of the Literature and Implications for State Policy." *Journal of Public Health Policy* 19, no. 4 (1998): 420–46.

Oksala, Johanna. *Foucault, Politics, and Violence*. Evanston IL: Northwestern University Press, 2012.

Ollman, Bertell. *Alienation: Marx's Conception of Man in Capitalist Society*. 2nd ed. Cambridge: Cambridge University Press, 1976.

———. *Dance of the Dialectic: Steps in Marx's Method*. Urbana: University of Illinois Press, 2003.

———. "Marx's Dialectical Method Is More Than a Mode of Exposition: A Critique of Systematic Dialectics." In *New Dialectics and Political Economy*, edited by Robert Albritton and John Simoulidis, 173–84. New York: Palgrave Macmillan, 2003.

Opotow, Susan. "Reconciliation in a Time of Impunity: Challenges for Social Justice." *Social Justice Research* 14, no. 2 (2001): 149–70.

Otlowski, Margaret. "Mercy Killing Cases in the Australian Criminal Justice System." *Criminal Law Journal* 17, no. 1 (1993): 10–39.

Overall, Christine. "Old Age and Ageism, Impairment and Ableism: Exploring the Conceptual and Material Connections." *NWSA Journal* 18, no. 1 (2006): 126–37.

Pain, Rachel, Michael Barke, Duncan Fuller, Jamie Gough, Robert MacFarlane, and Graham Mowl. *Introducing Social Geographies*. New York: Oxford University Press, 2001.

Paolucci, Paul. *Marx's Scientific Dialectics: A Methodological Treatise for a New Century*. Chicago: Haymarket Books, 2009.

Paul, Diane B. *Controlling Human Heredity: 1865 to the Present*. New York: Macmillan, 1995.

Peck, Jamie. *Work-Place: The Social Regulation of Labor Markets.* New York: Guilford, 1996.

Peet, Richard. *Global Capitalism: Theories of Societal Development.* New York: Routledge, 1991.

———. "Materialism, Social Formation, and Socio-Spatial Relations: An Essay in Marxist Geography." *Cahiers de Géographie du Québec* 22, no. 56 (1978): 147–57.

———. *Theories of Development.* New York: Guilford, 1999.

Peters, Michael A. *Poststructuralism, Marxism, and Neoliberalism: Between Theory and Politics.* Lanham MD: Rowman & Littlefield, 2001.

Philo, Chris. "Sex, Life, Death, Geography: Fragmentary Remarks Inspired by Foucault's Population Geographies." *Population, Space and Place* 11, no. 4 (2005): 325–33.

Piore, Michael J. "Notes for a Theory of Labor Market Stratification." Working Paper Department of Economics Number 95, Massachusetts Institute of Technology, 1972.

Pollock, Joycelyn M. *Criminal Law.* 10th ed. Waltham MA: Elsevier, 2013.

Popenoe, Paul, and Roswell Hill Johnson. *Applied Eugenics.* 2nd ed. New York: Macmillan, 1918.

Porter, Ray. *Madness: A Brief History.* Oxford: Oxford University Press, 2002.

Postone, Moishe. *Time, Labor, and Social Domination: A Reinterpretation of Marx's Critical Theory.* Cambridge: Cambridge University Press, 1993.

Quinn, Warren S. "Actions, Intentions, and Consequences: The Doctrine of Doing and Allowing." In *Killing and Letting Die*, edited by Bonnie Steinbock and Alastair Norcross, 355–82. 2nd ed. New York: Fordham University Press, 1994.

Rachels, James. "Killing and Starving to Death." *Philosophy* 54, no. 258 (1979): 159–71.

Raz, Aviad E. "Eugenic Utopias/Dystopias, Reprogenetics, and Community Genetics." *Sociology of Health & Illness* 31, no. 4 (2009): 602–16.

Rees, John. *The Algebra of Revolution: The Dialectic and the Classical Marxist Tradition.* New York: Routledge, 1998.

Reese, Ellen. *Backlash against Welfare Mothers: Past and Present.* Berkeley: University of California Press, 2005.

Reiman, Jeffrey. "The Marxian Critique of Criminal Justice." *Criminal Justice Ethics* 6, no. 1 (1987): 30–50.

Reiman, Jeffrey, and Paul Leighton. *The Rich Get Richer and the Poor Get Prison: Ideology, Class, and Criminal Justice.* 10th ed. New York: Pearson, 2013.

Roberts, Dorothy. *Killing the Black Body: Race, Reproduction, and the Meaning of Liberty.* New York: Pantheon, 1997.

Robinson, Tom, Mark Callister, Dawn Magoffin, and Jennifer Moore. "The Portrayal of Older Characters in Disney Animated Films." *Journal of Aging Studies* 21, no. 3 (2007): 203–13.

Rock, Melanie. "Discounted Lives? Weighing Disability When Measuring Health and Ruling on 'Compassionate' Murder." *Social Science & Medicine* 51, no. 3 (2000): 407–17.

Rose, Nikolas. *The Politics of Life Itself: Biomedicine, Power, and Subjectivity in the Twenty-First Century*. Princeton NJ: Princeton University Press, 2007.

Rothman, David J. *The Discovery of the Asylum: Social Order and Disorder in the New Republic*. Boston: Little, Brown, 1971.

Ruppert, Evelyn. "Population Objects: Interpassive Subjects." *Sociology* 45, no. 2 (2011): 218–33.

Sarat, Austin, and Jennifer L. Culbert. "Introduction: Interpreting the Violent State." In *States of Violence: War, Capital Punishment, and Letting Die*, edited by Austin Sarat and Jennifer L. Culbert, 1–22. Cambridge: Cambridge University Press, 2009.

Saunders, Peter, and Peter Williams. "The Constitution of the Home: Towards a Research Agenda." *Housing Studies* 3, no. 2 (1988): 81–93.

Savulescu, Julian. "Deaf Lesbians, 'Designer Disability,' and the Future of Medicine." *British Medical Journal* 325, no. 7367 (2002): 771–73.

Scheerenberger, Richard C. *A History of Mental Retardation*. Baltimore MD: Paul H. Brookes, 1983.

Schiebinger, Londa. *Nature's Body: Gender in the Making of Science*. Boston: Beacon, 1993.

Schweik, Susan M. *The Ugly Laws: Disability in Public*. New York: New York University Press, 2009.

Sen, Amartya. *Identity and Violence: The Illusion of Destiny*. New York: Norton, 2006.

Singer, Peter. *Practical Ethics*. 2nd ed. New York: Cambridge University Press, 1993.

Smith, Adam. *The Wealth of Nations*. Edited by C. J. Bullock. 1776. New York: Barnes & Noble, 2004.

Smith, Anna Marie. "The Politicization of Marriage in Contemporary American Public Policy: The Defense of Marriage Act and the Personal Responsibility Act." *Citizenship Studies* 5, no. 3 (2001): 303–20.

Smith, David M. *Geography and Social Justice*. Cambridge MA: Blackwell, 1994.

Smith, Neil. *The Endgame of Globalization*. New York: Routledge, 2005.

Smith, Wesley J. *Culture of Death: The Assault on Medical Ethics in America*. New York: Encounter Books, 2000.

Snyder, Sharon L., and David T. Mitchell. *Cultural Locations of Disability*. Chicago: University of Chicago Press, 2010.

Somerville, John. "Marxist Ethics, Determinism, and Freedom." *Philosophy and Phenomenological Research* 28, no. 1 (1967): 17–23.

Spriggs, Merle. "Lesbian Couple Create a Child Who Is Deaf Like Them." *Journal of Medical Ethics* 28, no. 5 (2002): 283.

Springer, Simon. "Violence Sits in Places? Cultural Practice, Neoliberal Rationalism, and Virulent Imaginative Geographies." *Political Geography* 30, no. 2 (2011): 90–98.

Stainton, Tim. "Identity, Difference and the Ethical Politics of Prenatal Testing." *Journal of Intellectual Disability Research* 47, no. 7 (2003): 533–39.

Steger, Manfred B. *Globalism: Market Ideology Meets Terrorism.* 2nd ed. Lanham MD: Rowman & Littlefield, 2005.

Steger, Manfred B., and Ravi K. Roy. *Neoliberalism: A Very Short Introduction.* Oxford: Oxford University Press, 2010.

Steinbock, Bonnie. "Introduction." In *Killing and Letting Die*, edited by Bonnie Steinbock and Alastair Norcross, 24–47. 2nd ed. New York: Fordham University Press, 1994.

Stepan, Nancy Leys. *"The Hour of Eugenics": Race, Gender, and Nation in Latin America.* Ithaca NY: Cornell University Press, 1991.

Stoddard, Lothrop. *The Rising Tide of Color against White World-Supremacy.* New York: Scribner, 1920.

Strawson, P. F. *The Bounds of Sense: An Essay on Kant's Critique of Pure Reason.* London: Routledge, 1989.

Sutherland, Edwin H. "White-Collar Criminality." *American Sociological Review* 5, no. 1 (1940): 1–12.

Taylor, J. D. *Negative Capitalism: Cynicism in the Neoliberal Era.* Winchester UK: Zero Books, 2013.

Thurschwell, Adam. "Ethical Exception: Capital Punishment in the Figure of Sovereignty." *South Atlantic Quarterly* 107, no. 3 (2008): 571–96.

Trammell, Richard. "Saving Life and Taking Life." In *Killing and Letting Die*, edited by Bonnie Steinbock and Alastair Norcross, 290–97. 2nd ed. New York: Fordham University Press, 1994.

Trent, James W. *Inventing the Feeble Mind: A History of Mental Retardation in the United States.* Berkeley: University of California Press, 1994.

Tringo, John L. "The Hierarchy of Preference toward Disability Groups." *Journal of Special Education* 4, no. 3 (1970): 295–306.

Tucker, William. *The Science and Politics of Racial Research.* Urbana: University of Illinois Press, 1994.

Tyner, James A. *Genocide and the Geographical Imagination: Life and Death in Germany, China, and Cambodia.* Lanham MD: Rowman & Littlefield, 2012.

——. "Population Geography I: Surplus Populations." *Progress in Human Geography* 37, no. 5 (2013): 701–11.

——. *Space, Place, and Violence: Violence and the Embodied Geographies of Race, Sex, and Gender*. New York: Routledge, 2012.

Tyner, James A., and Donna Houston. "Controlling Bodies: The Punishment of Multiracialized Sexual Relations." *Antipode* 32, no. 4 (2000): 387–409.

Tyner, James A., and Joshua Inwood. "Violence as Fetish: Geography, Marxism, and Dialectics." *Progress in Human Geography* 38, no. 6 (2014): 771–84. doi:10.1177/0309132513516177.

United Nations Children's Fund/World Health Organization. *Diarrhoea: Why Children Are Still Dying and What Can Be Done*. Geneva: World Health Organization, 2009.

Wacquant, Loïc. *Punishing the Poor: The Neoliberal Government of Social Insecurity*. Durham: Duke University Press, 2009.

Weeks, Kathi. *The Problem with Work: Feminism, Marxism, Antiwork Politics, and Postwork Imaginaries*. Durham: Duke University Press, 2011.

Wikler, Daniel. "Personal and Social Responsibility for Health." *Ethics and International Affairs* 16, no. 2 (2002): 47–55.

Williams, Alan. "The Value of QALYs." *Health and Social Service Journal* (July 1985): 3–5.

Winston, George T. "The Relation of the Whites to the Negroes." *Annals of the American Academy of Political and Social Science* 18, no. 1 (1901): 103–18.

Wood, Ellen M. *Empire of Capital*. London: Verso, 2003.

World Health Organization. *The Global Burden of Disease: 2004 Update*. Geneva: World Health Organization, 2008.

Wright, Melissa W. "The Dialectics of Still Life: Murder, Women, and Maquiladoras." *Public Culture* 11, no. 3 (1999): 453–74.

Wrightson, Keith. *English Society, 1580–1680*. London: Hutchinson, 1982.

Young, Robert. "What Is So Wrong with Killing People?" *Philosophy* 54, no. 210 (1979): 515–28.

Zinn, Howard. *Just War*. Milan: Edizioni Charta, 2005.

Žižek, Slavoj. *Violence: Six Sideways Reflections*. New York: Picador, 2008.

INDEX

Cartwright, Wil, 206
child abuse, 28–29
Coady, C. A. J., 7
Coleman, Diane, 196
colonialism, 133
commodification, 34, 79; of society,
    95–106, 197
consumption, 110–14
contradictions, 12–13, 27, 111, 186
crime, 34, 42, 45, 84–95, 138, 142; and
    capitalism, 54–62, 202
criminal act, 88–89, 168
criminal justice, 14, 34, 35–36, 59–62,
    88–89
Curtis, Bruce, 61

Dalla Costa, Mariarosa, 108
D'Amato, Paul, 76–77
Darwin, Charles, 136–37, 139
Davenport, Charles, 139
deafness, 176–77
Dean, Mitchell, 62, 80
Dear, Michael, 161
death: management of, 81–86, 179–
    97; premature, 171–79
degeneration, 139–40
designer babies, 172
determinism, 36–37, 45
dialectics, 12, 15–16, 19–31
disability, 157, 160, 162–71, 182, 191;
    and pregnancy, 171–79
discipline, 54–62, 200
disposability, 133, 163
domestic violence, 29–30, 101
Dore, Margaret, 192
Down syndrome, 172, 174–76, 178
Dranove, David, 157
Dubow, Saul, 142

Dugdale, Richard, 138
duties, 87–95, 118, 140, 208
Duty to Die', 182–97

Ekland-Olson, Sheldon, 142
empiricism, 19
ethics, 86–95, 150, 154
eugenics, 133–51, 164–65; positive/
    negative, 145
euthanasia, 179–97, 206
evolution, 135–37
evolutionary psychology, 8, 20
exploitation, 107, 113–15, 129, 211

family, 108–9, 138, 139, 142; values,
    116–17, 123
Federici, Silvia, 49, 51, 53, 54
Fletcher, Joseph, 177
Foot, Philippa, 90–92
Ford, Lynne Spalding, 205–6
Fortunati, Leopoldina, 53
Foucault, Michel, 10–11, 54–62, 80,
    81–83, 86, 166, 200–201, 203
freedom, 47, 71, 77, 100, 174, 200,
    206; and euthanasia, 179–97

Galton, Francis, 136, 140
Galtung, Johan, 5–6, 32, 206
Galvin, Rose, 92, 182, 208
Garland, David, 56
Garver, Newton, 6
gender, 52–53
genetic screening, 172–74
Giffords, Gabby, 30
Gilbert, Melissa, 123
Giroux, Henry, 117–18
Glover, Johnathan, 160, 163, 172, 175,
    178

www.ingramcontent.com/pod-product-compliance
Lightning Source LLC
Chambersburg PA
CBHW030356270326
41926CB00009B/1128